Christ Before the Manger

Christ Before the Manger

The Life and Times
of the Preincarnate Christ

Ron Rhodes

BAKER BOOK HOUSE
Grand Rapids, Michigan 49516

Copyright © 1992 by
Baker Book House Company
P.O. Box 6287
Grand Rapids, MI 49516-6287

Second printing, February 1993

Printed in the United States of America

Library of Congress Cataloging-in-Publication Data

Rhodes, Ron.
    Christ before the manger: the life and times of the preincarnate Christ / Ron Rhodes.
    p. cm.
    Includes bibliographical references.
    ISBN 0-8010-7766-4
    1. Jesus Christ—Pre-existence. 2. Jesus Christ—Person and offices. I. Title.
BT202.R46 1992
232′ .8—dc20   92-23993

With much gratitude,
this book is affectionately dedicated
to my parents
Tom and Alpha Rhodes

Contents

Acknowledgments

I want to thank Norman Geisler for critically reading the book manuscript prior to publication. His theological suggestions were invaluable. Thanks also go to Ken Samples for the same.

My wife, Kerri, deserves special mention for meticulously proofreading the manuscript for readability purposes. Her suggestions were gladly incorporated into the book.

Finally, I want to thank my children David and Kylie—my cheering squad. What a blessing from the Lord they are!

Introduction

For as long as I can remember, I have been inquisitive about the eternal nature of God. As a youngster, I recall approaching my mother one day while she was ironing my father's shirts and asking, "When was God born, and who were his parents?" She responded the way most mothers do when trying to explain the unexplainable eternality of God to their children: "God wasn't born. He's always been there—and he has no parents." To which I replied, "Oh, okay."

After giving this some thought for a time, I went back to her and asked, "Well, when is God going to die?" As you might expect, she simply responded, "He's not going to die. He'll always be there." To which I replied, "Oh, okay."

Not long after this, however, I decided I wanted some *real* answers! So I went to her yet again and asked, somewhat defiantly: "How come God was never born, and how come he'll never die?" She reflected for a few moments, took a deep breath, and said, "Because—God is God." I hesitated a little after hearing that answer. Not knowing what else to say, I mumbled, "Oh, okay." And I left it at that—for the time being.

During my college years, I remember taking an introductory religion course that had as its focus the divine attributes of God. Not fully grasping the doctrine of God's eternality and how it related to his foreknowledge, I raised my hand one day in class and made a grand display of my ignorance by saying to the instructor, "I know that God's 'foreknowledge' means that he fully knows all that will transpire in the future. But

11

how does this relate to God's actual process of thinking? Surely he doesn't know what he's going to think before he thinks it, does he?" I wasn't sure what to make of the look on the instructor's face. But after he cleared his throat a few times, he said, "God is in the realm of eternity. The past, present, and future are simultaneously present to him. Therefore [cough, cough] your question doesn't apply." Somewhat befuddled, I sank into my chair, but I was more resolved than ever to explore and understand God's eternality.

While enrolled at Dallas Theological Seminary, one of my first-year professors gave a lecture on "the cosmological argument." This argument says that every *effect* must have an adequate *cause*. Viewed as an effect, the world—so the argument goes—must have a cause sufficient to have produced it. God's existence is thereby proven. Since the world exists, something greater than the world (that is, God) must have created it.

"Prof," I said, "that makes a lot of sense. But if *every* effect *must* have a sufficient cause, then how does this argument relate to God's existence? Certainly, *he* was not 'caused'!" The professor was ready for that one. He responded with a deep, professorial tone of voice: "God is eternal. Hence, he is the uncaused First Cause." With widened eyes, I nodded my head and said, "Ahhh."

And so it goes. The eternality of God! During my seminary years, I discovered that I wasn't the only one interested in this subject. In fact, man's fascination with the doctrine is as old as human history. Yet, in his finiteness, man can only see as "in a mirror dimly" (1 Cor. 13:12 NASB). Man's temporality will allow for nothing more. Thankfully, however, God has given us in his Word at least a passing glimpse of his eternal nature. And what his Word reveals to us is truly staggering.

Before a single star burst into being, before our own sun emitted its first flood of light and energy, before any galaxies were formed from absolute nothingness, there God was. The eternal one without beginning. The living one. The self-existent one who is above and beyond the whole course of time.

Prior to the Creation, *God was all there was*. Just God! The blessed Trinity—Father, Son, and Holy Spirit—had, for eternity past, existed in a state of uninterrupted fellowship. The Father and the Holy Spirit enjoyed an eternal loving intercourse with each other and with the Son. So momentous was this divine love that near the close of his three-year ministry on earth, Jesus—in his prayer to the Father—spoke of eternity past as a matter of memory: ". . . Thou didst love Me before the foundation of the world" (John 17:24 NASB). Augustine once commented: "If God is love, then there must be in Him a Lover, a Beloved, and a Spirit of love; for no love is conceivable without a Lover and a Beloved." A captivating thought, to be sure! If there is a weakness in this statement, it is that some may wrongly conclude from it that the Holy Spirit is just a "Spirit of love" between the Father and Son. This is not the case, however, for the Holy Spirit is himself one of the persons loving the other two in the Trinity and himself being loved by them.

Most people acquainted with Scripture have little trouble accepting that "God" is an eternal being. Some, however, are surprised to discover that the Christ of the Gospels is an eternal being. When these individuals reflect on the person of Jesus, they see in their mind's eye the nativity scenes so popular at Christmas time. Jesus is portrayed as a baby wrapped in swaddling clothes in a lowly manger, often inadvertently implying that this scene represents the actual beginnings of Jesus Christ.

Contrary to this misconception, both the Old and New Testaments virtually shout the eternality of Christ. Isaiah 9:6 refers to him as "Everlasting Father," or, as it is better translated, "Father of Eternity." This verse does *not* mean that Jesus is *the* Father, that the *second* person of the Trinity is the *first* person. The Hebrew word for "Father" in this verse simply indicates that Christ is the *author* or *eminent possessor* of eternity (see chapter 2 for a full explanation of this verse). This is in perfect accord with Revelation 1:17, where Christ tells us, "I am the First and the Last." The prophet Micah likewise describes Christ as one whose "goings forth are from long ago, From the days of eternity" (Mic. 5:2 NASB). The writer of Hebrews uses the phrase, "yesterday and today and forever," as a way of describing the eternality of Christ (Heb. 13:8). Earlier in Hebrews, the Father is quoted as saying to the Son: "Your throne, O God, will last for ever and ever . . . you laid the foundations of the earth, and the heavens are the work of your hands. They will perish, but you remain. . . . you remain the same, and your years will never end" (Heb. 1:8–12).

Jesus often attested to his eternality in the Gospel records. For example, he revealed his true identity to a group of hostile Jews by saying, "Before Abraham was born, I am!" (John 8:58). The expression "I am" clearly echoes the words of God in Exodus 3:14: "I AM WHO I AM." This name conveys the idea of eternal self-existence. Jesus' use of this name constituted a claim to be eternal—to exist without ever having experienced a beginning—in contrast to Abraham, who had a beginning. It is this timeless, self-existing Christ who enjoyed an eternal loving intercourse with the Father and the Holy Spirit before the beginning of time.

Also prior to the beginning of time, God conceived a grand and glorious plan for humankind (Eph. 1:11). The plan was conceived *in eternity*, but would be carried out by God *in time*. That which was eternally determined *before the ages* would be brought to fruition *in the ages*.

We learn from Scripture that this eternal plan was colossal in scope. According to the plan, the Father chose the Son as the Redeemer (1 Peter 1:18–21), and determined, among other things, to "send" him into the world of humanity. This is what Jesus was referring to when he told Nicodemus: "For God did not send his Son into the world to condemn the world, but to save the world through him" (John 3:17). On another occasion, Jesus told a large gathering: "For I have come down from heaven not to do my will but to do the will of him who sent me" (John 6:38). Galatians 4:4–5 tells us that "when the time had fully come, God sent his Son, born of a woman, born under law, to redeem those under law, that we might receive the full rights of sons." Truly, the Incarnation—the event in which the preexistent, eternal Christ took upon himself a human nature—was a supreme moment in the outworking of God's eternal plan.

In addition to the Incarnation, God's eternal plan apparently called for many *preincarnate* appearances of Christ as the "Angel of the Lord" to various men and women in Old Testament times. It would seem from the scriptural evidence that the Father appointed Jesus to be *the visible manifestation of God* among people in both the Old and New Testaments. (Note that the Angel of the Lord *and* Jesus were both sent by the Father—one in the Old Testament [Judg. 13:8–9], the other in the New [John 3:17].) And, as we shall see in this book, Christ's activities among people in the Old Testament were similar in many ways to those described in the New Testament.

In view of these astounding facts, it is obvious that any study of Christ that begins with the Gospel accounts of Christ's birth in Judea is, to some extent, a shallow appreciation of the true Christ of Scripture. More often than not, books on "the life of Christ" assume that what Christ was *before* the Incarnation is either not sufficiently revealed in Scripture or is not important enough to warrant serious study. Either way, the result is an incomplete knowledge and appreciation of the person of Jesus Christ.

Please don't misunderstand what I am saying. Christ's work on the cross as God-incarnate is indisputably the greatest single event of all human history. Without Christ's sacrificial death on the cross, we would all be lost. But Scripture attests that this is *one of many* accomplishments of our eternal Lord and Savior. After recounting some of Christ's more notable miracles, the apostle John said: "Jesus did many other things as well. If every one of them were written down, I suppose that even the whole world would not have room for the books that would be written" (John 21:25). Using this same analogy, how much room would be required to contain the books if all Christ's works *throughout eternity past* were recorded alongside his works on earth? The whole universe?

The question is unanswerable. One thing we can be certain of, however, is that a study of Christ's eternality and preexistence lays an indispensable foundation for understanding the Christ of the New Testament. Consider for a moment: How can a Christian conceive of the inestimable condescension and humiliation Christ voluntarily took upon himself in the Incarnation unless he sees from what dazzling heights Christ came? Moreover, can a Christian fully appreciate the deity of Christ as portrayed in the New Testament unless he also sees him as *Yahweh*, the "I AM WHO I AM," of the Old Testament (Exod. 3:14)?

And what about the practical implications of Christ's eternality as related to the Incarnation? If one does not see the entry of eternal, undiminished deity into permanent union with humanity in the Incarnation, what kind of "incarnation" is left? Obviously, if Christ was not God *before* his human birth in Judea, then he was not God *afterward*. Moreover, if Jesus in the Incarnation is not eternal God *and* perfect humanity (completely human, though without a sin nature), then you and I have little to feel secure about. After all, it is upon the Incarnation that Christianity's most important doctrines depend (for example: salvation, resurrection, and glorification).

Seen in this light, a study of the eternality and preexistence of Christ, and of his appearances and activities in Old Testament times, is clearly one of monumental importance—for by it we catch a glimpse of Christ's true identity. He is eternal God and is without beginning. Like the Father and the Holy Spirit, Jesus is everlastingly the living one. And precisely because Christ *is* eternal God, all that he has accomplished in our behalf assumes proportions that are as limitless as infinity.

The shelves of our libraries are filled with tens of thousands of volumes written on both the words and works of Jesus

Christ. Even with all this, surprisingly little attention has been given to the appearances and activities of the preexistent Christ in Old Testament times. This is astonishing, for this doctrine is among the most exciting in the Bible.

This doctrine has a history of causing excitement in people. Recall that after his resurrection from the dead, Jesus appeared to two disciples on the road to Emmaus and spoke to them about his true identity: "And beginning with Moses and all the Prophets, he [Jesus] explained to them what was said in *all* the [Old Testament] Scriptures concerning himself" (Luke 24:27, insert mine, italics added). Christ's words to the disciples, in my view, cannot be limited in scope to Old Testament prophecies of his future coming (see Appendix B for a listing of the major prophecies). His words likely included a recounting of his many preincarnate appearances to the Old Testament patriarchs.[1] Later, after the resurrected Christ departed, the two disciples asked each other: "Were not our hearts burning within us while he talked with us on the road and opened the [Old Testament] Scriptures to us?" (Luke 24:32, insert mine).

Viewing the Old Testament "Christocentrically" (that is, in a way that centers on Christ) is not an interpretive option. Indeed, for the Christian, it is a divine imperative.[2] On five different occasions, Jesus claimed to be the theme of the entire Old Testament: (1) Matthew 5:17; (2) Luke 24:27; (3) Luke 24:44; (4) John 5:39; and (5) Hebrews 10:7.[3] And, because Christ is the theme of the Old Testament, the relationship between the Old and New Testaments is inseparably connected in the person of Jesus Christ. Lewis Sperry Chafer, the founder of Dallas Theological Seminary, put it this way:

> The Bible, opening with the words, "In the beginning God" (Gen. 1:1), and closing with reference to "the Lord Jesus" (Rev. 22:20–21), is preeminently a revelation of Jesus Christ. Though the Bible obviously treats many subjects—including the history of man, the existence of angels, the revelation of God's purposes for the nations, Israel, and the church, and includes in

its revelation facts from eternity past to eternity future—Jesus Christ is revealed as the Center. He is presented as the Creator, the Messiah of Israel, the Savior of the saints, the Head of the church, and King of kings over all creation. As the theme of divine revelation, the person and work of Jesus Christ threads its way from the first to the last book of the Bible.[4]

In this book I shall examine some of the many passages in the Bible that speak of Christ's appearances and activities among his people of old. From these passages, we shall discover that Christ had a distinct personal existence during Old Testament times and that he had definite and repeated dealings with his people, the Israelites.[5]

Theologian John F. Walvoord once commented: "The riches of divine revelation embodied in Jesus Christ are as measureless as the ocean and His perfections as numberless as the stars. To attempt to state in complete theological form all that should be said about Jesus Christ leaves the writer with a sense of futility. He has dipped but a cup from the ocean of infinite glory and perfections of his Lord and Savior."[6] I echo these words. It is with a profound sense of inadequacy that I dip my cup in this vast ocean.

Nevertheless, this book is humbly presented with a hope and a prayer. My hope is that you will come to know more fully the glory and majesty of our eternal God and Savior, Jesus Christ. My prayer is that this knowledge would not become an end in itself, but that it would serve to draw you ever closer to his side.

Ron Rhodes, 1992
Mission Viejo, California

1

Knowing God:
Father, Son, and Holy Spirit

"What were we made for? To know God!" J. I. Packer affirms in his modern classic, *Knowing God*. "What aim should we set ourselves in life? To know God. . . . What is the best thing in life, bringing more joy, delight, and contentment, than anything else? Knowledge of God."[1]

God tells us through the mouth of his prophet Jeremiah: "Let not the wise man boast of his wisdom or the strong man boast of his strength or the rich man boast of his riches, but let him who boasts boast about this: *that he understands and knows me*" (Jer. 9:23–24a, italics added).

Knowing Christ takes on similar importance in the New Testament. The apostle Paul said: "But whatever was to my profit I now consider loss for the sake of Christ. What is more, I consider everything a loss compared to the surpassing greatness of knowing Christ Jesus my Lord, for whose sake I have lost all things" (Phil. 3:7–8).

To know God. This is a lofty goal. For God—the triune God—is high and exalted above the creation, and his glory and majesty surpass human comprehension. One theologian has described God as "the eternal without beginning, He who is above the whole course of time, He who in harmony beyond explanation possesses unity and life, the Father, the Son, and the Holy Spirit, the basis of eternity, the Living One, the only God."[2]

It is a mind-stretching exercise to ponder that before the creation—indeed, before time even began—the three persons of the Trinity enjoyed uninterrupted and blissfully loving fellowship for all eternity. John's Gospel tells us that Jesus the divine "Word" was both God and *with* God from all eternity (John 1:1). The Greek word for "with" *(pros)* in this verse indicates intimate, unbroken fellowship (see chapter 8 for more on this). There never was nor ever could be anything but a mutually satisfying communion between the persons of the Trinity.

Truly, it is impossible for finite minds to comprehend the intimate and enduring affection that infinite love has produced within the triune Godhead. Each was loving and each received love in return. The joy and fulfillment that resulted from this divine communion must have been utterly supreme. It is this loving, triune God whom believers are given the privilege of knowing and loving on a personal, intimate basis.

The Divine Self-Disclosure

I have chosen to begin this book on the life and times of the preincarnate Christ with a chapter on the Trinity. I have done this for several reasons. First, biblical evidence for the doctrine of the Trinity constitutes, in itself, powerful evidence for Christ's preexistence and eternality. One doctrine supports the other. Second, this chapter guards against the distorted views of certain groups, such as the Oneness Pentecostals, who deny the triune nature of God and say that the Father, Son, and Holy Spirit are three "manifestations" (*not* persons) of the one God. And third, the doctrine of the Trinity is foundational to a proper understanding of the nature, appearances, and activities of the *second person* of the Trinity (Jesus Christ)—in both the Old and New Testaments. As we shall see, trinitarian distinctions serve as the theological backdrop for every chapter in this book.

As we seek to explore what Scripture says about the mystery of the Trinity, we begin with the recognition that in the course of God's self-disclosure to humankind, he revealed his nature to man in progressive stages. First, God revealed his essential unity and uniqueness—that is, he revealed that he is *one* and that he is the only true God. This was a necessary starting point for God's self-revelation, for throughout history Israel was surrounded by nations deeply engulfed in *polytheism* (the belief in many gods). Through the prophets, God communicated and affirmed to Israel the truth of *monotheism* (the belief that there is only one true God).

While God's unity and oneness is the clear emphasis in Old Testament revelation, this is not to say that there are no hints or shadows of the doctrine of the Trinity there, for indeed there are (we shall look at some examples shortly). But God did not reveal the fullness of this doctrine until New Testament times. It is by reading the Old Testament under the illumination of the New Testament that we find supporting evidences for the Trinity there. Indeed, as theologian Benjamin Warfield notes,

> The Old Testament may be likened to a chamber richly furnished but dimly lighted; the introduction of light brings into it nothing which was not in it before; but it brings out into clearer view much of what is in it but was only dimly or even not at all perceived before. The mystery of the Trinity is not [explicitly] revealed in the Old Testament; but the mystery of the Trinity underlies the Old Testament revelation, and here and there almost comes into view. Thus the Old Testament revelation of God is not corrected by the fuller revelation which follows it, but only perfected, extended and enlarged.[3]

Because God's triune nature is just as much a part of his self-revelation to man as his oneness is, a proper concept of God must include the idea of three persons in the one Godhead.

God is *by nature* triune. As Reformed theologian Louis Berkhof has observed, "this tri-personal existence is a necessity in the Divine Being, and not in any sense the result of a choice of God. He could not exist in any other than the tri-personal form."[4] Each person of the Trinity is thus essential to a correct and full definition of God.

As noted earlier, the doctrine of the Trinity is an appropriate starting point for a discussion of the eternality of Jesus Christ. But beyond the importance of the trinitarian doctrine as it relates to Christ, there are other ways in which the doctrine is important. As theologian Millard Erickson puts it, the doctrine of the Trinity is concerned with "who God is, what he is like, how he works, and how he is to be approached."[5] Moreover, the position we take on the Trinity will answer several questions of a practical nature. "Whom are we to worship—the Father only, Son, Holy Spirit, or the Triune God? To whom are we to pray? Is the work of each to be considered in isolation from the work of the others, or may we think of the atoning death of Jesus as somehow the work of the Father as well? Should the Son be thought of as the Father's equal in essence, or should he be relegated to a somewhat lesser status?"[6] Obviously, how one answers these questions will have a substantial impact on one's daily spiritual life.

Let us now seek to expand our understanding of the triune God of Scripture, and, in the process, understand more about the eternality of Christ. Let us seek to more fully *know* the God of the Bible. For, the higher and more worthy our views of him, nineteenth-century pastor Marcus Rainsford suggested, "the greater will be our appreciation of His salvation; and the more we understand Him who loved us, the greater will be our confidence and the repose of our souls in Him."[7]

The Triune God—The Only True God

The doctrine of the Trinity is based on (1) evidence that there is only one true God; (2) evidence that there are three persons who are God; and (3) scriptural indications for three-in-oneness within the Godhead.

Before we examine these three lines of evidence, it is important that we clarify what we do *not* mean by the word *Trinity*. In attempting to understand God's triune nature, two errors must be avoided. First, we must not conclude that the Godhead is composed of three separate and distinct individuals such as Peter, James, and Paul, each with his own unique characteristics or attributes. Such a concept would lead to what is known as "tritheism"—the belief that there are three Gods rather than three persons within the Godhead. Second, we must not conclude that the Godhead is *one person only* and that the triune aspect of his being is no more than three fields of interest, activities, or modes of manifestation—a view known as "modalism." The fallacy of these errors will become clearer as we examine the biblical evidence for the Trinity.

Evidence for One God

The fact that there is only one true God is the consistent testimony of Scripture from Genesis to Revelation. It is like a thread that runs through every page of the Bible. An early Hebrew confession of faith, the Shema, is an example of this consistent emphasis: "Hear, O Israel: The LORD our God, the LORD is one" (Deut. 6:4). In my view, this verse is better translated from the Hebrew, "Hear, O Israel! The Lord is our God, *the Lord alone.*" In a culture saturated with false gods and idols, the Shema would have been particularly meaningful for the Israelites. The importance of the Shema is reflected in the Hebrew practice of requiring children to memorize it at a very early age.

In the Song of Moses, which Moses recited to the whole assembly of Israel following the exodus from Egypt, we find God's own words worshipfully repeated: "See now that I myself am He! There is no god besides me. I put to death and I bring to life, I have wounded and I will heal, and no one can deliver out of my hand" (Deut. 32:39). The God of the Bible is without rival!

After God had made some astonishing promises to David (see the Davidic Covenant in 2 Sam. 7:12–16), David responded by offering praise to God: "How great you are, O Sovereign LORD! There is no one like you, and there is no God but you . . ." (2 Sam. 7:22). Later, in the form of a psalm, David praised God with similar words: "For you are great and do marvelous deeds; you alone are God" (Ps. 86:10).

God positively affirmed through Isaiah the prophet: "I am the first and I am the last; apart from me there is no God" (Isa. 44:6b; cf. 37:20; 43:10; 45:5, 14, 21–22). God later said, "I am God, and there is no other; I am God, and there is none like me" (46:9b). God often demonstrated that he alone is God by foretelling the future, something that false gods could never do (46:8–10).

The oneness of God is also often emphasized in the New Testament. In 1 Corinthians 8:4, for example, the apostle Paul asserted that "an idol is nothing at all in the world and that there is no God but one." James 2:19 likewise says, "You believe that there is one God. Good! Even the demons believe that—and shudder." These and a multitude of other verses (including John 5:44; 17:3; Rom. 3:29–30; 16:27; Gal. 3:20; Eph. 4:6; 1 Thess. 1:9; 1 Tim. 1:17; 2:5; 1 John 5:20–21; Jude 25) make it absolutely clear that there is one and only one God.

Evidence for Three Persons Who Are Called God

Though Scripture is clear that there is only one God, in the unfolding of God's revelation to humankind it also becomes clear that there are *three distinct persons* who are called God.[8] For example, Peter refers to the saints "who have been chosen according to the foreknowledge of God *the Father*" (1 Peter 1:2, italics added). When Jesus made a postresurrection appearance to doubting Thomas, Thomas worshipfully responded by addressing him as "my Lord and my God" (John 20:28). As well, the Father said to the Son, "Your throne, O God, will last for ever and ever" (Heb. 1:8a). In Acts 5:3–4, we are told that lying to the Holy Spirit is equivalent to lying to

God: Peter said, "Ananias, how is it that Satan has so filled your heart that you have *lied to the Holy Spirit* and have kept for yourself some of the money you received for the land? Didn't it belong to you before it was sold? And after it was sold, wasn't the money at your disposal? What made you think of doing such a thing? *You have not lied to men but to God"* (italics added).

Besides being called God, each of the three persons on different occasions is seen to possess the attributes of deity. For example:

- All three persons possess the attribute of *omnipresence* (that is, all three are everywhere-present): the Father (Jer. 23:23–24), the Son (Matt. 18:20; 28:20), and the Holy Spirit (Ps. 139:7).
- All three have the attribute of *omniscience* (all-knowing-ness): the Father (Rom. 11:33), the Son (Matt. 9:4), and the Holy Spirit (1 Cor. 2:10).
- All three have the attribute of *omnipotence* (that is, all three are all-powerful): the Father (1 Peter 1:5), the Son (Matt. 28:18), and the Holy Spirit (Rom. 15:19).
- *Holiness* is ascribed to each of the three persons: the Father (Rev. 15:4), the Son (Acts 3:14), and the Holy Spirit (John 16:7–14).
- *Eternity* is ascribed to each of the three persons: the Father (Ps. 90:2), the Son (Mic. 5:2; John 1:2; Rev. 1:8, 17), and the Holy Spirit (Heb. 9:14).
- And each of the three persons is individually described as *the truth*: the Father (John 7:28), the Son (Rev. 3:7), and the Holy Spirit (1 John 5:6).

In addition to having the attributes of deity, each of the three persons was involved in doing the *works* of deity. For example, all three were involved in the creation of the world: the Father (Gen. 2:7; Ps. 102:25), the Son (John 1:3; Col. 1:16; Heb. 1:2), and the Holy Spirit (Gen. 1:2; Job 33:4; Ps. 104:30).

A fact often overlooked in theological discussions is that all three persons of the Trinity were sovereignly involved in the Incarnation. In Luke 1:35 we find an angel informing Mary, "The Holy Spirit will come upon you, and the power of the Most High will overshadow you. So the holy one [Jesus Christ] to be born will be called the Son of God" (insert mine). Though the Holy Spirit was the primary agent through whom the Incarnation was brought about, we are told in Hebrews 10:5 that it was the Father who prepared a human body for Christ. Moreover, Jesus is said to have taken upon himself flesh and blood—as if it were an act of his own individual sovereign will (Heb. 2:14).

The three persons of the Trinity were also involved in Jesus' resurrection from the dead. God the Father is often said to have raised Christ from the dead (Acts 2:32; 13:30; Rom. 6:4; Eph. 1:19–20). But without diminishing the Father's key role in the resurrection, it is just as clear from Scripture that Jesus raised himself from the dead. Recall that in John 2:19 Jesus told some Jews who were looking for a divine sign, "Destroy this temple [my physical body], and I will raise it again in three days" (insert mine). Then, in John 10:17–18, Jesus said of his life: "I lay down my life—only to take it up again. No one takes it from me, but I lay it down of my own accord. I have authority to lay it down and authority to take it up again." The Holy Spirit was also involved in Christ's resurrection, for it was "through the Spirit of holiness" that Jesus was "declared with power to be the Son of God by his resurrection from the dead" (Rom. 1:4).

In view of all the above, it seems clear that within the triune Godhead, never is a single act performed by one person without the instant acquiescence of the other two. This is not to deny that each of the three persons has distinctive ministries unique to himself. But clearly, the three persons always act in harmonious unity in all the mighty works wrought by God throughout the universe.

Scriptural Indications for Three-in-Oneness

There are many scriptural indications for three-in-oneness in the Godhead. For example, when God was about to create man, he said: "Let *us* make man in *our* image, in *our* likeness, and let them rule over the fish of the sea and the birds of the air, over the livestock, over all the earth, and over all the creatures that move along the ground" (Gen. 1:26, italics added). Though scholars have offered different suggestions as to what may be meant by the plural pronouns in this verse,[9] there is good reason to interpret it as a reference to the Trinity.[10] (Note that the phrase "our image" in this verse is explained in verse 27 as "God's image.") Commenting on this verse, Bible scholar Gleason Archer notes that "the one true God subsists in three Persons, Persons who are able to confer with one another and carry their plans into action together—without ceasing to be one God."[11]

After Adam and Eve had been created and fell into sin in the Garden of Eden, God said: "The man has now become like *one of us*, knowing good and evil. He must not be allowed to reach out his hand and take also from the tree of life and eat, and live forever" (Gen. 3:22, italics added). Note that the phrase "like one of us" in this verse refers back to verse 5, "like God." As is true with Genesis 1:26, this verse supports plurality within the Godhead.

Later, when sinful human beings were attempting to erect the Tower of Babel, God said: "Come, let *us* go down and confuse their language so they will not understand each other" (Gen. 11:7, italics added). Again, plurality within the Godhead.

Many centuries later, Isaiah had a vision in the temple in which God commissioned him to service. God asked Isaiah, "Whom shall *I* send? And who will go for *us*?" And Isaiah said, "Here am I. Send me!" (Isa. 6:8, italics added).

We find the three persons of the Trinity manifested when Jesus was baptized by John the Baptist: "As soon as Jesus was baptized, he went up out of the water. At that moment heaven was opened, and he saw the Spirit of God descending like a dove and lighting on him. And a voice from heaven [the Father's voice] said, 'This is my Son, whom I love; with him I am well pleased'" (Matt. 3:16–17, insert mine).

Three years later, just prior to his crucifixion, Jesus spoke of the three persons of the Trinity in his Upper Room Discourse. Jesus said to the disciples: "And I will ask the Father, and he will give you another Counselor to be with you forever—the Spirit of truth. The world cannot accept him, because it neither sees him nor knows him. But you know him, for he lives with you and will be in you" (John 14:16–17). Jesus also said that "the Counselor, the Holy Spirit, whom the Father will send in my name, will teach you all things and will remind you of everything I have said to you" (14:26). Still again, Jesus said, "When the Counselor comes, whom I will send to you from the Father, the Spirit of truth who goes out from the Father, he will testify about me" (15:26).

After Jesus had resurrected from the dead, he again referred to all three persons of the Trinity. Jesus instructed the disciples: "Therefore go and make disciples of all nations, baptizing them in the name of the Father and of the Son and of the Holy Spirit" (Matt. 28:19). It is highly revealing that the word *name* is singular in the Greek, indicating that there is one God, but three distinct persons within the Godhead—the Father, the Son, and the Holy Spirit.[12] Theologian Robert Reymond draws our attention to the importance of this verse for the doctrine of the Trinity:

> Jesus does not say, (1) "into the names [plural] of the Father and of the Son and of the Holy Spirit," or what is its virtual equivalent, (2) "into the name of the Father, and into the name of the Son, and into the name of the Holy Spirit," as if we had to deal with three separate Beings. Nor does He say, (3) "into the name of the Father, Son, and Holy Spirit," (omitting the three recurring articles), as if "the Father, Son, and Holy Ghost" might be taken as merely three designations of a single person. What He does say is this: (4) "into the name [singular] of *the* Father, and of *the* Son, and of *the* Holy Spirit," first assert-

ing the unity of the three by combining them all within the bounds of the single Name, and then throwing into emphasis the distinctness of each by introducing them in turn with the repeated article.[13]

Still further evidence for God's three-in-oneness is found in Paul's benediction in his second letter to the Corinthians: "May the grace of the Lord Jesus Christ, and the love of God [the Father], and the fellowship of the Holy Spirit be with you all" (2 Cor. 13:14, insert mine). This verse shows the intimacy that each of the three persons has with the believer.

Trinitarian language virtually permeates the writings of Paul. Consider this brief excerpt from his first letter to the Thessalonians:

> We always thank *God* [the Father] for all of you, mentioning you in our prayers.
>
> We continually remember before our *God and Father* your work produced by faith, your labor prompted by love, and your endurance inspired by hope in our *Lord Jesus Christ.*
>
> For we know, brothers loved by *God* [the Father], that he has chosen you, because our gospel came to you not simply with words, but also with power, with *the Holy Spirit* and with deep conviction. You know how we lived among you for your sake.
>
> You became imitators of us and of *the Lord* [Jesus Christ]; in spite of severe suffering, you welcomed the message with the joy given by *the Holy Spirit.*
>
> And so you became a model to all the believers in Macedonia and Achaia.
>
> The *Lord's* [Christ's] message rang out from you not only in Macedonia and Achaia—your faith in *God* [the Father] has become known everywhere. Therefore we do not need to say anything about it, for they themselves report what kind of reception you gave us. They tell how you turned to *God* [the Father] from idols to serve the *living and true God* [the Father], and to wait for his *Son* from heaven, whom he raised from the dead—*Jesus,* who rescues us from the coming wrath. (1 Thess. 1:2–10, italics added, inserts mine)

It is interesting to observe that Paul and other New Testament writers felt no incongruity whatever between their doctrine of the Trinity and the Old Testament conception of God. "The New Testament writers certainly were not conscious of being 'setters forth of strange gods.' . . . The God of the Old Testament was their God, and their God was a Trinity, and their sense of the identity of the two was so complete that no question as to it was raised in their minds."[14] In other words, we do not find in the New Testament the birth of a new and novel concept of God. Indeed, "the doctrine of the Trinity does not appear in the New Testament in the making, but as already made."[15]

To sum up, we have seen that the doctrine of the Trinity is firmly based on (1) evidence that there is only one true God; (2) evidence that there are three persons who are God; and (3) scriptural indications for three-in-oneness within the Godhead. In view of this evidence, we may conclude that to deny belief in the Trinity is equivalent to denying belief in the God of the Bible.

Jesus: The Eternal Son of God

Perhaps no name or title of Christ has been so misunderstood as the title *Son of God*.[16] Some have taken this term to mean that Christ came into existence at a point in time and that he is in some way inferior to the Father. Some believe that since Christ is the Son of God, he cannot possibly be God in the same sense as the Father.

Such an understanding is based on a faulty conception of what "Son of . . ." meant among the ancients. Though the term *can* refer to "offspring of" in some contexts, it carries the more important meaning, "of the order of."[17] The phrase is often used this way in the Old Testament. For example, "sons of the prophets" (1 Kings 20:35) meant "of the order of prophets." "Sons of the singers" (Neh. 12:28 NASB) meant "of the order of singers." Likewise, the phrase "Son of God" means "of the order of God" and represents a claim to undiminished deity.

Ancient Semitics and Orientals used the phrase "Son of . . ." to indicate likeness or sameness of nature and equality of being.[18] Hence, when Jesus claimed to be the Son of God, his Jewish contemporaries fully understood that he was making a claim to be God in an unqualified sense. Benjamin B. Warfield affirms that, from the earliest days of Christianity, the phrase "Son of God" was understood to be fully equivalent to God.[19] This is why, when Jesus claimed to be the Son of God, the Jews insisted: "We have a law, and according to that law he [Christ] must die, because he claimed to be the Son of God" (John 19:7, insert mine). Recognizing that Jesus was identifying himself as God, the Jews wanted to put him to death for committing blasphemy (see Lev. 24:16).

Scripture indicates that Christ's Sonship is an *eternal* Sonship.[20] It is one thing to say that Jesus *became* the Son of God; it is another thing altogether to say that he was *always* the Son of God. We must recognize that if there was a time when the Son was not the Son, then, to be consistent, there was also a time when the Father was not the Father. If the first person's designation as "Father" is an eternal title, then the second person's designation as "Son" must be so regarded. Seen in this way, Christ's identity as the Son of God does not connote inferiority or subordination either of essence or position.

"Sonship" Prior to the Incarnation

Clear evidence for Christ's eternal Sonship is found in the fact that he is represented as already being the Son of God before his human birth in Bethlehem. Recall Jesus' discussion with Nicodemus in John 3, for instance, when he said: "For God so loved the world that he *gave* his one and only Son, that whoever believes in him shall not perish but have eternal life. For God did not *send* his Son *into* the world to condemn the world, but to save the world through him" (John 3:16–17, italics added). That Christ, as the Son of God, was *sent into* the world implies that he was the Son of God *before* the Incarnation.

This is also seen in John 11, where we find Jesus comforting Martha and Mary over the death of their brother Lazarus. Before Jesus brought Lazarus back to life, he said to Martha: "I am the resurrection and the life. He who believes in me will live, even though he dies; and whoever lives and believes in me will never die. Do you believe this?" (John 11:25–26). Martha responded: "Yes, Lord, I believe that you are the Christ, the Son of God, who was to come into the world" (v. 27). Lest Martha's words be misunderstood, we must emphasize that her statement reflects a sense of movement of the Son of God—*from* the realm of heaven and eternity *to* the realm of earth and time.

The Son of God in the Book of Proverbs

Chapter 30 in the Book of Proverbs was authored by a godly man named Agur. In the first four verses of this chapter, Agur reflects on man's inability to comprehend the infinite God. Because of this inability, he abases himself and humbly acknowledges his ignorance. He effectively communicates the idea that reverence of God is the beginning of true wisdom.

In verse 4, Agur's reflections are couched in terms of a series of questions. He asks:

> "Who has gone up to heaven and come down?
>   Who has gathered up the wind in the hollow of his hands?
> Who has wrapped up the waters in his cloak?
>   Who has established all the ends of the earth?
> What is his name, and the name of his son?
>   Tell me if you know!"

Many scholars—including renowned Old Testament scholars F. Delitzsch and A. R. Fausset—concede to the likelihood of this being an Old Testament reference to the first and second persons of the Trinity, the eternal Father and the eternal Son of God.[21] And it is highly significant that this portion of Scripture is not predictive prophecy speaking about a *future* Son of God. Rather, it speaks of God the Father and God the Son in *present-tense terms* during *Old Testament times*.

Obviously, the answer to each of the questions in verse four must be God. And the very fact that Agur asked about the name of God's Son seems to imply a recognition, by divine inspiration, of plurality within the Godhead.[22]

Further evidence for Christ's eternal Sonship is found in the fact that Hebrews 1:2 says God created the universe *through* his "Son"—implying that Christ was the Son of God *prior* to the Creation. Moreover, Christ *as the Son* is explicitly said to have existed "before all things" (Col. 1:17; cf. vv. 13–14). As well, Jesus, speaking as the Son of God (John 8:54–56), asserts his eternal preexistence before Abraham (v. 58).

Clearly, then, in view of all the above, the scriptural view is that Jesus is *eternally* the Son of God. Any attempt to relegate Christ to a position *less* than God simply because of his title "Son of God" is to woefully misunderstand what the term really meant among the ancients.

The Triune God and the Eternal Plan of Salvation

We shall discuss the triune God and the eternal plan of salvation in detail in chapter 7, "Christ the Savior." For now, however, it is important to grasp that before the world began—indeed, in eternity past—the triune God had already settled the issue of salvation for those who would trust in him in the space-time world. And each person of the Trinity *has been* and *continues to be* intimately involved in the outworking of this eternal plan (Rom. 8:29; Eph. 1:4; 1 Peter 1:19–20).

Scripture tells us that the Lamb of God "was slain from the creation of the world" (Rev. 13:8). And God "chose us in him before the creation of the world to be holy and blameless in his sight. In love he predestined us to be adopted as his sons through Jesus Christ, in accordance with his pleasure and will" (Eph. 1:4–5). Indeed, God promised eternal life to his people "before the beginning of time" (Titus 1:2). God has "saved us and called us to a holy life—not because of anything we have done but because of his own purpose and grace. This grace was given us in Christ Jesus before the beginning of time" (2 Tim. 1:9). Therefore, to the sheep of his pasture, Christ says: "Come, you who are blessed of My Father, inherit the kingdom prepared for you from the foundation of the world" (Matt. 25:34 NASB).

What God determined *before* time is being carried out *in* time. That which was eternally determined *before the ages* is being brought to fruition *in the ages*. For this reason, God's plan of salvation is called his "eternal purpose" (Eph. 3:11). And this eternal purpose is being carried out on earth, a seemingly insignificant planet when compared to the whole of God's glorious creation.

In view of the fact that the plan of salvation was formulated in eternity past and is worked out in human history, we must come to regard human history from the standpoint of eternity. A uniform plan, guided by God, has in the course of human history been unfolded—through Old and New Testament times and up to the present day—and will one day find its culmination when Christ comes again and sets up his glorious millennial kingdom (a 1000-year period on earth during which Christ will rule—Rev. 20). Following this, in the eternal state, we shall dwell in the unveiled presence of the triune God.

But we are getting ahead of ourselves. Our purpose in this book is to take a *backward* look, not a *forward* look, regarding Christ's role in the outworking of the eternal plan of salvation. More specifically, we will focus our attention on the life and times of the preincarnate Christ. Put another way, we shall focus our attention in this book on Christ before the manger.

2

The Preexistent, Eternal Christ

Only of Christ can it be said that his birth did not signal the beginning of his existence. Prior to his birth, he had existed for all eternity with the Father and the Holy Spirit. Jesus, with the Father and the Spirit, is everlastingly the living one.

Far, far before the manger, Christ created the universe in all its vastness, continually sustained it by his own intrinsic power, made many preincarnate appearances to Old Testament saints, helped his people in time of need, and much, much more. In fact, the scriptural testimony is that Christ was exceedingly active prior to his becoming a man in the Incarnation.

The doctrines of the preexistence and eternality of Christ are immeasurably important. Indeed, as popular theologian Charles C. Ryrie has pointed out, "if Christ came into existence at His birth, then no eternal Trinity exists. . . . If Christ was not preexistent then He could not be God, because, among other attributes, God is eternal. . . . If Christ was not preexistent then He lied, because He claimed to be. Then, the question arises, what else did He lie about?"[1]

In this chapter, I will focus on what the Old and New Testaments have to say about Christ's preexistence and eternality. The scriptural evidence in this regard is truly immense—far beyond what a single chapter can accommodate. For this reason, we shall focus our attention on only the more significant passages.

When Did Time Begin?

Related to the issue of the preexistence and eternality of Christ is this question: When did time begin? Scripture is not clear about the relationship between time and eternity. Some prefer to think of eternity as time—a succession of moments—without beginning or ending. However, there are indications in Scripture that time itself may be a created reality, a reality that began when God created the universe.

The Book of Hebrews contains some hints regarding the relationship between time and eternity. Hebrews 1:2 tells us that the Father "has spoken to us by his Son, whom he appointed heir of all things, and *through whom he made the universe*" (italics added). The last part of this verse is rendered more literally from the Greek, "through whom he made *the ages*." Likewise, Hebrews 11:3 tells us that "by faith we understand that *the universe* was formed at God's command" (italics added). This is more literally from the Greek, "By faith we understand that *the ages* were formed at God's command."

Scholars have grappled with what may be meant here by the term "ages." Lutheran scholar R. C. H. Lenski says the term means "not merely vast periods of time as mere time, but 'eons' with all that exists as well as all that transpires in them."[2] New Testament scholar F. F. Bruce says that "the whole created universe of space and time is meant."[3] From this verse, theologian John MacArthur concludes that "Jesus Christ is responsible for creating not only the physical earth but also time, space, force, action, and matter. The writer of Hebrews does not restrict Christ's creation to this earth; he shows us that Christ is the Creator of the entire universe and of existence itself. And Christ made it all without effort."[4]

Church father and philosopher Augustine (A.D. 354–430) held that the universe was not created in time, but that time itself was created along with the universe.[5] Reformed theologian Louis Berkhof agrees, and concludes: "It would not be correct to assume that time was already in existence when God created the world, and that He at some point in that existing time, called 'the beginning,' brought forth the universe. The world was created *with* time rather than *in* time. Back of the beginning mentioned in Genesis 1:1 lied a beginningless eternity."[6]

In view of the above, we may conclude that when the apostle John said, "In the beginning was the Word, and the Word was with God, and the Word was God" (John 1:1), the phrase *in the beginning* has specific reference to the beginning of time when the universe was created. When the time-space universe came into being, Christ the divine Word *was already existing* in a loving, intimate relationship with the Father and the Holy Spirit.

Having established this as a backdrop, let us now examine some specific passages of Scripture that clearly point to the preexistence and eternality of Christ.

The Testimony of John the Baptist

The Old Testament prophet Isaiah spoke of an individual who would prepare the way for the coming of the Messiah (Isa. 40:3). This prophecy was fulfilled seven hundred years later in the ministry of John the Baptist. John, who was born six months before Jesus was born, proclaimed, "I am the voice of one calling in the desert, 'Make straight the way for the Lord'" (John 1:23).

The Gospel of John tells us that God the Son had existed for all eternity in loving communion with God the Father (John 1:1). At the appointed time, Jesus "became flesh and made his dwelling among us" (v. 14a). This was in accord with the plan of salvation formulated by God in eternity past, which called for Jesus to take on a human nature and die on the cross for the sins of man (1 Peter 1:19–20).

After Jesus "became flesh," John the Baptist testified, "This is the one I meant when I said, 'A man who comes after me has surpassed me *because he was before me*" (John 1:30, italics added). This is an extremely significant statement by John. For it indicates that even though Christ in his humanity was born six months *after* John the Baptist, as the eternal Son of God he *preceded* John. "Christ's preexistence makes plain how one and the same person could come later than the Baptist and yet have come earlier than he; could be both his successor *and* his predecessor."[7]

F. F. Bruce notes that "the Coming One appeared later in history than John did, but he took precedence over John (the one whose way is being prepared is greater than his forerunner). His precedence over John, however, is expressed in exceptionally emphatic terms. John does not simply say [in the Greek] *pro mou en* ('he was before me') but *protos mou en* (literally 'he was first in respect of me'); that is to say, 'he had absolute primacy over me,' or better, as the New English Bible renders it, 'before I was born, he already was.'"[8]

The Testimony of Micah

Micah, a Judean who was one of the so-called minor prophets, was born in a little country village known as Moresheth in the southwest of Palestine (Mic. 1:1). His devotion to God is reflected in the meaning of his name, for Micah means "who is like God?"

Micah uttered his prophecies to the common people of Judah at a time when corruption was at an all-time high. Micah loathed social wrong and felt a special compassion for the poor (Mic. 7:2ff). He also loathed the hireling prophets whose words were anything *but* from God (3:5f). Most important, Micah's little book speaks of a coming Deliverer, a King who would redeem his people (7:7).

In Micah 5:2, we are told regarding the city of Bethlehem: "Though you are small among the clans of Judah, out of you will come for me one who will be ruler over Israel, *whose ori-*

gins are from of old, from ancient times" (italics added). This is clearly a prophecy of Christ and his approaching birth in Bethlehem. More important than his birthplace, however, is Micah's affirmation of Christ's eternal nature.[9]

Since the same Hebrew word that is translated "from of old" in Micah 5:2 is used in Habakkuk 1:12 to describe *God's* eternal nature (translated "from everlasting,"), we may conclude that Micah's use of the term points to *Christ's* eternal nature. Moreover, the phrase, "from ancient times," is literally "days of immeasurable time."[10] The terms convey "the strongest assertion of infinite duration of which the Hebrew language is capable."[11] Hence, these terms place Christ beyond time altogether. He is, along with the Father and the Holy Spirit, the eternal one—and his rule reaches back into eternity.

It is critical to understand what the Hebrew for "origins" means in the phrase, "whose origins are from old, from ancient times." It does not mean that Christ had an origin in the sense that he had a beginning. Rather, the Hebrew term literally means "goings out" or "goings forth." The last part of the verse could thus be rendered, "whose *goings out* are from of old, from ancient times." Old Testament scholar John A. Martin notes that these "goings out" probably refer to Christ's "victories in Creation, theophanies [preincarnate appearances], and providential dealings" in the universe.[12] Robert Reymond likewise relates Christ's "goings out" to the creation and sustenance of the universe.[13] Charles C. Ryrie says the phrase "refers primarily to Christ's preincarnate appearances as the Angel of the Lord, thus affirming the existence of Christ before His birth in Bethlehem."[14] Clearly, Micah 5:2 constitutes a powerful evidence for the preexistence and eternality of Christ.

The Testimony of Isaiah

The Book of Isaiah is one of the best-loved prophetic books in the Old Testament. The main reason for this is that it contains more references to the person and work of Jesus Christ than any other book in the Old Testament.

Isaiah is often referred to as "the messianic prophet"—and for good reason. He predicted the Messiah's virgin birth (Isa. 7:14), his deity and kingdom (9:1–7), his reign of righteousness (11:2–5), his suffering and death on the cross for the sins of man (52:13–53:12), and much more. No wonder the great composer Handel based so much of his musical masterpiece, "The Messiah," on the Book of Isaiah.

The authors of the New Testament quote from Isaiah quite often (twenty-one times). They obviously thought it was a very important book. Jesus thought it was important, too, for he inaugurated his public ministry with a quotation from Isaiah (Luke 4:17–21).

The person of the Messiah is described in detail in Isaiah 9:6–7. Pertinent to our study on the preexistence and eternality of Christ is the fact that the Messiah is called "Everlasting Father" in verse 6. This name has caused some confusion for Christians. In the Trinity, Jesus (the second person) is always distinguished from the Father (the first person). So why does Isaiah refer to Jesus the Messiah as "Everlasting Father"?

As we seek to interpret the meaning of this phrase, it is critical to keep in mind what other Scriptures have to say about the distinction between the Father and the Son. For example, the New Testament calls Jesus "the Son" over 200 times. Moreover, the Father is considered by Jesus as someone other than himself over 200 times in the New Testament. And over 50 times in the New Testament the Father and Son are seen to be distinct within the same verse (see, for example, Rom. 15:6; 2 Cor. 1:4; Gal. 1:1, 3; Phil. 2:10–11; 1 John 2:1; 2 John 3).[15]

Now, if the Father and the Son are distinct, then in what sense can Jesus be called "Everlasting Father"? "Everlasting Father" in this verse is better translated "Father of eternity." The words "Father of" in this context carry the meaning "possessor of eternity." *Father of eternity* is here used "in accordance with a custom usual in Hebrew and in Arabic, where he who possesses a thing is called the father of it. Thus, *the father of strength* means strong; *the father of knowledge*, intelligent; *the father of glory*, glorious."[16] Along these same lines, "the father of peace" means peaceful; "the father of compassion" means compassionate; and "the father of goodness" means good.[17] According to this common usage, the meaning of "Father of eternity" in Isaiah 9:6 is "eternal." Christ as the *Father of eternity* is an eternal being.[18] John A. Martin thus rightly concludes that the phrase *Everlasting Father* is simply "an idiom used to describe the Messiah's relationship to time, not His relationship to the other Members of the Trinity."[19]

Further support for this view is found in "the Targums"— simplified paraphrases of the Old Testament Scriptures utilized by the ancient Jews. It is highly revealing that the Targum of Isaiah renders Isaiah 9:6: "His name has been called from of old, Wonderful Counselor, Mighty God, *He who lives forever*, the Anointed One (or Messiah), in whose days peace shall increase upon us."[20] Clearly, the ancient Jews considered the phrase "Father of eternity" as indicating the eternality of the Messiah. There can be no doubt that this is the meaning Isaiah intended to communicate to his readers.

The Testimony of Jesus

Jesus often indicated his eternality to those around him. A good example of this is an occasion in which he found himself in a confrontation with a group of hostile Jews. Someone in the group had said to him: "Abraham died and so did the prophets, yet you say that if anyone keeps your word, he will never taste death. Are you greater than our father Abraham?" (John 8:52b–53a). Jesus responded: "Your father Abraham rejoiced at the thought of seeing my day; he saw it and was glad" (v. 56). The Jews mockingly replied: "You are not yet fifty years old and you have seen Abraham!" (v. 57). To which Jesus replied, "I tell you the truth, before Abraham was born, I am!" (v. 58).

The Jews immediately picked up stones with the intention of killing Jesus, for they recognized he was implicitly identifying himself as *Yahweh*—the "I AM WHO I AM" of Old Testament Scripture (see Exod. 3:14). They were acting on the prescribed penalty for blasphemy in Old Testament Law: death by stoning (Lev. 24:16).

We shall discuss the meaning of "Yahweh" in detail in chapter 9, "Christ and His Divine Names." At this early juncture, it is enough to know that the name *Yahweh* conveys the idea of *eternal self-existence*. *Yahweh* never came into being at a point in time, for he has always existed. He was never born. He will never die. He does not grow older, for he is beyond the realm of time altogether. To know *Yahweh* is to know the eternal one.

Besides implicitly identifying himself as *Yahweh*, Jesus consistently testified to his eternality in the many statements he made to people about his being "sent from God," or his having "come from above" to minister to God's people. Consider the following sampling of statements from Jesus as recorded in John's Gospel:

- "No one has ever gone into heaven except the one who came from heaven—the Son of Man" (3:13).
- "For the bread of God is he who comes down from heaven and gives life to the world" (6:33).
- "For I have come down from heaven not to do my will but to do the will of him who sent me" (6:38).
- "No one has seen the Father except the one who is from God; only he has seen the Father" (6:46).
- "I am the living bread that came down from heaven. If anyone eats of this bread, he will live forever. This bread is my flesh, which I will give for the life of the world" (6:51).
- "What if you see the Son of Man ascend to where he was before!" (6:62).

- But he continued, "You are from below; I am from above. You are of this world; I am not of this world" (8:23).
- Jesus said to them, "If God were your Father, you would love me, for I came from God and now am here. I have not come on my own; but he sent me" (8:42).
- "No, the Father himself loves you because you have loved me and have believed that I came from God. I came from the Father and entered the world; now I am leaving the world and going back to the Father" (16:27–28).

By such statements, Jesus clearly communicated to those around him that his human birth did not represent his actual beginnings. Indeed, he consistently startled his listeners with claims of deity and eternality.

Jesus Christ: Perfect Deity

In addition to Christ's preexistence and eternality, there are many other evidences in Scripture that Jesus Christ was (is) fully God. To complete our portrait of Christ as eternal God, we shall now examine some of these evidences (see also Appendix A).

Though most of the verses I shall examine in this section are in the context of Christ's three-year ministry, they are relevant to our study of Christ in his *preexistent* state since they describe his unchanging divine nature. In other words, the divine attributes Jesus so clearly displayed during his earthly ministry are the same divine attributes he has exercised for all eternity. We thus gain insights about the nature of Christ as he appeared to and interacted with Old Testament personalities by studying his nature as described in the New Testament.

Self-Existence

As the Creator of all things (John 1:3; Col. 1:16; Heb. 1:2), Christ himself must be *un*-created. Indeed, he is the uncaused First Cause. "If God exists endlessly," Charles C. Ryrie comments, "then He never came into existence nor was He ever caused to come into existence. He is endlessly self-existent."[21]

Colossians 1:17 tells us that Christ is "before all things, and in him all things hold together." Obviously, if Christ is "before all things," he does not depend on anyone or anything outside himself for his own existence. This theme is emphasized in John 5:26, where we are told that the Son has "life in himself" (see also John 1:4). How comforting to know that the one who bestows eternal life on us is the one who has life in himself!

Immutability

That Christ is immutable simply means that he—as God— is unchangeable, and thus unchanging. "This does not mean that He is immobile or inactive, but it does mean that He is never inconsistent or growing or developing."[22]

A key passage relating to the immutability of Christ is Hebrews 1:10–12, where the Father speaks of the Son's unchanging nature: "In the beginning, O Lord, you laid the foundations of the earth, and the heavens are the work of your hands. They will perish, but you remain; they will all wear out like a garment. You will roll them up like a robe; like a garment they will be changed. But you remain the same, and your years will never end."

Hebrews 1:10–12 is actually a quotation from Psalm 102:25– 27. It is highly revealing that the words in this psalm are addressed to *Yahweh* (God), but are directly applied to Jesus Christ in Hebrews 1:10–12, thus indicating Christ's full deity.

These verses teach that even when the present creation wears out like an old garment, Jesus will remain unchanged. The reference here is to "the transformation of the heavens and earth which will occur after the Millennium [Christ's future 1000-year rule on earth] and will introduce the eternal state (2 Peter 3:10–13). Yet even after those cataclysmic events the Son's years will never end."[23]

Christ's immutability is also affirmed in Hebrews 13:8, where we are told that "Jesus Christ is the same yesterday and today and forever." It is true that in the Incarnation, Christ took on a human nature. But orthodox scholars have always held that it is the *divine* nature of Christ that remains unchanged and is therefore immutable.[24]

Christ's immutability has great significance for us as Christians. Among other things, Christ's unchangeableness means that he will never fail in the promises he has made to us in his Word. Moreover, that Christ is immutable means that he will never alter his outlook on his hatred of sin and his love of righteousness. We as God's children will therefore never be able to coax Christ into going along with our compromises. He ever calls us to holiness.

Omnipresence

To say that Christ is omnipresent does not mean that Christ in his divine nature is diffused throughout space as if part of him is here and part of him is there. Rather, it means that Christ is everywhere-present with the totality of his being at all times (cf. Jer. 23:24).

How does Christ's omnipresence relate to his human body in the Incarnation? The fact that Christ is everywhere-present does not contradict the concept that he also has locality. "While living on earth, He also was omnipresent in His deity. At the present time, Christ is at the right hand of the Father (Mark 16:19; 1 Peter 3:22) although at the same time omnipresent."[25]

Christ's omnipresence is demonstrated in several ways in the New Testament. For example, one day Jesus saw a man by the name of Nathanael approaching, and Jesus said, "Here is a true Israelite, in whom there is nothing false." Nathanael responded, "How do you know me?" Jesus answered, "I saw you while you were still under the fig tree before Philip called you." Then Nathanael declared, "Rabbi, you are the Son of God; you are the King of Israel" (John 1:47–49). Though bodily removed from Nathanael and his situation at the fig tree, the omnipresent Lord was with him all the time.

Further evidence for Christ's omnipresence is found in the fact that he promised his disciples that "where two or three come together in my name, there am I with them" (Matt. 18:20). Obviously, there are people all over Planet Earth who gather in Christ's name. The only way he could be present with them all is if he is truly omnipresent.[26]

As well, after giving the disciples the Great Commission (to bring the gospel to all nations), Jesus assured them: "Surely I am with you always, to the very end of the age" (Matt. 28:20). Jesus could not have made this promise unless he possessed the attribute of omnipresence. With disciples taking the gospel all over the world, the only way Christ could be with them all at the same time would be if he was everywhere-present (see Eph. 1:23; 4:10; Col. 3:11).

How comforting to know that we will never escape the presence of our beloved Savior. Because of Christ's omnipresence, we can be confident of his real presence wherever we go. Like a good shepherd never leaves his sheep, so Christ our Good Shepherd never leaves us alone. He is with us always.

Omniscience

All those who came into close contact with Jesus seemed to sense that he was omniscient or all-knowing. The apostle John said that Jesus "did not need man's testimony about man, for he knew what was in a man" (John 2:25). Jesus' disciples said, "Now we can see that you know all things and that you do not even need to have anyone ask you questions. This makes us believe that you came from God" (16:30). After the resurrection, when Jesus asked Peter for the third time if Peter loved him, Peter responded: "Lord, you know all things; you know that I love you" (21:17).

Bible scholar Thomas Schultz has provided an excellent summary of the massive evidence for Christ's omniscience:

> First, He knows the inward thoughts and memories of man, an ability peculiar to God (1 Kings 8:39; Jeremiah 17:9–16). He saw the evil in the hearts of the scribes (Matthew 9:4); He knew

beforehand those who would reject Him (John 6:64) and those who would follow Him (John 10:14). He could read the hearts of every man and woman (Mark 2:8; John 1:48; 2:24, 25; 4:16–19; Acts 1:24; 1 Corinthians 4:5; Revelation 2:18–23). A mere human can no more than make an intelligent guess as to what is in the hearts and minds of others.

Second, Christ has a knowledge of other facts beyond the possible comprehension of any man. He knew just where the fish were in the water (Luke 5:4, 6; John 21:6–11), and He knew just which fish contained the coin (Matthew 17:27). He knew future events (John 11:11; 18:4), details that would be encountered (Matthew 21:2–4), and He knew that Lazarus had died (John 11:14).

Third, He possessed an inner knowledge of the Godhead showing the closest possible communion with God as well as perfect knowledge. He knows the Father as the Father knows Him (Matthew 11:27; John 7:29; 8:55; 10:15; 17:25).

The fourth and consummating teaching of Scripture along this line is that Christ knows all things (John 16:30; 21:17), and that in Him are hidden all the treasures of wisdom and knowledge (Colossians 2:3).[27]

Certainly a key evidence for Christ's omniscience is the fact that he hears and answers the prayers of his people. "When Jesus claimed for Himself the prerogative to hear and to answer the prayers of His disciples," New Testament scholar Robert Reymond suggests, "He was claiming omniscience. One who can hear the innumerable prayers of His disciples— offered to Him night and day, day in and day out throughout the centuries—keep each request infallibly related to its petitioner, and answer each one in accordance with the divine mind and will would need Himself to be omniscient."[28]

One of the great things about Christ's omniscience, insofar as Christians are concerned, is that he can never discover anything in our lives that will cause him to change his mind about our being in his family. When we trusted in him for salvation, he was fully aware of every sin we had ever committed and ever *would* commit in the future. "No talebearer can inform on us, no enemy can make an accusation stick; no forgotten skeleton can come tumbling out of some hidden closet to abash us and expose our past; no unsuspected weakness in our characters can come to light to turn God away from us, since He knew us utterly before we knew Him and called us to Himself in the full knowledge of everything that was against us."[29]

Omnipotence

Christ's omnipotence (the attribute of being *all-powerful*) is demonstrated in many ways in the New Testament. For example, Christ created the entire universe (John 1:3; Col. 1:16; Heb. 1:2). He sustains the universe by his own power (Col. 1:17; Heb. 1:3). During his earthly ministry, Christ exercised power over nature (Luke 8:25), over physical diseases (Mark 1:29–31), over demonic spirits (Mark 1:32–34), and over death by raising people from the dead (John 11:1–44). Moreover, Jesus' omnipotence was displayed in his own resurrection from the dead, for John 2:19 tells us that Christ *raised himself from the dead*. (This, of course, is not to deny the roles of the Father [Eph. 1:19–20] and the Holy Spirit [Rom. 1:4] in Christ's resurrection.) Clearly, Christ exercised powers that can only be described as omnipotence.

There are many practical ramifications regarding Christ's omnipotence. Not only does he have the power to fulfill all the promises he has made to us, but he has the power to see us securely into heaven without allowing us to fall away. As Jesus himself has said, "My sheep listen to my voice; I know them, and they follow me. I give them eternal life, and they shall never perish; *no one can snatch them out of my hand*" (John 10:27–28, italics added). Moreover, the same awesome power that raised Jesus from the dead will one day raise us from the dead. We may rest serenely in the knowledge that all is in the hands of our omnipotent Savior.

Sovereignty

Christ also possesses sovereignty that can only belong to God. Peter speaks of Christ presently at the right hand of God the Father, "with angels, authorities and powers in submission to him" (1 Peter 3:22). When Jesus comes again in glory, he will be adorned with a majestic robe, and on the thigh-section of the robe will be the words, "KING OF KINGS AND LORD OF LORDS" (Rev. 19:16)—a title indicating absolute sovereignty. Philippians 2:9–10 tells us that one day every knee in heaven and on earth and under the earth will bow in humble submission before Christ the Lord. And one day, all people will be judged before the King of kings (John 5:27; 1 Cor. 3:10–15; 2 Cor. 5:10–13; Rev. 20:11–15). These facts have caused Robert Reymond to comment:

> In claiming the authority to reveal the Father to whomever He chose (Matt. 11:27) and to give life to whomever He chose (John 5:21), in claiming both the prerogative and the power to call all men someday from their graves (5:28–29) and the authority to judge all men (John 5:22, 27), in claiming the authority to lay down His life and the authority to take it up again (John 10:18), in declaring he would return someday "in power and great glory" (Matt. 24:30), and in claiming that all authority in heaven and on earth had been given to Him by the Father (Matt. 28:18), Jesus was claiming, implicitly and explicitly, an absolute sovereignty and power over the universe. If any other man made such claims, we would rightly regard him as insane; but Jesus, because He is the divine Son, deserves men's adoration and praise.[30]

It should bring supreme peace to every believing soul to know that Christ the Lord is sovereign over the affairs of heaven and earth. No matter what punches life may throw us, and no matter how much we may fail to understand *why* certain things happen in life, the knowledge that Christ is in control is like an anchor that keeps us from going adrift in the ocean of earthly adversity.

Image of the Invisible God

Jesus is described by the apostle Paul as the "image of the invisible God" (Col. 1:15). In the present context, the Greek

word for image *(eikon)* indicates a *perfect* image. Theologian
Norman Geisler notes that the word *eikon* literally means "the
very substance or essential embodiment of something or
someone."[31] Hence, Colossians 1:15 indicates that Jesus is the
very substance or essence of God. Indeed, "to call Christ the
Eikon of God means He is the exact reproduction of God."[32]
God's nature and being "are perfectly revealed in him."[33] As
Jesus himself said, "Anyone who has seen me has seen the Father" (John 14:9b).

The Fullness of Deity in Bodily Form

Paul also tells us that "in Christ all the fullness of the Deity
lives in bodily form" (Col. 2:9). According to New Testament
scholar Joseph B. Lightfoot, the phrase "fullness of the deity"
means "the totality of the divine powers and attributes."[34]
Other scholars have noted that the phrase indicates the very
divine essence of God.[35] Theologian Benjamin B. Warfield
thus concludes that "the very deity of God, that which makes
God God, in all its completeness, has its permanent home in
our Lord, and that in a 'bodily fashion,' that is, it is in Him
clothed with a body."[36]

In Colossians 2:9 the "fullness of deity" refers to "the whole
glorious total of what God is, the supreme Nature in its infinite entirety."[37] This means that Christ in the Incarnation was
just as divine as the Father, and was in no sense *less* than God
as a result of taking on a human nature. Indeed, Paul is declaring in this verse that in the Son there dwells all the fullness of
absolute divinity; "they were no mere rays of divine glory
which gilded Him, lighting up His Person for a season and
with splendor not His own; but He was, and is, absolute and
perfect God."[38]

It is significant that the verb *lives* ("in Christ all the fullness
of the Deity *lives* in bodily form") is a present-tense verb, indicating continuing, durative action. The thought is that in
Christ the fullness of deity *permanently resides*. We might paraphrase the verse this way: "In him there is continuously and

permanently at home all the fullness of the Godhead in bodily fashion." Even today, Jesus in his glorified human body is the fullness of deity in bodily form. "The fullness of the Godhead ... dwells in the once mortal, now glorified body of Christ."[39]

The Exact Representation of God

Jesus is called the "radiance of God's glory and the exact representation of his being" in Hebrews 1:3. The word *radiance* is literally "effulgence" or "shining forth." The word indicates not a reflection but an outshining of resplendent light. It indicates a shining forth to the world of the very character, attributes, and essence of God in Jesus Christ (see John 1.14). Jesus is not just a reflection of the Father's glory; Jesus' glory is radiating from within his very being.

Interestingly, the phrase "exact representation" was used among the ancients of an engraving tool or a stamp, often in reference to the minting of coins. In common usage, however, it came to refer to the actual mark engraved or the impression made by the tool itself. The word thus indicates an "exact expression." In the present context, Jesus is portrayed as the absolute authentic representation of God's being (see John 14:9). The writer of Hebrews could not have affirmed Christ's deity in any stronger terms. Christ is "the 'exact representation of God's real being,' and all the essential characteristics of God are brought into clear focus in Him."[40] Indeed, "all that God is—not merely in His ways, but in His being—is expressed absolutely by the Son."[41]

To sum up, then, Christ in his essential being is self-existent, immutable, everywhere-present, all-knowing, all-powerful, and sovereign. In short, Christ is eternal God in an absolute, unqualified sense. In the next chapter, we shall examine how Christ—far before the manger—demonstrated his divine wisdom, power, and sovereignty by bringing the universe into being.

3

Christ the Creator

As a young shepherd, David must have spent many a night under the open sky as he led his sheep across vast fields of green. As he looked up to the starry heavens at night, waves of emotion must have swept through him as he contemplated how the Lord—his divine Shepherd—had created all of it. On one such night, David penned Psalm 19. Listen to his words:

> The heavens declare the glory of God;
>   the skies proclaim the work of his hands.
> Day after day they pour forth speech;
>   night after night they display knowledge.
> There is no speech or language
>   where their voice is not heard.
> Their voice goes out into all the earth,
>   their words to the ends of the world. [vv. 1–4]

David considered the magnificence of stellar space a universal testimony to the glory of the Creator. And this glory is visible to people all over the world. We, too, catch a glimpse of the Creator's greatness by observing the greatness of what he has made.

The Majesty of the Stellar Universe

Only about four thousand stars are visible to the human eye without a telescope. However, as creation scientist Henry M. Morris tells us, the creation's true vastness becomes evident when it is realized that with the giant telescopes now available, astronomers have statistically estimated that there are about 10^{25} stars (that is, 10 million billion billion) in the known universe. "One can also calculate that this is about the number of grains of sand in the world. In any case, it is not possible to count either number. If one could count even as many as twenty numbers per second, it would still take him at least 100 million billion years to count to 10^{25}."[1]

And who but God knows how many stars exist beyond the reach of our finite telescopes? Morris comments, "Since God is infinite, and He is the Creator of the universe, there is no reason to assume that either our telescopes or our relativistic mathematics have penetrated to its boundaries."[2]

What is truly fascinating is that even though the stars are innumerable from man's perspective, God knows precisely how many exist and has even assigned a name to each one of them (Ps. 147:4; Isa. 40:26). In the same way that Adam named animals based upon the characteristics of those animals (Gen. 2:19–20), so God in his infinite wisdom named each star according to its particular characteristics. "This can only mean that, despite the immensity of their number, each has been created for a particular purpose, with distinctive characteristics and attributes of its own, to be discovered or revealed in God's good time."[3]

The grandeur of the created universe is evident not only in the number of stars, but in their incredible distances from each other. Theologian John MacArthur did some scientific digging and discovered the following facts about the vastness of the universe:

> If you could bore a hole in the sun and somehow put in 1.2 million earths, you would still have room for 4.3 million moons.

The sun is 865,000 miles in diameter and 93 million miles away from earth. Our next nearest star is Alpha Centauri, and it is five times larger than our sun. The moon is only 211,453 miles away, and you could walk to it in twenty-seven years. A ray of light travels at 186,000 miles per second, so a beam of light would reach the moon in only one-and-a-half seconds. If we could travel at that speed, we would reach Venus in two minutes and eighteen seconds because it's only 26 million miles away. After four-and-one-half minutes we would have passed Mercury, which is 50 million miles away. We could travel to Mars in four minutes and twenty-one seconds because it's only 34 million miles away. The next stop would be Jupiter—367 million miles away—and it would take us thirty-five minutes. Saturn is twice as far as Jupiter—790 million miles—and it would take one hour and eleven seconds. Eventually we would pass Uranus, Neptune, and finally Pluto—2.7 billion miles away. Having gotten that far, we still haven't left our solar system, which moves in a multimillion-mile orbit through endless space. The nearest star is ten times further than the boundaries of our solar system—20 billion miles away. The North Star is 400 hundred billion miles away, but that still isn't very far compared with known space. The star called Betelgeuse is 880 quadrillion miles from us and has a diameter of 250 million miles, which is greater than the earth's orbit. . . . Where did it all come from? Who made it? It can't be an accident. Someone made it, and the Bible tells us it was Jesus Christ.[4]

Earth: A Center of Divine Activity

In view of the sheer vastness of the stellar universe, it is truly amazing that God sovereignly chose our tiny planet as a center of divine activity. Relatively speaking, the earth is but an astronomical atom among the whirling constellations, only a tiny speck of dust among the ocean of stars and planets in the universe. To the naturalistic astronomer, the earth is but one of many planets in our small solar system, all of which are in orbit around the sun. But Planet Earth is nevertheless the center of God's work of salvation in the universe. "On *it* the Highest presents Himself in solemn covenants and Divine appearances; on *it* the Son of God became man; on *it* stood the cross of the Redeemer of the world; and on *it*—though indeed on the new earth, yet still on the earth—will be at last the throne of God and the Lamb (Rev. 21:1, 2; 22:3)."[5]

The centrality of the earth is also evident in the creation account, for God created the earth *before* he created the rest of the planets and stars. Bible scholar John Whitcomb thus asks this penetrating question: "Why did God create the sun, moon, and stars on the fourth day rather than the first day? One possible explanation is that in this way God has emphasized the supreme importance of the earth among all astronomical bodies in the universe. In spite of its comparative smallness of size, even among the nine planets, to say nothing of the stars themselves, it is nonetheless absolutely unique in God's eternal purposes."[6]

The Triune God Prior to the Creation

In one moment there was no physical substance anywhere. In the next moment the stars and planets sprang into existence at God's command. Theologians have called this event *creatio ex nihilo*—which means "creation out of nothing." The question that comes to the inquisitive mind is, What was it like among the three persons in the Godhead *prior* to the creation of the universe?

We have already briefly touched on this issue in chapter 1, where we noted the incredibly rich love that existed among the persons of the Trinity in eternity past. Beyond this, theologians have suggested that prior to the moment of creation, God existed in self-sufficient and majestic fellowship. Indeed, "within the fundamental unity of His Godhead there exists a Trinity of Persons; He contains within Himself three centers of personal activity, each capable of being denoted by personal pronouns. This means that there is an incomprehensible richness in the inner life of God."[7] Passages such as John 17:24 indicate that the persons of the Trinity enjoyed intimate, unbroken fellowship in eternity past—a fellowship that was immeasurably fulfilling to each of them.

Having existed in sovereign self-sufficiency and love for all eternity past, the triune God sovereignly and eternally determined to create and project into being that which was not himself and yet which was utterly dependent on him for its continuing existence.[8] We must emphasize that God's production of the universe was not dependent in any way on an inherent necessity or intrinsic need in the divine being. Indeed, the triune God would have remained sovereignly self-sufficient and self-fulfilled for all eternity had he *not* created the universe. That he *did* create it was simply an outworking of his sovereign, loving will.

The Roles of the Father, Son, and Holy Spirit

Though this chapter focuses on Christ's role as the Creator, I do not want to give the impression that the other persons in the Trinity were uninvolved in the work of creation. The Father, the Son, *and* the Holy Spirit were each intimately involved in bringing the universe into being.

Many Old Testament references to the creation attribute it simply to "God," rather than to the individual persons of the Father, Son, or Holy Spirit (for example, Gen. 1:1; Ps. 96:5; Isa. 37:16; 44:24; 45:12; Jer. 10:11–12). Other passages—in both the Old and New Testaments—relate the creation specifically to the *Father* (Ps. 102:25; 1 Cor. 8:6), to the *Son* (Col. 1:16; Heb. 1:2; John 1:3), or to the *Holy Spirit* (Job 26:13; 33:4; Ps. 104:30; Isa. 40:12–13).

How do we put all these passages together into a coherent whole? Theologians have attempted to answer this question in various ways. Millard Erickson, for example, suggests that creation is "from" the Father, "through" the Son, and "by" the Holy Spirit.[9] Theologian Louis Berkhof suggests that "all things are at once *out of* the Father, *through* the Son, and *in* the Holy Spirit."[10] A passage that has bearing on this issue is 1 Corinthians 8:6, which describes the Father as the one "from whom all things came" and the Son as the one "through whom all things came."

Based on this and other passages, many have concluded that while the Father may be considered Creator in a broad, general sense, the Son is the *agent* or *mediating cause* of creation. *Through* the Son, all things came into being. Creation is said to be "in" the Holy Spirit in the sense that the *life* of creation is found in the Holy Spirit.

Though breaking down the creative roles of the persons of the Trinity may be helpful in some ways, we must be careful not to make these distinctions absolute. For example, though the Holy Spirit's role may have involved the bestowing of life, we are told elsewhere in Scripture that life is *in Christ* (John 1:4). Moreover, we must be careful to avoid thinking that the Son's role as a mediating agent ("through whom" the universe came into being) means that the Son had a lesser role than the Father. Indeed, the same Greek word for "through" [*diá*] that is used of Christ's work of creation is used elsewhere in Scripture of the Father's work of creation (Rom. 11:36; Heb. 2:10).

Whatever one concludes about the roles of each divine person in the work of creation, the New Testament is absolutely clear that the Son's role was not secondary but *primary*. The Son's role as Creator is at the very heart of New Testament revelation. This will become abundantly clear as we examine John 1:3, Colossians 1:16, and Hebrews 1:2.

The significance of the work of creation as ascribed to Christ is that it reveals his divine nature. "There is no doubt that the Old Testament presents God alone as Creator of the universe (Gen. 1, Isa. 40, Ps. 8). And when the disciples of Christ declare Jesus to be the one through whom all things were created, the conclusion that they were thereby attributing deity to him is unavoidable."[11]

John 1:3—In the Beginning

John's Gospel tells us, "In the beginning was the Word, and the Word was with God, and the Word was God. He was with

God in the beginning. Through him all things were made; without him nothing was made that has been made" (John 1:1–3).

How John must have exulted as he walked by Jesus' side, knowing that next to him stood the Creator of the universe in all of its vastness! Surely he must have marveled at how the stars above him were the handiwork of his friend, companion, and Savior, Jesus Christ. No wonder John had such a worshipful attitude toward Jesus (John 1:14; 2:11; 20:30–31).

Notice that John states Christ's creative work both positively and negatively: *positively*, "through him all things were made"; *negatively*, "without him nothing was made that has been made" (John 1:3). That John states this truth both positively and negatively is significant, for John wanted the reader to fully grasp that Christ himself is the sovereign Creator of all things.

Let us examine the positive statement first: "through him all things were made." The Greek word for "through" is *diá*, a preposition that indicates that Christ is the agent or mediating Cause of "all things"—that is, Christ is the Cause of every infinite detail of creation. This same word is used elsewhere of Christ's role as Creator of the universe (1 Cor. 8:6; Col. 1:16; Heb. 1:2). However, as noted earlier, the New Testament also states that the world came into being through [*diá*] God (Rom. 11:36), specifically through [*diá*] the *Father* (Heb. 2:10). Hence, the word cannot be taken to indicate a secondary, lesser role.

It is with this fact in mind that Bible expositor R. C. H. Lenski affirms that our passage must not be read as though Christ "was a mere tool or instrument. The act of creation . . . is ascribed to the three persons of the Godhead and thus to the Son as well as to the Father."[12] Indeed, "the existence of all things is due to the Logos [Christ], not, indeed, apart from the other persons of the Godhead but in conjunction with them."[13]

To drive his point home, John then states the same truth negatively: "without him nothing was made that has been made." No matter where one looks, even with the most pow-

erful of telescopes, one will never discover anything anywhere that was *not* created by Christ.

It is interesting that both John's Gospel and Genesis begin
with the words, "In the beginning . . ." As we examine the
Genesis account of creation, we see that it was "Elohim" who
brought the universe into being: "In the beginning God *[Elo-
him]* created the heavens and the earth" (Gen. 1:1). The name
Elohim is rich with meaning. It emphasizes God's might and
sovereignty (Gen. 24:3; Isa. 37:16; 54:5); his majesty and glory
(Isa. 40:28; 65:16); his role as the Savior God (Gen. 17:8; 26:24;
28:13); his intimacy with his people (Gen. 48:15; Ps. 4:1; Jer.
23:23), and his role as Judge (Pss. 50:6; 58:11; 75:7).

We know from other passages of Scripture that the name
Elohim can be used explicitly of Christ alone (Isa. 9:6). But in
many passages we are not given any indication as to which
of the three divine persons is meant by the name. Unless the
context of any given passage explicitly limits the usage of
the word *Elohim* to the Father or the Holy Spirit or Christ,
the conclusion should be reached that the triune God—including Christ, the second person—is meant.[14] Seen in this
light, the Genesis account of creation clearly includes the
work of Christ, the second person, and is in perfect harmony
with John 1:3 and other passages that speak of Christ as the
Creator.

Based on a survey of key passages, it seems clear that when
Christ did the work of creation, he did so in an instantaneous
fashion. Psalm 33 tells us, "By the word of the Lord were the
heavens made; and all the host of them by the breath of his
mouth. . . . for he spake, and it was done; he commanded, and
it stood fast" (vv. 6, 9 kjv; cf. Gen. 1:3, 6, 9, 14, 20, 24). Hebrews
11:3 likewise tells us that "the universe was formed at God's
command." John Whitcomb comments that "it is quite impossible to imagine a time interval in the transition from nonexist-
ence to existence! 'And God said, Let there be light: and there
was light' (Gen. 1:3). At one moment there was no light; the
next moment there was!"[15]

Colossians 1:16—Christ the Creator of All Things

In keeping with John's testimony, the apostle Paul affirms that by Christ "all things were created: things in heaven and on earth, visible and invisible, whether thrones or powers or rulers or authorities; all things were created by him and for him. He is before all things, and in him all things hold together" (Col. 1:16–17).

The little phrase "all things" means that Christ created the whole universe of things. "Every form of matter and life owes its origin to the Son of God, no matter in what sphere it may be found, or with what qualities it may be invested. . . . Christ's creative work was no local or limited operation; it was not bounded by this little orb [earth]."[16] Everything—whether simple or complex, visible or invisible, heavenly or earthly, immanent or transcendent—is the product of Christ.

It is highly revealing that Paul says that Christ created "thrones," "powers," "rulers," and "authorities." In the rabbinic (Jewish) thought of the first century, these words were used to describe different orders of angels (cf. Rom. 8:38; Eph. 1:21; 3:10; 6:12; Col. 2:10, 15; Titus 3:1). Apparently, there was a heresy flourishing in Colossae (to whom Paul wrote "Colossians") that involved the worship of angels. In the process of worshiping angels, Christ had been degraded. So, to correct this grave error, Paul emphasizes in this verse that Christ is the one who created all things—including all the angels—and hence, he is supreme and is alone worthy to be worshiped.

Paul also states of Christ that "all things were created by him and *for him*." The universe was created *for* Christ's glory; *for* such purposes as he sovereignly designed.[17] Indeed, "the universe was built solely by the Creator to be his own property; to be the theatre on which he could accomplish his purposes, and display his perfections."[18] Moreover, creation is "for" Christ in the sense that he is the end for which all things exist, the goal toward whom all things were intended to move. "They are meant to serve His will, to contribute to His glory. . . . Their whole being, willingly or unwillingly, moves to Him;

whether, as His blissful servants, they shall be as it were His throne; or as His stricken enemies, His footstool."[19]

Hebrews 1:2—The Supremacy of Christ

The writer of Hebrews tells us, "In the past God spoke to our forefathers through the prophets at many times and in various ways, but in these last days he has spoken to us by his Son, whom he appointed heir of all things, and through whom he made the universe" (Heb. 1:1–2).

One of the goals of the writer of Hebrews was to demonstrate the superiority of the New Covenant (as set forth in the New Testament) over the Old Covenant (as set forth in the Old Testament).[20] To accomplish this, the author throughout the book presents a series of comparisons between the Old and New covenants and between Jesus Christ and the prophets.

In our passage, we are told that in the past God spoke through his prophets. But now, all prior revelation is superseded by the greater revelation that has come through Jesus Christ (Heb. 1:1–3). One way Jesus is superior to the prophets is that *he* is the Creator of the universe whereas *they* are mere creatures. Therefore, the revelation that Christ brings is more important than the revelation brought by the prophets.

In the middle of verse two, we are told that Christ is the "heir of all things." This is as it should be, since Christ is also the maker of all things. Since Christ is the Creator, all in the universe is his by divine right.

In our discussion in chapter 2 regarding the question of when time was created, we noted that the phrase in Hebrews 1:2, "through whom he made *the universe*," is more literally rendered from the Greek, "through whom he made *the ages*." It is not necessary to repeat this earlier material. It is enough to recall here that Jesus was responsible for creating not only the physical universe but also time itself. The entirety of the space-time universe was brought into being at Christ's sovereign command.

Hebrews 1:10—The Work of Christ's Hands

Psalm 102:25 says of *Yahweh:* "In the beginning you laid the foundations of the earth, and the heavens are the work of your hands." As we noted in chapter 2, the writer of Hebrews directly applies this verse to Jesus Christ (Heb. 1:10). Here we can do no better than to quote Robert Reymond, who in his book *Jesus, Divine Messiah: The Old Testament Witness,* comments:

> We have to acknowledge that, apart from the use to which it is put in Hebrews 1, we probably would not have been quickly drawn to this psalm and to this particular passage in order to find a direct allusion to the divine Messiah. But the writer of Hebrews having done so, we not only can see immediately his rationale for doing so, but are also instructed by his method regarding the correct way to read and to interpret the Old Testament. What he ascribes to Christ by applying these verses in Psalm 102 to Jesus accords perfectly with what Paul (Col. 1:16–17) and John (John 1:3, 10–11) teach elsewhere; and here he simply affirms what he himself had earlier affirmed in Hebrews 1:2: ". . . through whom [the Son] He made the universe." The Christian is thus reminded that the Old Testament Creator is the Son of God who acted as the Father's agent in creation. . . . We can only guess how many other such references there are to the divine Messiah in the Old Testament corpus.[21]

Certainly there are other passages in the New Testament that speak of Christ as the Creator of the universe.[22] But the above passages more than adequately demonstrate the centrality of Christ's role in the Creation, and that it is to him that we owe our very existence.

Bowing Before Christ the Creator

Psalm 19:1 tells us that "the heavens declare the glory of God." Romans 1:20 likewise says, "For since the creation of the world God's invisible qualities—his eternal power and divine nature—have been clearly seen, being understood from what has been made, so that men are without excuse."

There can be no question that Jesus Christ is clearly revealed in the majesty of creation. Jesus is the Creator (John 1:3; Col. 1:16; Heb. 1:2), and his glory is seen in what he has made. As Henry Morris observes, "while we may wonder at the divine function commissioned by God for each individual star out of the almost infinitely great number of stars in the universe, one major purpose of all of them is certainly that of praising their Creator."[23]

David pondered, "When I consider your heavens, the work of your fingers, the moon and the stars, which you have set in place, what is man that you are mindful of him?" (Ps. 8:3–4). As David beheld the greatness of God's creation, he sensed his own smallness and insignificance. In short, David was humbled. It should humble every thoughtful person to ponder the greatness of Christ the Creator.

Scripture is resoundingly clear about the attitude that God desires human beings to have toward him. Indeed, they are to recognize that they are creatures who are responsible to him, their Creator. As the psalmist says, "Know that the LORD is God. It is he who made us, and we are his; we are his people, the sheep of his pasture" (Ps. 100:3).

This recognition of creaturehood should, like David of old, lead to humility and a worshipful attitude toward God. Again, it is the psalmist who tells us: "Come, let us bow down in worship, let us kneel before the LORD our Maker; for he is our God and we are the people of his pasture, the flock under his care" (Ps. 95:6–7).

In the beginning of this chapter, we touched on the magnificence of the stellar universe that Christ himself created. But as glorious as the stellar universe is, it is dim in comparison to the glory of the divine abode. Indeed, "the light in which He dwells is superior to all things visible; it is something other than the radiance of all suns and stars. It is not to be beheld by earthly eyes; it is 'unapproachable' (1 Tim. 6:16), far removed from all things this side (2 Cor. 12:4). Only the angels in heaven can behold it (Matt. 18:10); only the spirits of the perfected in the eternal light (Matt. 5:8; 1 John 3:2; Rev. 22:4); only the pure and holy, even as He Himself is pure (1 John 3:2, 3)."[24]

One day, we shall dwell with Christ face to face in his unveiled, glorious presence. Even now, Christ is preparing an eternal, glorious dwelling place for us (John 14:1–3). If the present created universe is any indication of what Christ can do, this eternal dwelling place must be truly astounding.

4

Christ the Preserver

When we say that Christ is the Preserver of the universe, we mean that everything in the universe owes the continuation of its existence to his sustaining power and will. Jesus personally monitors and sustains the movements and developments of the entire universe. Indeed, the creation in all of its vastness "hangs on the arm of Jesus," so to speak.

From a theological perspective, preservation is "that omnipotent energy of God by which all created things, animate and inanimate, are upheld in existence with all the properties and powers with which He has endowed them."[1] This means that without Christ's preserving and sustaining activities, the entire universe would simply collapse into chaos. Were the divine providence withheld, the created world and all existence would spin utterly out of control.

The flip side of this truth is that there is no part of God's creation that is self-sufficient. Some people tend to think that creation marked the end of God's "work." They suppose that following the creation, all things have remained in existence simply by virtue of some innate power. Scripture is clear, however, that the origination *and* continuation of all things are a matter of divine will and activity, not by virtue of some innate power in the creation itself. God alone is absolutely independent and self-existent.

What would our universe be like, especially as related to human existence on earth, if Christ were not its Preserver? John MacArthur offers these insights:

> Consider what would happen if things changed. The sun has a surface temperature of twelve thousand degrees Fahrenheit. If it were any closer to earth, we'd burn; and if it were any further, we'd freeze. Our globe is tilted on an exact angle of 23 degrees, which enables us to have four seasons. If it weren't tilted, vapors from the ocean would move north and south, eventually piling up monstrous continents of ice. If the moon did not remain a specific distance from the earth, the ocean tide would completely inundate the land twice a day. If the ocean floor merely slipped a few feet deeper, the carbon dioxide and oxygen balance in the earth's atmosphere would be completely upset, and no vegetable or animal life could exist on earth. If our atmosphere suddenly thinned out, the meteors that now harmlessly burn up when they hit our atmosphere would constantly bombard us.[2]

How does the universe stay in this kind of incredibly delicate balance? It is all due to the moment-by-moment preserving and sustaining activities of Jesus Christ. Jesus is not like the distant, spectator God of the deists who created the world and left it to its own like a watchmaker manufactures a watch and then lets it go on ticking on its own. "The reason the universe is a cosmos and not chaos—an ordered and reliable system instead of an erratic and unpredictable muddle—is the upholding power of Jesus Christ."[3]

The Triune God and Preservation

Many of the hundreds of Scripture passages that deal with preservation and providence involve the triune God and not any one person in the Trinity. In the Old Testament, *Yahweh* and *Elohim* are the names frequently associated with the preserving work of God. And, as we noted in chapter 3, unless these names are related to a specific person in the Trinity, they should be taken as a reference to the triune God.[4] Of course, as the work of the triune God, preservation and providence is a work also of Christ. In fact, *all* that is said of the triune God—*Yahweh* or *Elohim*—may rightly be said of Christ as well.[5]

A quick perusal of Scripture indicates that the triune God sustains human life (Deut. 30:20; Ps. 63:8; Dan. 5:23), animal life (Job 12:7–10), and the stellar heavens (Neh. 9:6; Ps. 148). God bestows rain upon the earth (Job 5:10), provides food for his creatures (Pss. 104:27; 145:15), quenches their thirst (Ps. 107:9), sustains people in old age (Ruth 4:15; Isa. 46:4), and provides for their clothing needs (Neh. 9:21).

God sustains his people when they are sick (Ps. 41:3), gives enduring strength to them (Ps. 89:21), and provides special sustenance to the fatherless and widows (Ps. 146:9). God protects his people from their enemies, from harm, and destruction (Ps. 91), provides help in time of need (Deut. 33:25–28), and rescues them when it seems there is no chance of deliverance (Exod. 14:29–30). In short, God's preserving and sustaining activities touch virtually every conceivable aspect of existence.

Christ and Preservation

Despite the fact that the triune God is involved in the work of preservation and providence, there is scriptural evidence that Jesus—the second person of the Trinity—is specifically and uniquely active in the work of preservation. Theologian John F. Walvoord, in his excellent book *Jesus Christ Our Lord*, notes that there are at least three evidences for this in Old Testament Scripture:

> First, the work of the Angel of Jehovah [the preincarnate Christ] . . . presents monumental proof that the Son of God preserved and guided Israel. Second, the various references to Jehovah as the Shepherd of Israel may be taken as specific references to

Christ (cf. Gen. 49:24; Ps. 23:1; 80:1; Isa. 40:11; Jer. 31:10; Ezek. 34:11–12, 23; 37:24). Although these references contextually could refer to God as a Trinity, the fact that Christ is specifically the Good Shepherd in John 10 would give some justification for this identification. As the Good Shepherd, He died for His sheep as prophesied in Psalm 22; as the Great Shepherd (Heb. 13:20), He fulfills Psalm 23; as the Chief Shepherd (1 Peter 5:4), He will come to reign as the King of glory (Ps. 24). Third, the language of Isaiah 63:9 specifically refers to the Son of God under the title "the angel of his presence": "The angel of his presence saved them: in his love and in his pity he redeemed them; and he bare them, and carried them all the days of old."[6]

This reference to "the angel of his presence" in Isaiah 63:9 is especially relevant to our study, for many scholars agree with Walvoord that this is in fact a reference to the preincarnate Christ.[7] It was *Christ himself* who "bare" the Israelites and "carried them all the days of old." The phrase, "all the days of old," indicates that Christ was involved in sustaining the Israelites from the very beginning of Israel's history.

I shall discuss in some detail Christ's ministry as Angel of the Lord in chapter 5, and his ministry as Shepherd of his people in chapter 6. But besides these evidences for Christ's sustaining activities, there are also several key passages in the New Testament that specifically relate the work of preservation to Jesus Christ. It is to these passages that we now turn our attention.

Colossians 1:17—In Christ All Things Hold Together

We noted in chapter 3 that Colossians 1:16 is a key text regarding Christ as the *Creator* of the universe: "For by him all things were created: things in heaven and on earth, visible and invisible, whether thrones or powers or rulers or authorities; all things were created by him and for him." In verse 17, we are told that Christ is the *Preserver* of the universe: "He is before all things, and in him all things hold together." These verses clearly show that the Creator himself sustains that which he sovereignly brought into being.

When the apostle Paul said that Christ is "before all things," the word *before* primarily has reference to the fact that Christ existed before all things in point of time. "Priority of existence belongs to the great FIRST Cause. He who made all necessarily existed before all. Prior to His creative work, He had filled the unmeasured periods of an unbeginning eternity. Matter is not eternal. . . . He pre-existed it, and called it into being."[8]

Some scholars find significance in the fact that a present tense is used in the phrase "he *is* before all things." Were Christ merely preexistent, one might say that Christ "*was* before all things." The present tense seems to indicate eternal, unending existence. The sense of the phrase is, "he eternally existed before all things."

Paul then makes an astounding statement: "In him all things hold together." Athanasius, early church father and champion of orthodoxy (A.D. 296–373), explained the gist of this verse by suggesting that Christ

> spreads His power over all things everywhere, enlightening things seen and unseen, holding and binding all together in Himself. Nothing is left empty of His presence, but to all things and through all, severally and collectively, He is the giver and sustainer of life. . . . He holds the universe in tune together. He it is who, binding all with each, and ordering all things by His will and pleasure, produces the perfect unity of nature and the harmonious reign of law.[9]

Truly, Christ's powerful arm upholds the universe in all of its grandeur. If he were to withdraw his sustaining power for even just a moment, all things would collapse into chaos. Without denying the validity and use of "secondary causes" (such as the law of gravity,[10] which he himself ordained), it is Christ who maintains the universe in continuous stability. "His great empire depends upon Him in all its provinces— life, mind, sensation, and matter; atoms beneath us to which geology has not descended, and stars beyond us to which astronomy has never penetrated."[11] Indeed, "the immaterial bonds which hold together the atom as well as the starry heavens are traced in this passage to the power and activity of the Son of God."[12]

Hebrews 1:3—Christ the Sustainer

As was true in Colossians, so in Hebrews we find a verse regarding Christ as the Creator (Heb. 1:2—"He made the universe") immediately followed by a verse pointing to Christ as the Preserver and Sustainer of the universe: "The Son is the radiance of God's glory and the exact representation of his being, *sustaining all things by his powerful word*" (Heb. 1:3a, italics added).

The word *sustaining* in this verse is rich with meaning. It doesn't refer to a mere passive support—like an Atlas supporting the weight of the world in his hands. Nor does the word merely indicate the idea of *maintenance*. Rather, the word carries the idea of *movement toward a final goal*.[13] In other words, Christ "carries all things forward on their appointed course."[14] The word in this context "expresses that 'bearing' which includes movement, progress, towards an end."[15] Hence, taking verses 16 and 17 together, the author of Hebrews "pictures the Son as in the first instance active in creation and then as continuing his interest in the world he loves and bearing it onward towards the fulfillment of the divine plan."[16]

It is significant that the word *sustaining* here is in the present tense. This indicates continuous action on the part of the Son of God. Everything in the universe is preserved and sustained moment by moment by the power of Jesus Christ.

To grasp the full significance of Christ's sustaining activities, it is important to understand the all-inclusive nature of the phrase "all things" ("sustaining *all things* by his powerful word") in the Greek. New Testament scholar Leon Morris tells us that this phrase indicates "the totality, the universe considered as one whole. Nothing is excluded from the scope of the

Son's sustaining activity."[17] Indeed, "not for an instant could the universe, the worlds, the heavenly bodies, the seasons, the waters, vegetation, the laws of nature, or man himself subsist apart from Him."[18]

And Christ accomplishes all this "by his powerful word." God is often seen accomplishing things by his "powerful word" in Scripture. The creation of the universe is an example: "Let there be light. . . . Let there be an expanse between the waters to separate water from water. . . . Let the water under the sky be gathered to one place, and let dry ground appear. . . . Let the land produce vegetation. . . . Let there be lights in the expanse of the sky to separate the day from the night. . . . Let the water teem with living creatures, and let birds fly above the earth across the expanse of the sky. . . . Let the land produce living creatures according to their kinds" (Gen. 1:3, 6, 9, 11, 14, 20, 24). In each case, God uttered a command, and what he commanded became reality. Of course, God's words were miraculously effective *not* because words are intrinsically powerful in and of themselves (as some have wrongly surmised), but because the one who spoke them (God) is all-powerful and is the sovereign of the universe.

During his three-year ministry, Jesus likewise accomplished tremendous miracles by his "powerful word." To Lazarus lying dead in a tomb, Jesus said: "Lazarus, come out!" And "the dead man came out, his hands and feet wrapped with strips of linen, and a cloth around his face" (John 11:43–44). In a town called Nain, Jesus encountered a woman whose son had died. Having compassion on the woman, Jesus went over to the dead man and said, "Young man, I say to you, get up!" and the dead man came back to life (Luke 7:11–17). The centurion mentioned in Matthew 8 understood the authority of Jesus' word, for he went to Jesus on behalf of his sick servant and said: "Lord, I do not deserve to have you come under my roof. But just say the word, and my servant will be healed." Jesus spoke the word, and the servant was healed (Matt. 8:8–13).

In the same way that God's powerful word brought the universe into being, and Jesus' word accomplished many miracles during his three-year ministry, so the universe is sustained moment by moment by the powerful word of Jesus. It is highly revealing that the phrase, "by his powerful word," is literally "by the word of his power." The word "power" translates the Greek word *dynamis,* from which we get the English word, "dynamite." Christ's omnipotent word, however, is much more powerful than dynamite, for his word has the power to sustain the entire creation.

Christ's Preservation of His People

Besides sustaining the entire universe as a whole, Christ has also consistently been the Preserver and Sustainer of his people. This is illustrated for us numerous times throughout both the Old and New Testaments. Let us briefly consider two examples.

Christ the Rock

In Paul's first letter to the Corinthians, we find some very interesting words regarding Christ's activities during Israel's time in the wilderness following her exodus from Egypt. Paul said: "For I do not want you to be ignorant of the fact, brothers, that our forefathers were all under the cloud and that they all passed through the sea. . . . They all ate the same spiritual food and drank the same spiritual drink; for they drank from the spiritual rock that accompanied them, and that rock was Christ" (1 Cor. 10:1–4).

Many scholars see this as a clear reference to Christ's sustaining activities in Old Testament times, and I am convinced that this view is correct.[19] *The International Bible Commentary* notes that "Paul's usage goes beyond a mere typological reference—that Rock was Christ, not 'is,' or, 'is a type of'—and is a clear statement to the preexistence of Christ."[20] R. C. H. Lenski notes that "this supernatural rock that never allowed Israel to perish of thirst in the desert—as any other similar expedition would quickly have perished—was Christ, the Son of God, who later became incarnate for our salvation. . . . Let no one imagine that the Israelites just happened to find water whenever it was needed. . . . A wondrous provider accompanied them."[21] Indeed, "Christ the Rock was constantly with His people, the true source of every provision."[22]

Notice that our text says the Israelites "*drank from* the spiritual rock." The imperfect tense used in the Greek of this phrase indicates continued action—as if this "rock" sustained the people throughout the entire journey. "Not once, but, as the imperfect states, continually the Israelites were drinking, and from no mere natural rock, although the water was twice made to gush out of such a rock [see Exodus 17:1–9; Numbers 20:1–13], but out of a spiritual rock which was supernatural, divine, and not left behind in the desert as those two natural rocks were but accompanied the Israelites wherever they went in their wanderings."[23]

Moreover, since the Israelites obtained this water in the early years of their wilderness wanderings (Exod. 17:1–9) *and* in the closing years (Num. 20:1–13), it is only natural to infer that Christ—the Supplier of the water—was with them all along the way. As Leon Morris puts it, "Paul understands Christ to have been the source of all the blessings the Israelites received as they journeyed. So he can think of the Rock, Christ, as following them, and continually giving them drink."[24]

In the Book of Daniel

In the Book of Daniel, God's (and, I believe, Christ's) work of preservation is very striking. Recall that when Daniel's three companions—Shadrach, Meshach, and Abednego—refused to worship the image of gold set up by King Nebuchadnezzar, they were threatened with being thrown into a blazing fire (Dan. 3:15). But the three brave lads responded: "If we are thrown into the blazing furnace, the God we serve is able to save us from it, and he will rescue us from your hand, O king" (v. 17). This comment made the king so mad that he heated the furnace seven times hotter than usual and commanded his strongest soldiers to toss Daniel's three friends into the flames (vv. 19–20).

As the king was observing what should have been an instant incineration, he was suddenly startled by what he saw and exclaimed: "Look! I see four men walking around in the fire, unbound and unharmed, and *the fourth looks like a son of the gods*" (Dan. 3:25, italics added). The king then commanded the three to come out of the flames, and after seeing that they were completely unharmed, exclaimed: "Praise be to the God of Shadrach, Meshach and Abednego, who has *sent his angel* and rescued his servants! They trusted him and defied the king's command and were willing to give up their lives rather than serve or worship any god except their own God" (v. 28, italics added).

Though we are not explicitly told that it was Christ as the Angel of the Lord who sustained Daniel's three friends through the fiery trial, many scholars believe that it was (see chapter 5 for more on this). Bible expositor J. Dwight Pentecost, for example, comments that "this One was probably the preincarnate Christ. Though Nebuchadnezzar did not know of the Son of God, he did recognize that the Person appearing with the three looked supernatural."[25] Theologian Robert D. Culver likewise affirms that "this person may indeed have been the preincarnate Son of God."[26] Certainly this view is compatible with what we know of the Angel of the Lord from other passages. Christ the divine Angel is often seen functioning as Sustainer of his people in Old Testament times (Gen. 16:10f; 22:17f; Exod. 3:1f; 23:21; Josh. 5:14; Zech. 1:12f).

Living in Confidence

To sum up, we have seen that Christ is not only the Creator of the universe, but is its Sustainer and Preserver as well. The closer we look at the pages of Old Testament Scripture, the more evidence we find regarding Christ's sustaining activities. Indeed, Walvoord notes:

A careful study will reveal that Christ was very active in the Old Testament and an integral factor in every page of Israel's history. The work of the Son of God did not begin when He died on the cross or when He ministered to men in His public ministry as recorded in the Gospels, but is an essential ingredient in all the work of God throughout the pages of human history. Taken as a whole, the work of the preincarnate Christ in providence includes all the major features of the doctrine, and the Son of God is seen preserving, guiding, delivering, and governing His creatures.[27]

In view of all this, how amazing it is that Christ—the Creator and Preserver of the universe—stepped out of his glorious existence and became a man to die on our behalf. "Are we not entranced with the dignity of our Redeemer, and are we not amazed at His condescension and love? That the creator and upholder of the universe should come down to such a world as this, and clothe Himself in the inferior nature of its race, and in that nature die to forgive and save it, is the most amazing of revelations."[28]

Of course, Christ did not cease his sustaining and preserving activities following his death and resurrection from the dead. He is today just as much the Sustainer of the universe as ever. And this has great implications for you and me as Christians, for Christ is *our* Sustainer (see Jude 24–25).

Because Christ is our Sustainer, we can rest assured that he will see us into eternity. He upholds us and preserves us, and will do so until we enter into glory (Phil. 1:6). Jesus said, "My sheep listen to my voice; I know them, and they follow me. I give them eternal life, and they shall never perish; no one can snatch them out of my hand" (John 10:27–28).

And until we are with him in glory, his sustaining power will enable us to accomplish his will. As Paul said, "I can do everything through him who gives me strength" (Phil. 4:13). Christ the Sustainer will see us through.

Psalm 91—A Psalm Praising the Sustainer

He who dwells in the shelter of the Most High
    will rest in the shadow of the Almighty.
I will say of the LORD, "He is my refuge and my fortress,
    my God, in whom I trust."
Surely he will save you from the fowler's snare
    and from the deadly pestilence.
He will cover you with his feathers,
    and under his wings you will find refuge;
    his faithfulness will be your shield and rampart.
You will not fear the terror of night,
    nor the arrow that flies by day,
nor the pestilence that stalks in the darkness,
    nor the plague that destroys at midday.
A thousand may fall at your side,
    ten thousand at your right hand,
    but it will not come near you.
You will only observe with your eyes
    and see the punishment of the wicked.
If you make the Most High your dwelling—
    even the LORD, who is my refuge—
then no harm will befall you,
    no disaster will come near your tent.
For he will command his angels concerning you
    to guard you in all your ways;
they will lift you up in their hands,
    so that you will not strike your foot against a stone.
You will tread upon the lion and the cobra;
    you will trample the great lion and the serpent.
"Because he loves me," says the LORD, "I will rescue him;
    I will protect him, for he acknowledges my name.
He will call upon me, and I will answer him;
    I will be with him in trouble,
    I will deliver him and honor him.
With long life will I satisfy him
    and show him my salvation."

5

Christ the Angel of the Lord

Who was it that suddenly appeared to Abraham and prevented him from sacrificing his son Isaac on an altar? Who spoke to Moses from the burning bush and commissioned him to lead the enslaved Hebrews out of Egypt? And who appeared to Hagar in her darkest hour, giving her encouragement, physical sustenance, and direction? Could it be that each of these were preincarnate appearances of our eternal God and Savior, Jesus Christ? Like a ray of sunlight piercing the clouds, did Christ on occasion step out of the eternal realm and appear to select human beings in order to accomplish his sovereign purposes?

The scriptural testimony is so plenteous on this that many Bible scholars have responded, "Surely it must be so." But like the Berean converts of the apostle Paul, you, the reader, are encouraged to examine the Scriptures for yourself to see if these things be true (see Acts 17:11).

We begin our journey through Scripture with the observation that appearances of Christ in the Old Testament are called theophanies. This word comes from two Greek words: *theos* ("God") and *phaino* ("to appear"). We might define a theophany as an appearance or manifestation of God, usually in visible, bodily form. (Some scholars define a theophany strictly in terms of the second person of the Trinity—that is, a theophany is defined as an appearance or manifestation of the preincarnate Christ.[1]) The principal theophany of the Old Testament is the *Angel of the Lord* (or, more literally, "Angel of *Yahweh*"), and—as I shall argue in this chapter—was the primary manifestation of Christ among people who lived prior to his incarnation. Used of Christ, the word *Angel* indicates not a created being but—true to its Hebrew root—a "Messenger," "One who is sent," or "Envoy" (more on this shortly).

Before we examine some of the ways Christ interacted with his people as the Angel of Yahweh, however, we must firmly settle in our minds that Jesus was, in fact, the Angel of Yahweh.[2] To do this, we will focus on three lines of argument: (1) this Angel is identified as being *Yahweh* (God); (2) though the Angel is identified as being *Yahweh*, he is also seen to be *distinct* from another person called *Yahweh*—thus implying plurality within the Godhead; and (3) the Angel of Yahweh must be Jesus Christ by virtue of what we learn from both the Old and New Testaments about the nature and function of each person in the Trinity. Once the evidence is in, you—the jury—must weigh it for yourself and render a verdict.

The Angel of Yahweh Is God

If the Angel of Yahweh in Old Testament times was really God, we would expect him to make a definite claim to deity and not leave us in the dark about his identity. The Angel accommodates us in this regard in a famous Old Testament passage. Recall the account of Moses and the burning bush: "Now Moses was tending the flock of Jethro his father-in-law, the priest of Midian, and he led the flock to the far side of the desert and came to Horeb, the mountain of God. There the angel of the LORD appeared to him in flames of fire from within a bush" (Exod. 3:1–2a). The Angel then made an astonishing assertion to Moses: "I am the God of your father, the God of Abraham, the God of Isaac and the God of Jacob" (v. 6a). Upon hearing the Angel's identity, "Moses hid his face, because he was afraid to look at God" (v. 6b). His fear was well-founded in view of the Old Testament teaching that no man can see God and live (Gen. 16:13; 32:30).

The purpose of the Angel's appearance to Moses was to commission him to lead the enslaved Hebrews out of Egypt. During the encounter, Moses expressed a clear recognition of the Angel's deity: ". . . Moses said *to God* [the Angel of the Lord], 'Suppose I go to the Israelites and say to them, "The God of your fathers has sent me to you," and they ask me, "What is his name?" Then what shall I tell them?'" (Exod. 3:13, insert mine, italics added). The Angel answered with a name that can only be used of God: "God [the Angel of the Lord] said to Moses, 'I AM WHO I AM. This is what you are to say to the Israelites: I AM has sent me to you'" (v. 14, insert mine). It is hard to conceive of how the Angel could have asserted his deity in any stronger way. As we will see in chapter 9, the name "I AM" communicates the idea of eternal self-existence.

A powerful evidence for the Angel's deity is found in Genesis 22, where we find God instructing Abraham, "Take your son, your only son, Isaac, whom you love, and go to the region of Moriah. Sacrifice him there as a burnt offering on one of the mountains I will tell you about" (v. 2). Abraham responded obediently, and just as he was about to slay Isaac, the Angel of the LORD appeared and said to him: "Do not lay a hand on the boy. . . . Do not do anything to him. Now I know that you fear God, because you have not withheld *from me* your son, your only son" (v. 12, italics added). Withholding Isaac *from the Angel of the Lord* and withholding him *from God* are seen as identical.

The Angel's deity was also evident in the encounter Jacob had with him at Bethel. Jacob had fallen asleep and, in a dream, *Yahweh* said to him: "I am the LORD, the God of your father Abraham and the God of Isaac. I will give you and your descendants the land on which you are lying" (Gen. 28:13). Upon awakening, Jacob named the place Bethel ("house of

God") because God had appeared to him there. Jacob also anointed a pillar and made a solemn vow to God (vv. 18–22). Some time later, the Angel of the Lord appeared to Jacob and said: "I am the God of Bethel, where you anointed a pillar and where you made a vow to me. Now leave this land at once and go back to your native land" (31:13).[3]

The Angel's deity was displayed on another occasion when he appeared to an Old Testament couple, Manoah and his sterile wife, informing them that she would conceive and bear a son (Judg. 13:3f). This son was to be the infamous Samson. Because of the humanlike appearance of the Angel of Yahweh when he manifested himself on this particular occasion, Manoah and his wife were initially unaware of his deity. Manoah therefore asked the Angel to reveal his name (v. 17). The Angel responded, "Why do you ask my name, seeing it is *wonderful?*" (v. 18 NASB, italics added). The Hebrew word for "wonderful" means "surpassing," "ineffable," or "beyond human capacity to understand."[4] This is the same word used in Isaiah's prophecy of Christ's future incarnation: "And he will be called '*Wonderful* Counselor, Mighty God, Everlasting Father, Prince of Peace'" (Isa. 9:6, italics added).

After the Angel departed, Manoah was paralyzed with fear: "'We are doomed to die!' he said to his wife. 'We have seen God'" (Judg. 13:22). Manoah, like Moses, was aware of the Old Testament teaching that no one could see God and live. In any event, they *did* live and Manoah's wife later gave birth to Samson, as the Angel had promised.

Further support for the Angel's deity is found in the several occasions where he displayed the attributes of deity. For example, going back to the Angel's appearance to Moses in the burning bush, recall that the Angel said to Moses: "Take off your sandals, for the place where you are standing is holy ground" (Exod. 3:5b). The intrinsic holiness of the Angel required that Moses not defile the surrounding area with his shoes.[5]

The Angel also demonstrated that he was *omniscient* (all-knowing) and *omnipotent* (all-powerful). These attributes are seen on several occasions where the Angel made promises by his own authority that only God could make.[6] The Angel, for example, appeared to Hagar after she had desperately fled into the desert to escape from Sarah (Abraham's wife) and promised her: "I will so increase your descendants that they will be too numerous to count" (Gen. 16:10). No ordinary angel could make such a promise, for the promise itself required the exercise of *omniscience* and fulfilling the promise would require *omnipotence.*[7] It is noteworthy that Hagar expressed an awareness of the Angel's deity, for she acted genuinely surprised that she was permitted to live after seeing God (v. 13).

The Angel made a similar promise to the patriarch Abraham: "I will surely bless you and make your descendants as numerous as the stars in the sky and as the sand on the seashore" (Gen. 22:17a). Again, no one but God could make such a promise. As was true in Hagar's case, the promise itself required the exercise of *omniscience* and fulfilling the promise would require *omnipotence.*

Aside from the Angel of Yahweh claiming to be God, possessing the attributes of deity, and being recognized as God, there are additional evidences for the Angel's deity. The Angel had the authority to forgive sins (Exod. 23:21a), something only God can do. God's *name* (representing all that God is[8]) was said to be in the Angel (Exod. 23:21b). "Nothing short of identification [with *Yahweh*] can be meant by [the fact that *Yahweh's* Name is in Him], for it is stated as the ground why sin committed against the Name-bearing Angel will not be pardoned by Him."[9] The Angel also received worship (Josh. 5:14; see also Exod. 3:5), and accepted sacrifices from people (Judg. 13:19–23). Moreover, he always spoke and acted in his own intrinsic authority (see, for example, Gen. 16:10).

These and other factors leave no doubt that appearances of the Angel of Yahweh in the Old Testament were, in fact, appearances of God. Despite our certainty on this, however, we have yet to see any indication about whether the Angel was an appearance of the triune God, or, perhaps, the Father, the Son, or the Holy Spirit. We will now begin to narrow the field.

The Angel of Yahweh Is Distinct from *Yahweh*

The Angel of the Lord is not only recognized as being *Yahweh*, he is also recognized as a person distinct from *Yahweh*. This may seem contradictory at first glance, but the problem is immediately resolved by recognizing trinitarian distinctions in the Godhead. Though the doctrine of the Trinity is not fully developed in Old Testament revelation, we see preliminary glimpses of the trinitarian God in several important passages.

Among these is Zechariah 1:12, where we find the Angel of the Lord (literally "Angel of Yahweh") interceding *to Yahweh* on behalf of the people of Jerusalem and Judah: "Then the angel of the LORD said, 'LORD Almighty, how long will you withhold mercy from Jerusalem and from the towns of Judah, which you have been angry with these seventy years?'" Here, the Angel of the Lord (one person of the Trinity) intercedes before God (another person in the Trinity) on behalf of the chosen people. The result of this intercession before the Father by the divine Angel was that the Father's intentions to bless and prosper the chosen people were reaffirmed.

We see further glimpses of the trinitarian God in Zechariah 3:1–2 where the Angel of Yahweh is seen calling on *Yahweh*. In this passage, Zechariah witnesses the Angel of Yahweh defending Joshua (the high priest) against the accusations of Satan in the presence of *Yahweh*.[10] Zechariah sees an Angel called *Yahweh* speaking to a separate person also called *Yahweh!* How can there be two different persons with the name *Yahweh?* The answer is found in the trinitarian God.[11] One person in the Trinity (the divine Angel) was addressing another person in the Trinity (the Father).

That the Angel of Yahweh interceded to or called on *Yahweh* in no way indicates that the Angel is less than deity. The Angel's intercessory prayer to *Yahweh* on behalf of Judah, and his calling on *Yahweh* on behalf of Joshua, is no more a disproof of his essential unity with *Yahweh* than the intercessory prayer of Christ to the Father in John 17 is a disproof of his divinity.[12]

In fact, Christ is often portrayed as interceding to the Father in the New Testament: ". . . he [Jesus] is able to save completely those who come to God [the Father] through him, because he always lives to intercede for them" (Heb. 7:25, inserts mine). In Jesus, "we have one who speaks to the Father in our defense—Jesus Christ, the Righteous One" (1 John 2:1).

To recap, then, we have seen that the Angel of Yahweh is *Yahweh*. We have also seen that the Angel of Yahweh is distinct from *Yahweh*. These are important foundational truths to keep in mind as we proceed to narrow our focus regarding the precise identity of the divine Angel.

The Angel of Yahweh: Jesus Christ

The conclusion that appearances of the Angel of Yahweh in the Old Testament were actually preincarnate appearances of Jesus Christ is the only sensible explanation of an otherwise confusing picture.[13] For how can a person who is clearly God (as the Angel of Yahweh) address *another* person who is just as clearly God *(Yahweh)?* Since there is only one God, the answer must lie in the personal distinctions of the Trinity. More specifically, the answer lies in recognizing the Angel as the second person of the Trinity, Jesus Christ.

This conclusion is based on six considerations. First, Jesus Christ is the visible God of the New Testament. Neither the Father nor the Holy Spirit characteristically manifest themselves visibly. Though the Father's voice is heard from heaven and the Holy Spirit is seen descending as a dove at Jesus' baptism (Matt. 3:16–17), Jesus Christ is the full manifestation of God in visible, bodily form: "The Word became flesh and made his dwelling among us" (John 1:14a; cf. Col. 2:9). It seems logical and consistent to assume that it is the second person's role to appear visibly in both Testaments.

From a theological perspective, it would seem unlikely that the Angel of the Lord was the Father or the Holy Spirit. Paul tells us that God the Father is invisible (Col. 1:15; 1 Tim. 1:17) and "lives in unapproachable light, whom no one has seen or can see . . ." (1 Tim. 6:16). John's Gospel tells us that "no one has ever seen God [the Father], but God the One and Only [Jesus Christ], who is at the Father's side, has made him known" (John 1:18, inserts mine). John 5:37 tells us that no one has ever seen God the Father's form. These passages indicate that it was the Son's unique function to make the Father, *who has never been seen*, known to man. We know that "the One and Only" is Jesus Christ, for John tells us: "The Word became flesh, and made his dwelling among us. We have seen his glory, the glory of the *One and Only*, who came from the Father, full of grace and truth" (1:14, italics added). This One and Only, Jesus Christ, was sent to reveal and manifest the invisible God to the world.

The Holy Spirit is also invisible. In the Upper Room Discourse, Jesus said of the Holy Spirit: "The world cannot accept him, because it neither sees him nor knows him. But you know him, for he lives with you and will be in you" (John 14:17). The invisible Holy Spirit is known by believers because *he indwells them*. Jesus also said: "The wind blows wherever it pleases. You hear its sound, but you cannot tell where it comes from or where it is going. So it is with everyone born of the Spirit" (3:8). The presence of the Holy Spirit is known not by a visible manifestation but by his *effect* on people.[14]

In view of the above factors, it is safe to assume that every visible manifestation of God in bodily form in Old Testament times was a preincarnate appearance of the second person of the Trinity—Jesus Christ.[15]

Second, both Christ in the New Testament and the Angel of the Lord in the Old Testament were sent by the Father. The divine pattern in Scripture is that the Father is the Sender and the Son is the Sent One.[16] This implies no superiority of the Father or inferiority of the Son. This is simply the eternal relationship of the first and second persons of the Trinity. That the Angel and Jesus were both sent by the Father—one in the Old Testament (Judg. 13:8–9), the other in the New (John 3:17)—lends support to the idea that they are one and the same person.

Third, as noted earlier, both Christ in the New Testament and the Angel of the Lord in the Old Testament interceded to and called on God the Father. The New Testament pattern is that the second person of the Trinity consistently intercedes to the first person (see John 17; Heb. 7:25; 1 John 2:1). This pattern is never reversed. The intercessory ministry of the Angel therefore points us to his identity as the preincarnate Christ.

Fourth, Christ in the New Testament and the Angel of the Lord in the Old Testament had amazingly similar ministries. In addition to their ministries of intercession, both were involved in revealing truth, leading Israel, commissioning people for service, comforting the downcast, delivering those in bondage, protecting servants of God, and judging sin (more on all this shortly).[17] Such similarities argue strongly that the Angel and Christ are the same person.

Fifth, the Angel of the Lord no longer appears after the Incarnation. In view of the substantial role played by the Angel throughout Old Testament history, his sudden disappearance after the Incarnation would be strange indeed unless he was a preincarnate manifestation of Jesus Christ. There is no other way to explain the Angel's complete inactivity among human beings in New Testament times unless he is recognized as *continuing* his activity as God-incarnate—that is, as Jesus Christ.

Some readers may respond, What about the references (albeit few) in the New Testament to an "angel of the Lord"? Theologian Norman Geisler responds:

> An angel of the Lord (Gabriel) appeared to Joseph (Matt. 1:20); *an* angel of the Lord spoke to Philip (Acts 8:26); and *an* angel of the Lord released Peter (Acts 12:7), but not *the* Angel of the Lord. Furthermore, the New Testament 'angel of the Lord,' unlike 'the Angel of the Lord' in the Old Testament, did not permit worship of himself (cf. Rev. 22:8–9), but 'the Angel of the Lord' in the Old Testament demanded worship (cf. Exodus 3:5; Joshua 5:15).[18]

This critical distinction between *an* angel of the Lord in the New Testament (a created angel) and *the* Angel of the Lord in the Old Testament (God) is recognized by many, many scholars.[19] The reader must be cautious not to get confused on this point.

Sixth, Christ in his glory and the Angel of the Lord are described in notably similar ways. Bible scholar Guy Funderburk offers this summary for us:

> His appearance to David and to Balaam was terrifying. He appeared to Moses in the midst of a fire, and vanished from Gideon with the holocaust fire. Daniel said His eyes were like flaming torches, and Ezekiel saw a brightness "like the appearance of fire" around one in "human form" seated on a throne (Dan. 10:6; Ezek. 1:26ff.). In comparison to these descriptions one can find striking similarities in John's vision of Jesus, a part of which is, "his eyes were like a flame of fire, his feet were like burnished bronze, refined as in a furnace, and his voice was like the sound of many waters" (Rev. 1:14, 16).[20]

In view of all the above considerations, there is very good reason to believe that appearances of the Angel of the Lord in Old Testament times were, in fact, appearances of the prein-

Table 5.1
The Angel of the Lord Is the Lord Jesus Christ[21]

Reference to the Angel of the Lord	Common Activity or Attribute	Reference to Christ
Genesis 16:7, 13	Called "Lord"	John 20:28
Genesis 48:15–16	Called "God"	Hebrews 1:8
Exodus 3:2, 5, 6, 14	Claimed to Be "I AM"	John 8:58
Judges 13:15, 18	His Name Was "Wonderful"	Isaiah 9:6
Exodus 23:20	Sent from God	John 5:30; 6:38
Exodus 14:19	Guides God's People	Matthew 28:20
Isaiah 63:9	Loved and Redeemed His Own	Ephesians 5:25
Joshua 5:13–15	Commander of the Lord's Army	Revelation 19:11–14

carnate Christ. This view best explains the biblical data within the framework of trinitarian theology.

The View of the Early Church

The view that the Angel of the Lord was actually the preincarnate Christ has been the view of many Christians throughout church history. For example, Irenaeus (ca. A.D. 125–200), a disciple of Polycarp, explained in his *Against Heresies* that Christ was often seen by Moses and that it was Christ who spoke to Moses from the burning bush.[22] Irenaeus affirmed that Christ is "implanted everywhere" throughout Moses' writings: "at one time, indeed, speaking with Abraham, when about to eat with him; at another time with Noah, giving to him the dimensions [of the ark]; at another, inquiring after Adam; at another bringing down judgment upon the Sodomites; and again, when He becomes visible, and directs Jacob on his journey, and speaks with Moses from the bush."[23]

Church father Justin Martyr (A.D. 110–166), an able defender of the Christian faith, said: "I have often said, often enough, that when My God says, 'God went up from Abraham,' or 'the Lord spake unto Moses,' and 'the Lord came down to see the tower which the sons of men had built,' or 'God shut Noah within the Ark,' you must not imagine that the unbegotten God himself went down or went up anywhere, nor walks, nor sleeps, nor rises up." Indeed, Martyr says, Abraham and Isaac and Jacob saw not the ineffable Father, but his Son, "who was also fire when He spoke with Moses from the bush." Martyr elsewhere said: "Our Christ conversed with Moses under the appearance of fire from a bush." It was not God the Father who spoke to Moses, but "Jesus the Christ," who "is also God," yea, "the God of Abraham, Isaac, and Jacob," and "the I am that I am."[24]

Church father and defender of the faith Tertullian (ca. A.D. 160–220) similarly stated in his *Against Praxeas*:

It is the Son, therefore, who has been from the beginning administering judgment, throwing down the haughty tower, and dividing the tongues, punishing the whole world by the violence of waters, raining upon Sodom and Gomorrah fire and brimstone, as the LORD from the LORD. For He is who was at all times came down to hold converse with men, from Adam on to the patriarchs and the prophets, in vision, in dream, in mirror, in dark saying.[25]

Other ancient writers who believed that theophanies in the Old Testament were actually appearances of the preincarnate Christ include Clement of Alexandria (ca. A.D. 150–220), Origen (ca. A.D. 185–254), Theophilus of Antioch (died A.D. 181), Cyprian (ca. A.D. 200–258), Hilary (ca. A.D. 315–367), and Saint Basil (ca. A.D. 330–379). The Synod of Antioch also believed the same.[26]

Did Jesus Speak of His Preincarnate Appearances?

The view that Christ was the Angel of the Lord warrants the suggestion that Jesus may have spoken of his activities *as* Angel of the Lord to the two disciples on the road to Emmaus following his resurrection from the dead: "And beginning with Moses and all the Prophets, he [Christ] explained to them what was said *in all the [Old Testament] Scriptures* concerning himself" (Luke 24:27, inserts mine, italics added). Surely his words to the two disciples would have included not only prophecies about his future incarnation and ministry, but also details about his many preincarnate appearances to various human beings.[27]

On a different occasion, Jesus told a group of Jews, "If you believed Moses, you would believe me, for he wrote about me. But since you do not believe what he wrote, how are you going to believe what I say?" (John 5:46–47). What Moses "wrote" (Genesis, Exodus, Leviticus, Numbers, and Deuteronomy) includes not only prophecies about Christ's future incarnation and ministry (e.g., Gen. 3:15; Deut. 18:18), but also some of Christ's preincarnate appearances to human beings (e.g., Gen. 16:7; 22:11).

The Meaning of "Angel"

If Christ was the Angel of Yahweh in Old Testament times, it is important for us to understand in what sense he can properly be called an "angel." In accordance with its Hebrew root, the word *Angel* was used of Christ in the sense of "Messenger," "One who is sent," or "Envoy"[28]—indicating that Christ was acting on behalf of the Father. Christ, as the Angel of the Lord, was a divine *intermediary* between God (the Father) and man. Famed Reformer John Calvin comments: "For even though he [Christ] was not yet clothed with flesh, he came down, so to speak, *as an intermediary,* in order to approach believers more intimately. Therefore this closer intercourse gave him the name of angel. Meanwhile, what was his he retained, that as God he might be of ineffable glory."[29] Calvin's point is well taken, for even though Christ may have *appeared* in the form of an angel, he would forever retain his intrinsic deity and glory.

This is why the qualifying phrase, "of Yahweh," was always attached to the word *Angel* when used of Christ. The name *Yahweh* was reserved *solely* for God, the eternal self-existent one who made heaven and earth. This name was never used in association with a mere created angel.

Parallel Ministries of Christ in the Old and New Testaments

We have already noted that the ministries of the Angel of the Lord in Old Testament times are amazingly parallel to Christ's ministries in the New Testament. This is one evidence that Christ himself was the divine Angel.

Though many parallel ministries could be cited, we will focus our attention on only eight: Christ as Revealer of God, Commissioner, Intercessor, Comforter, Deliverer, Protector, Companion, and Judge.

Christ the Revealer of God

Among the greatest of Christ's ministries in both Testaments was his role as the Revealer of God to the world of humanity. We noted earlier that appearances of Christ in Old Testament times are called theophanies. A theophany is an *appearance* or *manifestation* of God, usually in visible, bodily form. Hence, every appearance of Christ in Old Testament times as Angel of the Lord was a visible and concrete revelation of God. To encounter the Angel was to encounter God.

Without doubt, the theophany *par excellence* in the Old Testament was the preincarnate appearance of Christ in the burning bush to Moses. On this occasion, the Angel revealed his true identity to Moses: "I am the God of your father, the God of Abraham, the God of Isaac and the God of Jacob" (Exod. 3:6a).[30] The divine Angel also revealed his name to be "I AM" (v. 14), a name he would again apply to himself *after* the Incarnation: "Before Abraham was born, I am!" (John 8:58). As we shall see in chapter 9, "Christ and His Divine Titles," this particular name constitutes an immeasurably important revelation of the nature of God.

Christ continued his role as Revealer of God in New Testament times via the Incarnation. Indeed, Christ claimed that "anyone who has seen me has seen the Father" (John 14:9). Jesus affirmed that "when a man believes in me, he does not believe in me only, but in the one who sent me. When he looks at me, he sees the one who sent me" (12:44–45). Later, in his prayer to the Father before his crucifixion, Jesus said: "I have *revealed* you to those whom you gave me out of the world" (17:6a, italics added). Jesus also said that ". . . no one knows the Father except the Son and those to whom the Son chooses to reveal him" (Matt. 11:27b).

How comforting it is to know that Christ is the aggressor in making God known to us. He did not create us and then leave us to grope around in the dark searching for God. In both Testaments, Christ took the initiative in being the Revealer of God to his people.

Christ the Commissioner

In Old Testament times, Christ as the Angel of the Lord commissioned key individuals to specific acts of service. In Exodus 3:7–8, for example, he commissioned Moses to deliver God's people from Egyptian bondage and lead them to the Promised Land. In Judges 6:11–23, he commissioned Gideon to go in God's strength against the Midianites. In Judges 13:1–21, he commissioned the mighty Samson through his parents. In each of these cases, Christ commissioned and worked through chosen individuals to accomplish his sovereign purposes among human beings.

In New Testament times, Christ continued commissioning individuals for specific acts of service. For example, we read in Matthew 4:18–20: "As Jesus was walking beside the Sea of Galilee, he saw two brothers, Simon called Peter and his brother Andrew. They were casting a net into the lake, for they were fishermen. 'Come, follow me,' Jesus said, 'and I will make you fishers of men.' At once they left their nets and followed him." Peter and Andrew were commissioned to share the Good News of salvation with their fellow human beings.

Another notable commissioning took place when Saul, a persecutor of the church, was traveling on the road to Damascus. The risen Christ appeared to him from heaven and said: "Saul, Saul, why do you persecute me?" (Acts 26:14a). Saul responded: "Who are you, Lord?" (v. 15a). The Lord replied: "I am Jesus, whom you are persecuting. Now get up and stand on your feet. I have appeared to you to appoint you as a servant and as a witness of what you have seen of me and what I will show you. I will rescue you from your own people and from the Gentiles. I am sending you to them to open their eyes and turn them from darkness to light, and from the power of Satan to God, so that they may receive forgiveness of sins and a place among those who are sanctified by faith in me" (vv. 15b–18).

Jesus' most famous commission is appropriately known as "The Great Commission." Here, Jesus commissioned the disciples to "go and make disciples of all nations, baptizing them in the name of the Father and of the Son and of the Holy Spirit, and teaching them to obey everything I have commanded you . . ." (Matt. 28:19–20). This commission is one that all Christians should play a part in fulfilling.

Christ the Intercessor

We noted earlier that Christ, as Angel of the Lord, interceded before the Father on behalf of the Israelites when they were severely oppressed by their enemies (Zech. 1:12–13; see also 3:1–2). Such intercession no doubt continued throughout Israel's long history in the Old Testament.

Christ is portrayed as persevering in this intercessory ministry for the people of God in the New Testament. We see this in John 17, where Jesus prays that the Father would protect the disciples (v. 11a) and enable them to maintain their unity (v. 11b). He also prays for their joy (v. 13), their protection from Satan (v. 15), and their sanctification (v. 17). These verses tell us that Christ's intercession is not general, but *specific* and *purposeful*. By virtue of his omniscience, Christ knows the specific details of all our circumstances and needs, and intercedes for us according to that knowledge.

Even now, Christ is interceding for believers from the heavenly realm, for Christ "who died—more than that, who was raised to life—is at the right hand of God and is also interceding for us" (Rom. 8:34). Indeed, "he always lives to intercede for [us]" (Heb. 7:25). This should give every believer a profound sense of joy and security.

Christ the Comforter

It is highly revealing of Christ's nature that his first appearance as the Angel of the Lord in Old Testament times was to bring comfort to a downcast soul. Because of a brutal confrontation Hagar had with Sarah (Abraham's wife) over the issue of childbearing, Hagar had fled into the desert. She was emotionally devastated and spiritually wasted. After she stopped at a well of water, Christ appeared to her as the Angel of the

Lord to bring her comfort and physical sustenance (Gen. 16:7–14). He had heard her cry from the *eternal realm*, felt compassion for her, and came *in person* to minister to her needs in the *earthly realm*. It was at this time that he promised to bless her: "I will so increase your descendants that they will be too numerous to count" (v. 10). Recognizing that the Angel who had seen her in her distress and had come to comfort her was divine, "she gave this name to the LORD who spoke to her: 'You are the God who sees me,' for she said, 'I have now seen the One who sees me'" (v. 13).

Christ's compassion is revealed again in his appearance as Angel of the Lord to Elijah. Elijah had become so despondent after his frightening encounter with the wicked Queen Jezebel that he wanted to die. Elijah fled into the desert, sat down, and prayed: "I have had enough, LORD. . . . Take my life" (1 Kings 19:4). He then fell asleep in a deep state of depression. Completely unexpectedly, the preincarnate Christ appeared next to him as the Angel of the Lord, awakened him with a gentle touch, and provided food to strengthen him: "Get up and eat," the divine Angel said, "for the journey is too much for you" (v. 7). Because of Christ's personal intervention, Elijah's strength was renewed and he was able to continue in the work God called him to do (vv. 8–9).

We should not be surprised at such a ministry of compassion and comfort, for this is so like the Christ of the New Testament. Recall that after spending some time alone in a boat, "Jesus landed and saw a large crowd, [and] he had compassion on them and healed their sick" (Matt. 14:14).

Later, a crowd of four thousand people who had been listening to Jesus teach became hungry. Jesus called his disciples and said to them: "I have compassion for these people; they have already been with me three days and have nothing to eat. I do not want to send them away hungry, or they may collapse on the way" (Matt. 15:32). So Jesus multiplied seven loaves of bread and a few small fish so that everyone had plenty to eat (vv. 35–39).

Still later, when two blind men pleaded for mercy from Jesus, he did not need to be coerced to help them: "Jesus had compassion on them and touched their eyes. Immediately they received their sight and followed him" (Matt. 20:34).

Whether ministering as the Angel of the Lord in Old Testament times or as God-incarnate in New Testament times, the second person of the Trinity was preeminently concerned with displaying compassion and comfort to his people. He has the same kind of compassion for believers today. As was true with Hagar, Elijah, and all those he ministered to in New Testament times, Christ is fully aware of the tears we shed, and of all our frustrations and disappointments. And, as was true with the saints of old, Christ reaches out in compassion to meet all our needs and help us bear our troubles.

Christ the Deliverer

Another key ministry of Christ in both Testaments is that of being a Deliverer of his people. In the encounter Moses had with the divine Angel at the burning bush, the Angel said to him: "I have indeed seen the misery of my people in Egypt. I have heard them crying out because of their slave drivers, and I am concerned about their suffering. *So I have come down to rescue them* from the hand of the Egyptians and to bring them up out of that land into a good and spacious land, a land flowing with milk and honey . . ." (Exod. 3:8, italics added). Old Testament scholar John J. Davis comments that the divine Angel as Deliverer "was a God sensitive and aware of the deep need of His people. He was a merciful God. He had seen their affliction and heard their cry and knew their sorrows. . . . The description here is that of a God who acts not above history, but in and through history."[31]

Christ continues his role as Deliverer in the New Testament. Paul describes Jesus as the one "who gave himself for our sins to rescue us from the present evil age" (Gal. 1:4), and the one "who rescues us from the coming wrath" (1 Thess. 1:10). Paul tells young Timothy that "the Lord will rescue me from every evil attack and will bring me safely to his heavenly kingdom" (2 Tim. 4:18). The author of Hebrews says that Jesus shared in humanity "so that by his death he might destroy him who holds the power of death—that is, the devil—and free those who all their lives were held in slavery by their fear of death" (Heb. 2:14–15).

It is truly liberating to recognize that our deliverance from sin and Satan depends not on our own feeble efforts but on the great Deliverer of both the Old and New Testaments.

Christ the Protector

Psalm 34:7 tells us that "the angel of the LORD encamps around those who fear him. . . ." Like a powerful army encamped around a city to protect it, Christ *surrounds* those who reverence him with a divine, protective hedge. (Of course, this should not be construed to mean that Christians are utterly exempt from being hurt by others.[32])

We noted in chapter 3, "Christ the Preserver," that the divine Angel protected Daniel's colleagues from being incinerated in King Nebuchadnezzar's furnace (Dan. 3:15–20). Later, Daniel himself was rescued when he was thrown into the lions' den at the hands of King Darius. Though the king personally liked Daniel, the governmental leaders under Darius despised him. These unscrupulous men tricked the king into signing an irrevocable edict which decreed that no one could pray to any god or man except Darius for the next thirty days. Undaunted, Daniel continued his practice of praying three times a day to the true God. Upon being discovered by the scheming governmental leaders, Daniel was thrown into the lions' den overnight. Due to the irrevocable nature of the edict, Darius could not intervene, but the king admonished Daniel: "May your God, whom you serve continually, rescue you!" (6:16).

The following morning, the king rushed to the lions' den and shouted, "Daniel, servant of the living God, has your God, whom you serve continually, been able to rescue you from the

lions?" (Dan. 6:20). Daniel responded: "O king, live forever!
My God sent his angel, and he shut the mouths of the lions . . ."
(v. 22, italics added). Many scholars believe, as I do, that the
"angel" the Father sent was none other than the preincarnate
Christ.[33]

Christ continues his role as the faithful Protector of his people in New Testament times. One example of this is found in
Matthew 8, where we find Jesus and the disciples sailing on
the Sea of Galilee: "Without warning, a furious storm came up
on the lake, so that the waves swept over the boat. But Jesus
was sleeping. The disciples went and woke him, saying, 'Lord,
save us! We're going to drown!' He replied, 'You of little faith,
why are you so afraid?' Then he got up and rebuked the winds
and the waves, and it was completely calm" (vv. 24–26).

Perhaps the disciples did not have the same level of faith
Daniel did, but they learned the same lesson: "The angel of the
LORD encamps around those who fear him, and he delivers
them" (Ps. 34:7). We may rest secure in the knowledge that
God personally looks after each of us, for he himself has prom-
ised us: "Never will I leave you; never will I forsake you"
(Heb. 13:5).

Christ the Companion

Genesis 5:22 records the startling words, "Enoch *walked*
with God" (italics added). Most expositors interpret this verse
in a figurative way, meaning something such as, "Enoch
maintained continuous spiritual fellowship with God."
Kyle M. Yates's view is typical: "In a deteriorating age, Enoch
gave a remarkable demonstration of commendable piety. In
thought, word, deed, and attitude he was in accord with the
divine will; and he brought joy to the heart of his Maker."[34]
Certainly this interpretation has much to commend it, and all
these things must have been true of Enoch. But it is possible
that the word *walk* may indicate more in this case.

In view of what we have learned about the Angel of the
Lord and his visible appearances to people in Old Testament

times, it is entirely possible that Enoch literally (physically) walked with God. This is feasible especially since appearances by the Angel of the Lord were God's primary means of giving revelation in patriarchal days.[35] Old Testament scholars C. F. Keil and Franz Delitzsch note that the phrase "walked with God"

> denotes the most confidential intercourse, the closest communion with the personal God, a walking as it were by the side of God, who still continued His visible intercourse with men (*vid.* 3:8). It must be distinguished from "walking before God" (chapter 17:1; 24:40, etc.), and "walking after God" (Deuteronomy 13:4), both which phrases are used to indicate a pious, moral, blameless life under the law according to the directions of the divine commandments. The only other passage in which this expression "walk with God" occurs is Malachi 2:6, where it denotes not the piety of the godly Israelites generally, but the conduct of the priests, who stood in a closer relation to Jehovah under the Old Testament than the rest of the faithful, being permitted to enter the Holy Place, and hold direct intercourse with Him there, which the rest of the people could not do.[36]

If God was pleased to physically walk with Enoch, then—as a prerequisite—it would also have to be true that Enoch "walked" with God in the *spiritual* sense as well. The second person, as Angel of the Lord, could never physically walk in fellowship with one who was spiritually rebellious. It may be that the Holy Spirit purposefully chose this unique phraseology in describing Enoch because both the literal and spiritual senses of "walking with God" were completely true in his life.

In any event, we learn from the New Testament that believers of the present age are privileged to "walk" in spiritual fellowship with the risen Christ. John describes this as "walking in the light," a walk in which one's lifestyle is to be characterized by complete obedience to our Lord's Word (see 1 John 1:5–7). Such a walk of obedience is necessary to maintain spiritual fellowship with Christ, who himself is "the light of the world" (John 8:12; 9:5; cf. 12:46).

Of course, the choice to walk in fellowship with Christ is ours alone. It has always been this way. If we find ourselves out of fellowship with our Lord, it is of our own doing. But his invitation has not been withdrawn. From the depths of his compassionate heart, he ever calls to his children: "Walk with me."

Christ the Judge

Christians often speak of Christ in terms of being the humble and loving carpenter of Nazareth who was the Lamb of God, sacrificed on a cross for the sins of man. But many seem to wince at the suggestion that Christ is also a sovereign Judge who will send those who reject him into a suffering eternity apart from God.

Christ's role as Judge (and Executor of judgment) is the clear teaching of Scripture—in both the Old and New Testaments. In Old Testament times, Christ on occasion pronounced and executed judgment as the Angel of the Lord. An example of this is found in 1 Chronicles 21, where we read that David (at Satan's prompting) numbered Israel (v. 1), apparently so David could revel in his military might. God the Father was greatly displeased at this and sent the Angel of the Lord to execute judgment, even to the partial destruction of Jerusalem (vv. 14–15). David had the sobering experience of seeing the divine Angel with a drawn sword in his hand stretched out over Jerusalem, at which time David wisely fell on his face in repentance and intercession (vv. 16–17). The Angel then commanded David to build an altar, which was later to become the exact site of Solomon's great temple (see 21:18, 24–29; 22:1, 6).

Christ is also portrayed as a Judge in the New Testament. John 5:22 records Jesus as saying that "the Father judges no one, but has entrusted all judgment to the Son." Peter describes Christ as "the one whom God appointed as judge of the living and the dead" (Acts 10:42). Paul informs us that "we must all appear before the judgment seat of Christ, that each one may receive what is due him for the things done while in the body, whether good or bad" (2 Cor. 5:10).

Christ clearly perceived of himself as a divine Judge. Recall that when Caiaphas the high priest asked Jesus, "Are you the Christ, the Son of the Blessed One?" Jesus responded, "I am. And you will see the Son of Man sitting at the right hand of the Mighty One and coming on the clouds of heaven" (Mark 14:61–62).

In his answer to Caiaphas, Jesus was drawing on Old Testament imagery taken from Daniel 7. He informed Caiaphas that *he*—the Son of Man—will ultimately be the one to whom everlasting dominion is given. Jon A. Buell and O. Quentin Hyder comment that "the irony of Jesus' words should not be missed: although he is before them as one indicted and at their mercy, they, one day, will be at *his* tribunal, and he will be the judge."[37] In that day of judgment, it will be utterly horrific for those who have rejected Christ's gracious provision of salvation.

Close Encounters and Changed Lives

We have seen that Christ as the Angel of the Lord was extremely active among his people in Old Testament times. He provided for those in need, comforted the suffering, guided believers in the path of God's will, protected his people from their enemies, carried out the providence of God, and enjoyed fellowship with those obedient to his Word. This ministry of the second person was not occasional or exceptional, but was rather the common and continual ministry of a caring God to his people.

As we reflect on what we have learned about Christ as Angel of the Lord, it becomes overwhelmingly clear that he was in the business of changing lives. Through personal encounters with the divine Angel, *Abraham* became a man of faith (Gen. 12:7; 15; 17; 18); *Hagar's* sorrow turned to rejoicing (16:10); *Isaac's* fear was dispelled (26:2, 23–24); *Jacob's* life was changed from that of a cheater to a prince (32:24–32); and meek and lowly *Moses* was commissioned, empowered, and

emboldened to deliver God's people from Egypt (Exod. 3:1–
4:17).

Christ as God-incarnate continued changing lives in New
Testament times. Radical changes! Among the more notable
conversions are *Simon Peter* (Luke 5:4–11), *Levi* (5:27–28), *Zac-
chaeus* (19:1–10), *Nathanael* (John 1:46–51), and *Saul,* who became the apostle Paul (Acts 9:1–19). These all had varied
backgrounds and careers, but the one thing they all had in
common was that Christ came into their lives and brought
about dramatic, lasting changes.

How is it with you? Have you encountered the living
Christ?

6

Christ the Shepherd

In the New Testament, Christ is called the Good Shepherd (John 10), the Chief Shepherd (1 Peter 5:4), and the Great Shepherd (Heb. 13:20). When Christ was born, he was recognized as the direct fulfillment of the messianic prophecy in Micah 5:2: "But you, Bethlehem, in the land of Judah, are by no means least among the rulers of Judah; for out of you will come a ruler who will be the shepherd of my people Israel" (Matt. 2:6).

During his three-year ministry, Jesus thought of his people in terms of lost sheep, as is illustrated in Matthew 9:36: "When he saw the crowds, he had compassion on them, because they were harassed and helpless, like sheep without a shepherd." Jesus also used the shepherd/sheep motif in some of his parables (e.g., Matt. 18:10–14).

Toward the end of his three-year ministry, Jesus warned the disciples that his impending arrest and crucifixion would cause them (his sheep) to be scattered. Jesus told them, "This very night you will all fall away on account of me, for it is written: 'I will strike the shepherd, and the sheep of the flock will be scattered'" (Matt. 26:31). This prophecy was literally fulfilled. Peter even denied Christ three times in the process.

Just prior to his ascension into heaven following his resurrection, Jesus sought out Peter's restoration and told him to "take care of my sheep" (John 21:16). In the end times, Jesus will separate the "sheep" from the "goats" (Matt. 25:31–46). The sheep will enter into Christ's eternal kingdom, and the goats into the lake of fire. Clearly, Jesus' role as the Shepherd of his people is a major emphasis in the New Testament.

The shepherd motif is rich in meaning in Old Testament Scripture. Broadly speaking, Scripture indicates that the shepherd is simultaneously a *leader* and a *companion* to his sheep. The shepherd is typically a strong man capable of defending his flock against wild beasts (1 Sam. 17:34–37; cf. Matt. 10:16; Acts 20:29). He is also gentle with his flock, knowing their condition (Prov. 27:23), bearing them in his arms (Isa. 40:11), adapting himself to their needs (Gen. 33:13–14), cherishing each and every one of them "as his daughter" (2 Sam. 12:3). The shepherd was known for his seeking out the lost sheep (Ezek. 34:12) and for rescuing those that were attacked (Amos 3:12). In view of all this, the shepherd motif is certainly an appropriate way of describing the relationship Jesus Christ has with his people.

It is noteworthy that many Old Testament prophecies speak of the coming Messiah as the *single* Shepherd of his people (Ezek. 34:23; 37:22, 24; Zech. 11:4–14; 13:7). Christ specifically said he was the fulfillment of these prophecies (John 10:8, 11, 14).

The question of interest for our present study is: In view of the numerous New Testament verses that point to Jesus as the divine Shepherd, was Jesus *also* involved in shepherding his people in Old Testament times? It is to this issue that we now turn our attention.

Jesus a Shepherd in Old Testament Times?

Many biblical scholars believe that the Shepherd mentioned in Psalm 23 is none other than the preincarnate Christ.[1] Theologian John F. Walvoord suggests, for example, that "the various references to Jehovah as the Shepherd of Israel may be taken as specific references to Christ (see Gen. 49:24; Ps. 23:1; 80:1; Isa. 40:11; Jer. 31:10; Ezek. 34:11–12, 23; 37:24). Although these references contextually could refer to God as a Trinity, the fact that Christ is specifically the Good Shepherd in John 10 would give some justification for this identification."[2]

The suggestion that Christ is the divine *Shepherd* is certainly in keeping with the fact that Christ is the *Creator* (John 1:3; Col. 1:16; Heb. 1:2), for these two roles are, on several occasions, found side by side in Scripture. For example, Psalm 100:3 tells us, "Know that the LORD is God. It is he who made us, and we are his; we are his people, the sheep of his pasture." Psalm 95:6–7 likewise tells us, "Come, let us bow down in worship, let us kneel before the LORD our Maker; for he is our God and we are the people of his pasture, the flock under his care." These verses tell us that he who *created* human beings is also the one who *cares for* human beings as the divine Shepherd. Without denying the contributions of the Father and the Holy Spirit in this regard, the Son's respective roles as Creator and Shepherd are undeniably at the heart of scriptural revelation about Christ.

Some scholars have suggested that Psalms 22, 23, and 24 constitute a messianic triad. Each of these psalms points in some way to the person of Christ. "As the Good Shepherd, [Christ] died for his sheep as prophesied in Psalm 22 [*by crucifixion*—'they have pierced my hands and my feet'; v. 16]; as the Great Shepherd (Heb. 13:20), he fulfills Psalm 23; as the Chief Shepherd (1 Peter 5:4), he will come to reign as the King of glory (Ps. 24)."[3]

The Shepherd and Quiet Waters

In Psalm 23 the Shepherd is described as one who "leads me beside quiet waters" (v. 2). In remarkably similar language, we are told in Revelation 7:17—a verse describing a scene in heaven where the risen, glorified Jesus dwells—that "the Lamb [Christ] at the center of the throne will be their shepherd; he will lead them to springs of living water . . ." (insert mine). The fact that Christ in heaven is described as a shepherd who leads his people to springs of living water lends credence to the suggestion that Christ may be the Shepherd who led his people "beside quiet waters" in Old Testament times.

Later in the Book of Revelation, Jesus said to John: "It is done. I am the Alpha and the Omega, the Beginning and the End. To him who is thirsty I will give to drink without cost from the spring of the water of life" (Rev. 21:6). This must have brought back memories for John, for he well remembered the words from his own Gospel about the woman at Jacob's well to whom Jesus offered "the gift" of living water (John 4:10). It is interesting to note that "the offer John had just heard from the Alpha and Omega was the same now at the end of God's revelation in Jesus Christ as it had been at the very beginning. It was still a gift."[4] It seems to be one of the unique ministries of the second person—the divine Shepherd—to bring waters of spiritual refreshment to his people.

Jacob's Shepherd

Scriptural evidence was provided in chapter 5 that appearances of the Angel of the Lord in Old Testament times were actually appearances of the preincarnate Christ. It is therefore highly significant that Jacob, in blessing his son Joseph's children, said: "May the God before whom my fathers Abraham and Isaac walked, the God who has been my *shepherd* all my life to this day, the *Angel* who has delivered me from all harm—may he [note the singular *he*] bless these boys . . ." (Gen. 48:15–16, italics added, insert mine).

Since we have concluded that the Angel of the Lord was the preincarnate Christ, and since the Angel of the Lord and Jacob's Shepherd were one and the same, we may conclude that the preincarnate Christ was Jacob's Shepherd.[5] This same Angel of the Lord (Christ) had appeared earlier to Abraham to prevent him from slaying Isaac on the altar (Gen. 22:11–18). Now we are told that the Angel watched over and protected

Jacob from all harm (48:15–16). Among the occasions when Christ as the Angel of the Lord helped Jacob was when he informed Jacob that he would prosper him in the face of Laban's unfair dealings with him (see Gen. 31:11–13).

Jacob not only blessed the children of his son Joseph (in Gen. 48), he also blessed his *own* sons—including Joseph—in the following chapter (49:22–26). Verses 23 and 24 of Genesis 49 represent a mini-biography of Joseph: "With bitterness archers attacked him; they shot at him with hostility. But his bow remained steady, his strong arms stayed limber, because of the hand of the Mighty One of Jacob, because of the Shepherd, the Rock of Israel."

Now, keep in mind that Jacob equated the Angel of the Lord (the preincarnate Christ) and the Shepherd in the previous chapter (Gen. 48:15–16). We may therefore assume that Jacob was referring to the *same* Shepherd while pronouncing blessing upon his son Joseph (49:24). The hand of Christ the divine Shepherd protected Joseph from hostile arrows.

Further evidence for this view may be found in the fact that Jacob equated the Shepherd with "the Rock of Israel." While God is often equated with the Rock of Israel in Old Testament times (Deut. 32:4, 15, 18, 30, 31, 37; Ps. 18:2, 31; Isa. 30:29), it may be that "Rock" in our present context has explicit reference to Christ. We noted in chapter 4 that Paul said of the Israelites in their wilderness experience: "For I do not want you to be ignorant of the fact, brothers, that our forefathers were all under the cloud and that they all passed through the sea. . . . They all ate the same spiritual food and drank the same spiritual drink; for they drank from the spiritual rock that accompanied them, and *that rock was Christ*" (1 Cor. 10:1–3, italics added). Christ is also referred to as a "rock" elsewhere in Scripture (e.g., Isa. 28:16; Matt. 7:24; Rom. 9:33; 1 Peter 2:8).

In any event, since the Angel of the Lord was a preincarnate manifestation of Christ, and since the divine Angel was the Shepherd of Jacob, we may legitimately conclude that Christ himself was the Shepherd of both Jacob and Joseph.

Christ never left his people to themselves. Christ the Shepherd was constantly with his people, the true source of every provision.

The Shepherd of the Exodus

We find further evidence for Christ as Shepherd in Old Testament times in the Exodus account. Recall that in Exodus 3 it was the Angel of the Lord (the preincarnate Christ) who commissioned Moses to go to Egypt as a deliverer of the Israelites. Aware that Egypt's pharaoh would be unwilling to let the Israelites go, the divine Angel told Moses: "But I know that the king of Egypt will not let you go unless a mighty hand compels him. So *I will stretch out my hand* and strike the Egyptians with all the wonders that *I will perform* among them. After that, he will let you go" (Exod. 3:19–20, italics added).

In view of the fact that the divine *Angel* did these things, it is highly revealing that Psalm 78 tells us that it was the divine *Shepherd* who did these things—thus indicating their common identity. The psalmist tells us:

> How often they rebelled against him in the desert
>   and grieved him in the wasteland!
> Again and again they put God to the test;
>   they vexed the Holy One of Israel.
> They did not remember his power—
>   the day he redeemed them from the oppressor,
> the day he displayed his miraculous signs in Egypt,
>   his wonders in the region of Zoan.
> He turned their rivers to blood;
>   they could not drink from their streams.
> He sent swarms of flies that devoured them,
>   and frogs that devastated them.
> He gave their crops to the grasshopper,
>   their produce to the locust.
> He destroyed their vines with hail
>   and their sycamore-figs with sleet.
> He gave over their cattle to the hail,
>   their livestock to bolts of lightning.

> He unleashed against them his hot anger,
>   his wrath, indignation and hostility—
>   a band of destroying angels.
> He prepared a path for his anger;
>   he did not spare them from death
>   but gave them over to the plague.
> He struck down all the firstborn of Egypt,
>   the firstfruits of manhood in the tents of Ham.
> But he brought his people out *like a flock;*
>   *he led them like sheep* through the desert.
> *He guided them safely,* so they were unafraid;
>   but the sea engulfed their enemies.
>
> (Ps. 78:40–53, italics added)

Clearly, a comparison of Psalm 78 with Exodus 3 points to the common identity of the divine Shepherd and the divine Angel. And since the Angel of the Lord was the preincarnate Christ, we may surmise that Christ functioned in the role of a Shepherd for his people during the time of the Exodus.

"Yahweh Is My Shepherd"

In Psalm 23 David says, "the Lord is my shepherd." In the Hebrew this is literally, *"Yahweh* is my shepherd." Though the name *Yahweh* is most often used of the triune God in the Old Testament, a close look at Scripture reveals that there are many parallels between Jesus in the New Testament and *Yahweh* in the Old Testament, as the chart on the next page makes clear (see also chapter 9, "Christ and His Divine Titles").

In all of these passages, Jesus was either claiming (or acclaimed) to be exactly what is reserved solely for *Yahweh* in the Old Testament.[6] For example, in Isaiah 42:8, *Yahweh* claimed, "I am the LORD, that is my name; my glory I give to no other . . ." (RSV). And yet, Jesus shared in this glory even before the world was created (John 17:5), and John says that it was Jesus' glory of which Isaiah spoke (John 12:41). Evidence such as this has led John F. Walvoord to conclude that David in his assertion that *"Yahweh* is my shepherd" was "declaring his confidence in the preincarnate Son of God, the good Shepherd, to care for him as a shepherd cares for his sheep."[7]

We find further evidence for this in the fact that three of Jesus' parables—the parable of the lost sheep (Matt. 18:12–14), the parable of the good shepherd (John 10:1–5), and the parable of the hireling (John 10:11–13)—have direct parallels to the discussion of God as Shepherd in Ezekiel 34. Theologian Millard J. Erickson has provided this brief summary of some of the more notable parallels:

> Jesus on several occasions described himself as the good shepherd, evidently having in mind the imagery of Ezekiel 34. He depicts himself as performing the same acts the good shep-

Table 6.1
Parallels Between *Yahweh* and Jesus[8]

Yahweh in the Old Testament	Mutual Title or Act	Jesus in the New Testament
Isaiah 40:28	Creator	John 1:3
Isaiah 43:11; 45:22	Savior	John 4:42
1 Samuel 2:6	Raise Dead	John 5:21
Joel 3:12	Judge	John 5:27
Isaiah 60:19–20	Light	John 8:12
Exodus 3:14	I AM	John 8:58; see 18:5–6
Psalm 23:1	Shepherd	John 10:11
Isaiah 42:8; see 48:11	Glory of God	John 17:1, 5
Isaiah 41:4; 44:6	First and Last	Revelation 1:17; 2:8
Hosea 13:14	Redeemer	Revelation 5:9
Isaiah 62:5; Hosea 2:16	Bridegroom	Revelation 21:2
Psalm 18:2	Rock	1 Corinthians 10:4
Jeremiah 31:34	Forgiver of Sins	Mark 2:7, 10
Psalm 148:2	Worshiped by Angels	Hebrews 1:6
Throughout OT	Addressed in Prayer	Acts 7:59
Psalm 148:5	Creator of Angels	Colossians 1:16
Isaiah 45:23	Confessed as Lord	Philippians 2:11

herd, God, performs in the Old Testament: searching for the scattered sheep and bringing them back (Ezek. 34:11–13, 16, 22; the parable of the lost sheep); leading them into good pasture-land, feeding them, and being a good shepherd to them (Ezek. 34:13–15, 31; the parable of the good shepherd); caring for them and protecting them from prey (Ezek. 34:15, 22; the parable of the hireling); and judging the flock, separating the sheep from the goats (Ezek. 34:17–22; Matt. 25:31–33).[9]

These three parables, along with the other passages cited above, clearly point to Christ's identity as Shepherd of his people—even in Old Testament times. For those who disagree with this assessment, preferring instead to interpret Old Testament verses that speak of God as "Shepherd" as referring to the triune God, one further point bears mentioning. Even if the word *Yahweh* in Psalm 23 and other passages is referring not specifically to Christ but to the triune God, all that is said of *Yahweh* in these verses may also be rightly said of Christ, since Christ is the second person of the Godhead. Hence, any way one chooses to look at it, Christ was heavily involved in shepherding his people in Old Testament times.

Christ Our Shepherd

Christ did not cease his shepherding activities in biblical times. That Christ is *our* personal Shepherd is one of the most exciting and motivating truths in Scripture. He leads us day by day and calls us to follow his lead closely. Those who stay closest to the divine Shepherd are the healthiest of "sheep" (spiritually speaking), for they find themselves in rich "pastures." Those who find themselves in a barren wasteland, by contrast, have strayed from the Shepherd's side.

The remainder of this chapter will focus on Psalm 23 and John 10. Not only do these passages give us insights about Christ as Shepherd in Old and New Testament times, they give us insights on Christ as our Shepherd today. Indeed, these passages are rich in spiritual truths for those who seek intimacy with the Lord. May the following brief exposition draw you closer to his side.

Psalm 23—A Psalm of David

The LORD is my shepherd, I shall not be in want.
He makes me lie down in green pastures,
he leads me beside quiet waters,
    he restores my soul.
He guides me in paths of righteousness
    for his name's sake.
Even though I walk
    through the valley of the shadow of death,
I will fear no evil,
    for you are with me;
your rod and your staff,
    they comfort me.
You prepare a table before me
    in the presence of my enemies.
You anoint my head with oil;
    my cup overflows.
Surely goodness and love will follow me
all the days of my life,
and I will dwell in the house of the LORD
    forever.

"Three thousand years have passed since the psalmist David first sang the words of the Twenty-third Psalm," says theologian Haddon Robinson in his inspirational commentary on this classic psalm. "The sand of those thirty centuries has buried beneath it many of the relics of that distant day. The harp on which this ancient melody was played, the book of the law from which King David drew his meditations, the royal chamber in which the psalmist composed his song, are now all covered with the debris of the ages. Yet, the Twenty-third Psalm is still as fresh as the day it was first composed."[10]

David, himself once a shepherd who went to great lengths to care for his sheep, reflects in this psalm about how God has taken care of him throughout his life. Inspired by the Spirit, David exulted: "The LORD is my shepherd. . . ."

The LORD is my shepherd, I shall not be in want. [Ps. 23:1]

David had learned by experience that because the Lord was his shepherd, all of his needs would always be fully met. By the tone of the psalm, it is obvious that David was satisfied with the Lord's management of his life. David believed that the Lord had planned his life down to the details of his day, as a good shepherd would. It was in the knowledge that the Lord was at the helm of his life that David went about his days in joy, believing that any trials that came his way were taking place within his shepherd's sovereign plan. Whenever a difficult circumstance came up, David rested in the security that the Lord was with him every minute.

Implicit in his affirmation that the Lord was his shepherd is the fact that David likened himself to a sheep. Sheep are known to be defenseless, dependent, and foolish. David was thus acknowledging in this psalm that he was utterly dependent in every way upon the Lord.

Because the Lord was David's shepherd, David confidently affirmed: "I shall not be in want." We might paraphrase David's words this way: "Because the Lord is my shepherd, I shall never be in a state of lack at any time for anything I need."

Those involved in Christian ministry have often pointed out that we must be careful not to get sidetracked so that our focus is merely on the *benefits* of following the shepherd. Rather, our focus must ever be on the Shepherd himself; then, all else will follow. Haddon Robinson has observed that sometimes "we get so taken up with the details of this psalm that we actually ignore the Shepherd. We are delighted at the prospect of green pastures and quiet waters. We respond to the promise of an overflowing cup. Indeed, we are so eager for all the Shepherd *does*, we do not pay much attention to who the Shepherd *is*. Yet He is at the center of the entire psalm. All of these blessings are mine because I am one of His sheep."[11]

**He makes me lie down in green pastures, he leads me
beside quiet waters, he restores my soul. He guides me in
paths of righteousness for his name's sake. [Ps. 23:2–3]**

Just as a shepherd leads his sheep to green pastures and
quiet waters, so those who follow the Lord do not lack any
spiritual nourishment or refreshment. Because of this, contentment should be the hallmark of one who has put his or her
affairs in the hands of the Lord.

The phrase "quiet waters" can easily be translated "stilled
waters." As in most of this psalm, David is thinking of an inci-
dent that occurs in the shepherd life of Palestine. Haddon Robinson writes:

> Sheep are deeply afraid of running water. Instinctively they
> seem to realize that if water should get on their coats of wool,
> they would become waterlogged and sink beneath a stream. As
> a result, a flock tired and thirsty after making a difficult journey
> over the blistering sands will come to a running stream. The
> cool, crystal clear waters can quench the thirst of the weary an-
> imals, but the sheep will only stand beside the stream and look.
> Fear of the water keeps them from refreshment.[12]

Aware of the fear of his sheep, the shepherd—perhaps taking his rod and staff—might pry loose a few large stones to
dam up a quiet place where the sheep may drink. In the midst
of a rushing stream, he provides refreshment for the flock with
water that he has stilled.

A good Eastern shepherd will go to no end of trouble to
supply his sheep with the finest grazing, the richest pasturage,
and the cleanest water. He does all in his power to ensure the
highest possible quality of life for them. Likewise, our divine
Shepherd Jesus makes it his personal business to ensure that
those who follow him stay spiritually nourished and refreshed.

Throughout Scripture, the drinking of water is often used as
a way of indicating spiritual refreshment. For example, Jesus
told the woman at the well in Samaria that he could give her

"living water" (John 4:10). Jesus informed her that "whoever drinks the water I give him will never thirst. Indeed, the water I give him will become in him a spring of water welling up to eternal life" (v. 14). The phrase *will never thirst* is actually a double negative in the Greek. The verse carries the idea, "whoever drinks the water I give him *will by no means thirst, forever.*"[13]

Later in John's Gospel, we read that "on the last and greatest day of the Feast, Jesus stood and said in a loud voice, 'If anyone is thirsty, let him come to me and drink. Whoever believes in me, as the Scripture has said, streams of living water will flow from within him'" (John 7:37–38).

Still later, when John prophetically beheld the glorified Christ in a heavenly scene, we read of God's people:

> "Never again will they hunger;
>   never again will they thirst.
> The sun will not beat upon them,
>   nor any scorching heat.
> For the Lamb at the center of the throne
>   will be their shepherd;
>   he will lead them to springs of living water.
> And God will wipe away every tear from their eyes"
>   (Rev. 7:16–17).

Clearly, one of the goals of Christ our Shepherd is that we might have life more abundantly. Those who follow Christ's lead will find their souls refreshed and guided in paths of righteousness for his name's sake (Ps. 23:3). Christ our Shepherd will never lead us astray or on the wrong path. If we find ourselves in a barren wasteland spiritually, it is not because he has led us there, but because we have chosen to stop following his lead.

Human beings have a propensity to follow their *own* lead. Isaiah tells us: "We all, like sheep, have gone astray, each of us has turned to his own way" (Isa. 53:6). Proverbs 14:12 tells us that "there is a way that seems right to a man, but in the end it leads to death." Without a conscientious effort to stay close to our divine Shepherd, following *his* lead and not our own, we will likely end up somewhere out in the desert of life, torn and bleeding—like the unfortunate Israelites in their wilderness experience.

Perhaps, even now, you may feel that your spiritual life has been stagnating in a dry and barren wasteland. If so, take heart, for your Shepherd seeks your full restoration. His hands are opened wide, waiting to embrace you in unconditional love. His affection is as measureless as the sea. Turn to him without delay, and you will be able to exult with David, "The LORD is my shepherd; I shall not be in want" (Ps. 23:1).

Even though I walk through the valley of the shadow of death, I will fear no evil, for you are with me; your rod and your staff, they comfort me. [Ps. 23:4]

The "valley of the shadow of death" refers to a treacherous, dreadful place. In fact, many scholars believe the phrase is more accurately translated "the valley of deep darkness." It may be that David was thinking of an actual place in Palestine—"a chasm among the hills, a deep, abrupt, faintly lighted ravine with steep sides and a narrow floor."[14] This place is a home for vultures by day and a haven for wolves and hyenas by night. The danger for defenseless sheep is obvious.

Because he knew the Lord was with him, David feared no evil while passing through this dreadful valley. The truth we draw from this verse is that no matter what dark circumstances we might find ourselves passing through, Christ our Shepherd is with us and we need not ever fear. Just as a shepherd with his rod and staff comforts his sheep, so Christ our Shepherd comforts us, even in the midst of distressing circumstances.

The instruments used by ancient shepherds were highly effective. The *rod* is a great oak club about two feet long. It had a round head in which the shepherd had pounded sharp bits of metal. This rod was specifically used to protect the sheep from wild animals. "A skillful shepherd not only swung the club to smash the head of an attacker but he could also hurl the club like a missile over the heads of his flock to strike a wolf lurking in the distance."[15]

The *staff* was bent or hooked at one end. It was often used by shepherds to restrain a sheep from wandering off from the flock or to hook its legs to pull it out of a hole into which it had fallen. At other times, the shepherd would use the staff to pull branches aside when a sheep got entangled in the brush.

By using the rod and the staff, the shepherd brought "comfort" to the sheep. The Hebrew word for *comfort* literally means "to give strength" or "empower." In the presence of their shepherd, the sheep were strengthened and empowered because they knew they were secure in his presence.

The same is true of each of us as Christ's sheep. Knowing that he is with us every step of the way—that we are never alone—gives us strength to cope with whatever might come our way. We will never find ourselves in situations the Lord is not aware of, and he will never leave or forsake us (Heb. 13:5).

You prepare a table before me in the presence of my enemies. You anoint my head with oil; my cup overflows.
[Ps. 23:5]

Those who follow the Shepherd are spiritually well-nourished. We cannot repeat it too often—If any sheep in the flock of Christ finds himself or herself in a spiritually barren wasteland, it is because he or she is not following near the Shepherd or has strayed from his side. Those who follow the Lord will never find themselves in such a spiritual environment.

The ancient shepherd in the Near East would often pick a branch off a tree and, as he walked, hold the branch behind him so that the sheep could follow closely and nibble on the morsels. This illustrates a profound truth: Those who stay nearest a shepherd are the best nourished. The same is true of us. Those of us who stay nearest our divine Shepherd are the best-nourished spiritually.

Surely goodness and love will follow me all the days of my life, and I will dwell in the house of the LORD forever. [Ps. 23:6]

David closes this psalm with the simple recognition that in view of all that he has affirmed in verses 1 through 5 about the divine Shepherd, surely only goodness and love will prevail in his life. How could it be otherwise? For the Shepherd himself is utterly good and utterly loving. Those who stay near him therefore find themselves showered with his goodness and love.

David affirmed that he would "dwell in the house of the LORD forever." His commitment was not a fleeting one. His commitment was a *forever* commitment.

We, too, must be committed forever. We can intellectually *know* that the Lord is a shepherd, but that knowledge in itself will not do us much good. We can intellectually understand that the Lord *can*, if permitted, meet our needs. But it is only when we come before him and place our lives completely in his hands and confidently affirm, "The Lord is *my* Shepherd," that the blessings in this psalm become a reality in our lives. Then we will be able to say along with the psalmist, "I shall not be in want."

John 10:1–18—Christ the Good Shepherd

According to Psalm 23, Bible expositor J. Dwight Pentecost tells us, "the role of the Shepherd was to make the sheep lie down in green pastures, to lead them beside quiet waters, to restore their souls, and to guide them in paths of righteousness. All this the Good Shepherd did. Christ as the Good Shepherd was Himself the way to life; and those who entered through Him were saved. They entered into freedom and found that which satisfied their souls."[16]

In describing himself as the Good Shepherd to his disciples, Jesus began by pointing out that "the man who does not enter the sheep pen by the gate, but climbs in by some other way, is a thief and a robber" (John 10:1). The sheep pen—a place of refuge and protection for the flock—was a stone enclosure, roughly square in shape, that had an entrance on only one side. This single entrance was guarded by a watchman or doorkeeper, whose business it was to keep out intruders and admit only authorized shepherds. If anyone were seen climbing over one of the four walls and not coming in through the entrance, it was safe to assume that he was an intruder, up to no good. To help discourage just such an unauthorized entry, the tops of the walls on most sheep pens in the ancient Near East were lined with a thorn hedge.[17]

Christ spoke to his disciples of the intimate relationship the shepherd has with his sheep: "The man who enters by the gate is the shepherd of his sheep. The watchman opens the gate for him, and the sheep listen to his voice. He calls his own sheep by name and leads them out" (John 10:2–3).

It was common in ancient days for more than one flock to be accommodated in the same sheep pen. In such a situation, each respective shepherd would stand at the entrance and call his own sheep by name. Such names were based on some peculiar characteristic of the sheep. This shows a shepherd's intimate familiarity with his sheep and pictures Christ's intimate familiarity with all who follow him, the divine Shepherd.

When the shepherd brings all his sheep out of the pen, "he goes on ahead of them, and his sheep follow him because they know his voice" (John 10:4). In Western countries, shepherds drive their sheep from behind. But Eastern shepherds always lead their sheep from the front.[18] So it is with Jesus, our Shepherd.

Following the shepherd was an absolute necessity for the sheep, if only for reasons of survival. Indeed, sheep by themselves have no ability to find food, water, shelter, or protection and are hence totally dependent upon the shepherd. In the same way, we as Christians are utterly dependent on our divine Shepherd. To *not* follow our Shepherd is to stray off the path and end up in a spiritually barren wasteland (Isa. 53:6).

One of the characteristics of sheep is that they know their shepherd and hear his voice. Implicit in the word *hear* is the commitment to obey. When a sheep hears his shepherd's voice, he moves immediately. In the same way, Christians hear their divine Shepherd's "voice" (in the words of Scripture, for example) and must obey without hesitation. To do otherwise is to stray from the Shepherd onto a wrong and destructive path.

Not only do sheep follow their shepherd's voice, "they will never follow a stranger; in fact, they will run away from him because they do not recognize a stranger's voice" (John 10:5). The phrase "they will never follow a stranger" is actually a double negative in the Greek; it carries the meaning, "they *certainly will not* follow a stranger." It is interesting to observe that strangers, even when dressed in their own shepherd's clothing and attempting to imitate his call, succeed only in making the sheep run away.[19]

To clarify to his disciples just what he meant by the Shepherd/sheep figure of speech, Jesus told them: "I tell you the truth, I am the gate for the sheep" (John 10:7). In other words, Jesus is the only way by which people can enter into God's provision for them. There is no other way. In fact, Christ's statement, "I am the gate," is not unlike another statement by Christ: "I am the way . . ." (John 14:6). Both passages communicate that Jesus is *the* way to the exclusion of all other alleged ways.

Then Jesus said to the disciples, "All who ever came before me were thieves and robbers, but the sheep did not listen to them" (John 10:8). By the words *thieves* and *robbers*, Jesus was not referring to the Old Testament prophets. (His high regard for the prophets is more than clear in John 6:45 and 8:56.) Rather, Jesus was referring to the self-appointed religious leaders of Israel. Such leaders were not interested in the well-being of the "sheep" (God's people) but in their own advantage. "The Sadducees in particular were known to make quite a lot of money out of temple religion and there are denunciations of the Pharisees (Luke 16:14) and the scribes (Mark 12:40) for covetousness."[20] Such men were unworthy shepherds of God's people.

Christ therefore emphasized that "*I* am the gate," and positively affirmed that "whoever enters *through me* will be saved. He will come in and go out, and find pasture" (John 10:9, italics added). The words *through me* are in an emphatic position in the Greek. It is he and no other who enables men to enter salvation.[21] Christ is THE gate.

Those who enter through Christ have the privilege of "coming in and going out," and finding pasture. The phrase *coming in and going out* is simply an idiom that indicates free and secure movement. Christ is the Shepherd who liberates his people so that they are truly free and unfettered from the chains of any kind of bondage.

Moreover, Christ is the Shepherd who satisfies. His own sheep shall "find pasture," for he has "come that they may have life, and have it to the full" (John 10:10). The shepherd "is not content that they should eke out a bare and miserable existence; he wants them to live life to the full, to have plenty of good pasturage and enjoy good health."[22] What a contrast this freedom and liberation is to the heavy chains of bondage so common to the Judaism of Jesus' day!

To emphasize the contrast between himself and the false shepherds of Israel, Jesus said, "I am the good shepherd. The good shepherd lays down his life for the sheep" (John 10:11). This sacrifice of one's life was a genuine possibility for Eastern shepherds. "When evening settled over the land of Palestine, danger lurked. In Bible times lions, wolves, jackals, panthers, leopards, bears, and hyenas were common in the countryside. The life of a shepherd could be dangerous, as illustrated by David's fights with at least one lion and one bear (1 Sam. 17:34–35, 37). Jacob also experienced the labor and toil of being a faithful shepherd (Gen. 31:38–40)."[23]

When a Palestinian shepherd lost his life on behalf of the sheep, it was always unplanned—an accident. With Jesus, however, death for his beloved sheep was purposeful and planned. His death resulted in the atonement for man's sins. Moreover, while the death of the Palestinian shepherd meant disaster for the flock, the death of Jesus our Good Shepherd means life for his sheep. For he rose from the dead, and because of his victory over death, we, too, shall be resurrected and live eternally with him.

Jesus then emphasized to the disciples that the hired hand is not committed; he is more or less interested in making money and "saving his own hide" (see John 10:12–13). When danger draws near, the hired hand is more concerned for his own safety than for the sheep. He will not risk his life to defend them against intruding animals, as the true shepherd will.

By contrast, Jesus says he is the Good Shepherd, and that *he knows his sheep* and *his sheep know him* (John 10:14). This reciprocal knowledge between the Shepherd and the sheep is not superficial but intimate. Indeed, this knowledge is likened to the "knowing" wherewith Jesus knows the Father and the Father knows him (John 10:15a). This is intimacy at its deepest. So intimately does Christ the Shepherd care for his sheep that he laid his life down for them (v. 15b).

We close with the following observation. To argue that Christ is the Shepherd, as I have done in this chapter, is not to say that the Father is uninvolved. Indeed, in John 10:29, Jesus acknowledges that it is the Father who has given him all his sheep. Jesus often spoke of those who were "given" to him by the Father. An example of this is found in Jesus' high priestly prayer to the Father, uttered just prior to Jesus' crucifixion and resurrection: "Father, the time has come. Glorify your Son, that your Son may glorify you. For you granted him authority over all people that he might give eternal life *to all those you have given him.* . . . I have revealed you to *those whom you gave me out of the world. They were yours; you gave them to me* and they have obeyed your word. . . . Father, I want *those you have given me* to be with me where I am, and to see my glory, the glory you have given me because you loved me before the creation of the world" (John 17:1–2, 6, 24, italics added). Apparently, part of the eternal plan of salvation called for the Father—who elected certain individuals unto salvation (Rom. 8:29–30; 1 Peter 1:2)—to entrust the care of the sheep (the people of God) to the divine Shepherd, Jesus Christ.

Praise to Christ Our Shepherd

In both Psalm 23 and John 10, we have seen that Christ our divine Shepherd is with us at every moment and intimately cares about even the smallest details of our lives. He knows us intimately by name, leads us and guides us, protects us, spiritually nourishes and refreshes us, gives us abundant life, gives us liberty and freedom, provides for all our needs, comforts us during tough times, and bestows goodness and love upon us. Christ the divine Shepherd did all this in Old Testament times among the people of God (Gen. 48:15; 49:24; Ps. 78:40–55); he did all this in New Testament times among the people of God (John 10); and he does it among the people of God *today!*

A closing thought: When we consider that Christ is himself the Creator of the entire universe and sustains it by his powerful word, it is truly staggering to ponder that this same glorious being has become our personal Shepherd. "All this is a bit humbling," real-life shepherd Phillip Keller has observed. "It drains the 'ego' from a man and puts things in proper perspective. It makes me see myself as a mere mite of material in an enormous universe. Yet the staggering fact remains that Christ the Creator of such an enormous universe of overwhelming magnitude, deigns to call Himself my Shepherd and invites me to consider myself His sheep—His special object of affection and attention. Who better could care for me?"[24]

Christ wants to be *your* Shepherd. In both Psalm 23 and John 10, it is as if he is saying to you: "Entrust the keeping of your soul and life to Me. Let Me lead you gently in the paths of righteousness and peace. My part is to show the way. Your part is to walk in it. All will be well."[25]

7

Christ the Savior

Before the world began—indeed, in eternity past—the triune God fully settled the issue of salvation. Scripture tells us that the Lamb of God "was slain from the creation of the world" (Rev. 13:8). And God "chose us in him before the creation of the world to be holy and blameless in his sight. In love he predestined us to be adopted as his sons through Jesus Christ, in accordance with his pleasure and will" (Eph. 1:4–5).

God promised eternal life to his people "before the beginning of time" (Titus 1:2). God has "saved us and called us to a holy life—not because of anything we have done but because of his own purpose and grace. This grace was given us in Christ Jesus before the beginning of time" (2 Tim. 1:9). Therefore, to the sheep of his pasture, Christ says: "Come, you who are blessed of My Father, inherit the kingdom prepared for you from the foundation of the world" (Matt. 25:34 NASB).

Because God's plan of salvation is an *eternal* plan, it is clear that man's salvation was not an afterthought on God's part. Nor was it the only possible way out of a "hopeless dilemma" for God. God planned everything from the very beginning. In view of this, we must conclude that God in his omniscience (all-knowingness) was not shocked or surprised when Satan, and then man, fell. God's glorious plan—which encompasses even the Fall—is *from* eternity past *to* eternity future.

Only God Can Be Savior

A study of the Old Testament indicates that it is *only* God that saves. In Isaiah 43:11, God asserts: "I, even I, am the LORD, and apart from me there is no savior." This is an extremely important verse, for it indicates that (1) a claim to be Savior is, in itself, a claim to deity; and (2) there is only *one* Savior—God.

Against this backdrop, it is truly revealing of Christ's divine nature that the New Testament refers to Jesus Christ as the Savior. Following the birth of Christ, an angel appeared to some neighboring shepherds and said: "Today in the town of David a Savior has been born to you; he is Christ the Lord" (Luke 2:11). John's Gospel records the conclusion of the Samaritans: Jesus "really is the Savior of the world" (John 4:42).

In Titus 2:13, Paul encourages Titus to await the blessed hope, the "glorious appearing of our great God and Savior, Jesus Christ." An examination of Titus 2:10–13, 3:4, and 3:6 reveals that the phrases "God our Savior" and "Jesus our Savior" are used interchangeably four times. The parallel truths that *only* God is the Savior (Isa. 43:11) and that Jesus is himself the Savior constitute a powerful evidence for Christ's deity.

In view of such scriptural evidence, theologians have concluded that Jesus Christ is the Savior hoped for in both Testaments.[1] Indeed, "the important fact which stands out above all others is that the Savior of the Old Testament is the Savior of the New Testament. He was actively engaged in bringing salvation in its widest sense to those who trusted Him."[2] Certainly it was Christ who actually made salvation possible by his work on the cross. Indeed, "all salvation of God stems from the Savior, the Son of God, and His work on the cross."[3]

Charles Hodge agrees that "the Redeemer is the same under all dispensations [ages]. He who was predicted as the seed of the woman, the seed of Abraham, the Son of David, the Branch, the Servant of the Lord, the prince of Peace, is our

Lord Jesus Christ, the Son of God, God manifest in the flesh. He, therefore, from the beginning has been held up as the hope of the world."[4] That Christ is the Savior is reflected in the name *Jesus*—which means, "Yahweh is salvation."

Related to this is the fact that Jesus placed himself on an equal par with the Father as the proper object of men's trust. Jesus told the disciples: "Do not let your hearts be troubled. Trust in God; trust also in me" (John 14:1). Theologian Robert Reymond notes that "if Jesus was not in fact divine, such a saying would constitute blasphemy of the first order. . . . He cannot be a mere man and at the same time good while teaching men to trust Him as they would trust the Father."[5]

Christ the Savior: Central Theme of the Old Testament

Though the full revelation of Christ as Savior is found in the New Testament, it is highly revealing that Christ often indicated that he and his work of redemption was the theme of the Old Testament Scriptures. We have noted on several occasions that after his resurrection from the dead, Jesus explained all that was said about him in the Old Testament Scriptures to two disciples on the road to Emmaus (Luke 24:27).

Later, Jesus appeared to some of his frightened disciples and assured them that his suffering and crucifixion had been part of the eternal plan of salvation: "This is what I told you while I was still with you: Everything must be fulfilled that is written about me in the Law of Moses, the Prophets, and the Psalms" (Luke 24:44). Notice that Jesus said, "this is what I told you while I was *still with you*" (that is, *prior* to the crucifixion). Apparently, Jesus had explained to the disciples quite thoroughly what the Old Testament said about him and his role in the outworking of the plan of salvation—but Jesus' words didn't fully sink in. So now, to give his frightened disciples strength, the resurrected Jesus again "opened their minds so they could understand the [Old Testament] Scriptures" (v. 45, insert mine).

Jesus made this same point during his three-year ministry when he encountered a group of hostile Jews. Jesus said to them: "You diligently study the [Old Testament] Scriptures because you think that by them you possess eternal life. These are the Scriptures that testify about me, yet you refuse to come to me to have life" (John 5:39–40, insert mine). Though these Jewish leaders had studied the Old Testament Scriptures in minute detail, they had failed to recognize the one to whom it bears supreme testimony (see Appendix B for more on this). As Norman Geisler puts it, the Jewish leaders "knew the shell of the Bible but were neglecting the kernel within it."[6]

In light of all the above, viewing the Old Testament in a way that centers on Christ and his mission of salvation is not a mere option for the Christian. Indeed, for the Christian it is a divine imperative, since Christ himself claimed to be the theme of the Old Testament (Matt. 5:18).

Because Christ the Savior is the theme of the Old Testament Scriptures, the relationship between the Old and New Testaments is inseparably connected in the person of Jesus Christ. The two Testaments are mutually interdependent. Norman Geisler explains that "the Old Testament is incomplete without the New. What the Old Testament prepared for, the New Testament provides in Christ. Christ is the anticipation of the Old and the realization of the New. For what is commenced in the Old Testament is completed in the New Testament, and the fact of Christ in the New Testament cannot be understood apart from the foundation laid for Him in the Old Testament."[7]

The mutual interdependency of the Old and New Testaments is no accident. The fact that the Old Testament prepared for and laid the foundation for the New Testament is due to the fact that *God planned it that way*. Indeed, all that took place in Old Testament times in preparation for the coming of Christ in New Testament times—including all of Christ's preincarnate appearances—was simply an outworking of God's eternal plan of salvation. It is to this plan that we now turn our attention.

The Eternal Plan of Salvation

Even before the beginning of time, God the Most High concerned himself with our eternal benefit. Before the earth and the stellar universe were brought into being at God's command, *even then* he had thoughts on you and me. The thoughtful Christian can only respond with awe as he contemplates what God has done for him. As one Christian writer has put it, "truly these are depths not to be fathomed, and which the heart of every man despairs of being able to describe in words. Here we can only bow and worship, and lay our life at the feet of Him, the All-loving."[8]

Scripture indicates that each person of the Trinity had an important role to play in the outworking of God's eternal plan of salvation. In theological circles, God's plan of salvation for humanity is related to his "decree." God's decree may be defined as "his eternal purpose, according to the counsel of his will, whereby, for his own glory, he hath foreordained whatsoever comes to pass."[9] God's eternal decree relates to *all* of God's work, not simply to his work in saving humankind. The decree includes God's work of creation, providence, preservation, the permission of sin into the world, the provision of salvation, the judgment of all humankind, and the sovereign will of God as it is related to all events of time and eternity.[10]

There are literally hundreds of passages in Scripture related to the outworking of God's sovereign plan. A look at just a few of these shows that what he has planned will, in fact, be accomplished down to the smallest detail: "For the LORD Almighty has purposed, and who can thwart him? His hand is stretched out, and who can turn it back?" (Isa. 14:27); "I make known the end from the beginning, from ancient times, what is still to come. I say: My purpose will stand, and I will do all that I please" (46:10).

God's people in biblical times recognized the sure and certain nature of God's sovereign plan. Job said, "I know that you can do all things; no plan of yours can be thwarted" (Job 42:2).

Solomon said, "Many are the plans in a man's heart, but it is the LORD's purpose that prevails" (Prov. 19:21). David affirmed, "All the days ordained for me were written in your book before one of them came to be" (Ps. 139:16).

It is not surprising that our sovereign God, who controls all things in the universe, should have a specific plan according to which he works out his purposes in the universe. When God formulated his decree, he drew on his boundless knowledge and wisdom. This plan even includes and allows for the free-will decisions made by his creatures. As Reformed theologian Louis Berkhof has observed,

> [The inclusion of all things in God's decree] does not necessarily mean that He Himself will actively bring them into existence, but means in some cases that, with the divine permission and according to the divine plan, they will certainly be brought to realization by His rational creatures. The decree covers all the works of God in creation and redemption, and also embraces the actions of His free moral beings, not excluding their sinful actions. But while the entrance of sin into the world and its various manifestations in the lives of angels and men were thus rendered certain, this does not mean that God decided to effectuate these Himself. God's decree with reference to sin is a permissive decree.[11]

Charles Hodge, another Reformed theologian, adds this helpful insight about the relationship between God's sovereign decree and human free-will choices:

> All events embraced in the purpose of God are equally certain, whether He has determined to bring them to pass by His own power, or simply to permit their occurrence through the agency of His creatures. It was no less certain from eternity that Satan would tempt our first parents, and that they would fall, than that God would send His Son to die for sinners. . . . Some things He purposes to do, others He decrees to permit to be done. He effects good, He permits evil. He is the author of the one, but not of the other.[12]

Hence, when we speak of God's eternal decree, we are referring to his effective sovereign resolve or purpose, which is grounded in his free wisdom, and by which he eternally controls the creation. It encompasses all God's actions in the creation and direction of the world.

The Father's Role in the Eternal Plan of Salvation

A careful reading of Scripture shows that it was the Father who planned and ordained salvation (John 3:16; Isa. 53:6, 10). This plan was not an emergency response conceived as a plan of rescue after humankind fell, but rather was the Father's sovereign choice in eternity past.

"He who works in an orderly way in nature," theologian Henry C. Thiessen comments, "has not left the salvation of man to haphazard and uncertain experimentation. Scripture shows us that he has a definite plan of salvation. This plan includes the means by which salvation is to be provided, the objectives that are to be realized, the persons that are to benefit by it, the conditions on which it is to be available, and the agents and means by which it is to be applied."[13]

In the outworking of this eternal plan, the Father—with infinite love and compassion—acted on our behalf even before we were born. The apostle Paul told the Ephesian Christians that they had been *chosen* in Christ by the Father before the foundation of the world (Eph. 1:4). Paul likewise wrote to the Roman Christians about the Father's *foreknowledge, predestination,* and sovereign *calling* of certain individuals before time even began (Rom. 8:29–30). Peter, writing to saints scattered throughout Asia Minor, described them as *elect* of God the Father (1 Peter 1:1–2). From these and other verses, it is clear that within the eternal plan of salvation, it was the Father's unique role to elect and call certain individuals to salvation.

The Son's Role in the Eternal Plan of Salvation

The Son's task in the eternal plan of God included playing a key role in the creation of the universe (John 1:3; Col. 1:16; Heb. 1:2), making preincarnate appearances to the patriarchs in Old Testament times (Gen. 16:7; 22:11), coming to earth as God's ultimate revelation (John 1:18; Heb. 1:1–2), dying on the cross as a substitutionary sacrifice for man's sins (John 3:16), resurrecting from the dead (1 Peter 1:3; 3:21), and being the Mediator between the Father and humankind (1 Tim. 2:5). The eternal plan also called for the second coming of the Son in glory to consummate human redemption (Rev. 19–22).

In his sermon at Pentecost, Peter specifically spoke of Christ's suffering and crucifixion as a part of God's eternal plan of salvation. Peter said that "this man was handed over to you by God's set purpose and foreknowledge; and you, with the help of wicked men, put him to death by nailing him to the cross" (Acts 2:23). Some time later, Peter and John acknowledged that those who had crucified Christ were doing what the Father had determined in the eternal plan of salvation (Acts 4:28). Still later, Peter said that people are redeemed by "the precious blood of Christ, a lamb without blemish or defect. *He was chosen before the creation of the world . . .*" (1 Peter 1:19–20, italics added). Benjamin Warfield thus concludes that Jesus "was not the prey of chance or the victim of the hatred of men, to the marring of His work or perhaps even the defeat of His mission, but was following step by step, straight to its goal, the predestined pathway marked out for Him in the counsels of eternity."[14]

As Jesus was dying on the cross as a substitutionary sacrifice for the sins of humankind, he uttered the words: "It is finished" (John 19:30). This proclamation from the Savior's lips is fraught with meaning. "Surely the Lord was doing more than announcing the termination of his physical life. That fact was self-evident. What was not known by those who were carrying out the brutal business at Calvary was that somehow, in spite of the sin they were committing, God through Christ had completed the final sacrifice for sin."[15]

Actually, the phrase *it is finished* is better translated from the Greek, "it stands finished." Upon the cross, the Son of God was announcing that God's eternal plan of salvation had been enacted in time and space. And the sacrificial aspect of that plan was now completed.

In view of the above, it is clear that Christ's role in the out-working of the eternal plan of salvation was absolutely central. Indeed, as one Christian writer put it, "Jesus Christ is the innermost center of the whole divine counsel of salvation. Everything which came to pass before Him took place with a view to His coming; everything in the history of the kingdom of God which is later than His coming is wrought in His name."[16]

The Holy Spirit's Role in the Eternal Plan of Salvation

The Holy Spirit also played a key role in the outworking of the plan of salvation. A key aspect of the Holy Spirit's role involved ministering to Jesus Christ during his incarnate state. John Walvoord writes:

> In the plan, the Third Person [the Holy Spirit] undertook to be-get the Second Person (the Son) of the Virgin Mary, to fill Him, and to supply all necessary enablement to sustain the Son in the sphere of His humiliation and empower Him for His life among men. . . . The fact that the Holy Spirit undertook this ministry is not explicitly revealed, but may be concluded from the nature of the eternal purpose which is based on specific revelation (Acts 2:23; Rom. 8:29; 1 Cor. 2:7; 2 Tim. 1:9; Titus 1:2). As essential to the program of redemption and the salvation of the elect, the Holy Spirit must have assumed this part of the plan.[17]

Moreover, the Holy Spirit undertook the ministry of inspiring Scripture (2 Peter 1:21), regenerating believers (Titus 3:5), indwelling believers (1 Cor. 6:19), baptizing believers (1 Cor. 12:13), sealing believers (Eph. 4:30), and bestowing spiritual gifts upon believers (1 Cor. 12:11). It is obvious from these and many other passages that the third person was heavily involved in the outworking of the eternal plan of salvation.

Planned in Eternity; Carried Out in Time

All that the triune God determined *before* time was carried out *in* time. For this reason, God's plan of salvation is called his "eternal purpose" (Eph. 3:11), and God is praised as "the King of ages" (1 Tim. 1:17 RSV).

Human history in all its details, even the most minute, is but the outworking of the eternal purposes of God. Theologian Robert Lightner comments that "when viewed from the perspective of Scripture, history is more than the recording of the events of the past. Rather, what has happened in the past, what is happening now, and what will happen in the future is all evidence of the unfolding of the purposeful plan devised by the personal God of the Bible. All the circumstances of life—past, present, and future—fit into the sovereign plan like pieces of a puzzle."[18]

Since the plan of salvation was formulated in eternity past and is worked out in temporal history, we as Christians must come to regard history from the standpoint of eternity. We must recognize a uniform plan, guided by God, which in the course of human history has been steadily unfolded and will one day find its culmination when Christ comes again and sets up his glorious millennial kingdom. Following this, in the eternal state, we shall dwell in the unveiled presence of the triune God for all eternity!

The First Preaching of the Gospel: Genesis 3:15

The first preaching of the gospel took place in Genesis 3:15.[19] Adam and Eve had sinned against God by eating the forbidden fruit, having been deceived by the crafty serpent (vv. 1–7). Then Adam and Eve "heard the sound of the LORD God as he was walking in the garden in the cool of the day, and they hid from the LORD God among the trees of the garden" (v. 8). The almost casual way in which God walked in the garden has led some scholars to conclude that this was not the first time God had done this. "The assumption that God had repeatedly done this is quite feasible," Old Testament scholar H. C. Leupold suggests.[20]

As he was walking along, the Lord called for Adam and Eve, "Where are you?" (Gen. 3:9). "It is easy to imagine the sweetness of the divine voice, as it sounded forth through the trees in the stillness of the evening, calling, 'Where are you?' Of course, God knew where the man and woman were. But he was appealing to them, seeking through tenderness and love to win a favorable response."[21] And when Adam answered, he immediately confessed to eating the forbidden fruit, but "passed the buck" (or blame) to Eve, who had given him the fruit (v. 12). Eve promptly responded by saying that "the serpent deceived me, and I ate" (v. 13).

Following this disobedience, God had no choice but to pronounce judgment. Since the serpent was a prime culprit in the Fall, God pronounced judgment against him first: "And I will put enmity between you and the woman, and between your offspring and hers; he will crush your head, and you will strike his heel" (Gen. 3:15). In this pronouncement of judgment, the dawn of man's salvation is clearly evident. Walvoord tells us:

> It is a wonderful revelation of the mercy and love of God that in the Garden of Eden, before He pronounced judgment on Adam and Eve, God—it may have been the Son of God Himself—promised that the seed of the woman would bruise the head of the serpent (Gen. 3:15). Here was the ray of hope in the darkness of human sin and failure. God had a way of salvation. The reference to the seed of the woman is a prophecy of the birth of the Son of God. This is the point of Luke's genealogy (cf. Gal. 4:4). The coming Savior was to be the seed of the woman—human; and yet in the fact that He is not called the seed of man, we have the foreshadowing of the virgin birth (Isa. 7:14; Matt. 1:21–22). To Adam it was made very plain that his hope lay in this future Child of the woman, that through this Child salvation would come from God. God confirmed His mercy to Adam and Eve by driving them out of the garden—a judgment

for sin to be sure, but an act of mercy as well, lest they eat of the tree of life and live forever in bodies of sin.[22]

In view of the vast implications of this verse, famed preacher Charles H. Spurgeon commented that "this is the first gospel sermon that was ever delivered upon the surface of this earth. It was a memorable discourse indeed, with Jehovah himself for the preacher, and the whole human race and the prince of darkness for the audience. It must be worthy of our heartiest attention. . . . Is it not remarkable that this great gospel promise should have been delivered so soon after the transgression?"[23]

When Jesus came on the scene in the first century, he was clearly the fulfillment of the prophecy.[24] Indeed, Jesus said that he had come to destroy the works of the devil (John 12:31; 16:11; see Heb. 2:14 and 1 John 3:8), and he inflicted a mortal blow to the devil's domination over humankind (Acts 10:38; 26:15–18; Eph. 4:8; Col. 2:15; James 4:7). Following Christ's future millennial kingdom, Christ will once and for all do away with the devil by casting him into the lake of fire (Rev. 20:10).

Blood Sacrifices in Early Human History

Immediately following the Fall, we find clear evidence that God had communicated to Adam and his family about the need for blood sacrifices. Recall that when Cain, Adam's first son, offered a bloodless sacrifice (fruit) to God, God refused to receive it (Gen. 4:5). By contrast, Abel, Adam's second son, offered "fat portions from some of the firstborn of his flock," and God accepted this offering (v. 4).

It is likely that these respective offerings reflected the spiritual condition of both Cain and Abel. The key point to observe here is that God appealed to Cain on the basis of revelation God had previously provided. "Abel and Cain both knew that the sacrifice for sin should be a particular animal, a lamb; a particular lamb, the firstling; and a particular part of the lamb, the fat. Such knowledge could come only from revelation."[25]

We are told in Hebrews 11:4 that *"by faith* Abel offered God a better sacrifice than Cain did" (italics added). Abel's faith was based on the revelation that God must have provided Adam and his family regarding blood sacrifices and the fact that they point forward to the coming Savior. If revelation had *not* been given, how could Abel have responded in faith? (Faith always has objective content!) We can deduce from this verse that Cain *lacked* faith regarding what God revealed about the blood sacrifices.

The Savior and Old Testament Personalities

It is fascinating to ponder how key Old Testament personalities such as Moses and Abraham had some personal knowledge about Christ the Savior.[26] How *much* knowledge they possessed we cannot be sure. Walvoord notes that "it is clear that Old Testament saints did not believe in Christ in the same way and with the same comprehension that believers with the New Testament do for the simple reason that they were not in possession of the same information. In the nature of the case the issue of faith is to believe in the revelation given."[27]

Nevertheless, Scripture provides us with clear indications that some of the Old Testament saints were definitely aware of Christ and his ministry.

Moses and the Savior

Hebrews 11:24–27 tells us:

> By faith Moses, when he had grown up, refused to be known as the son of Pharaoh's daughter.
>
> He chose to be mistreated along with the people of God rather than to enjoy the pleasures of sin for a short time.
>
> He regarded disgrace for the sake of Christ as of greater value than the treasures of Egypt, because he was looking ahead to his reward.
>
> By faith he left Egypt, not fearing the king's anger; he persevered because he saw him who is invisible.

It is interesting that the writer of Hebrews said that Moses "regarded disgrace for the sake of Christ as of greater value than the treasures of Egypt," since Moses lived at least 1,500 years before Christ. It is difficult to ascertain how much Moses knew about Christ, but our text clearly indicates that Moses was declared to have had a personal faith in Christ on the basis of which he forsook Egypt. "God spoke to him, showing him things invisible to the natural eye, revealing another King, another kingdom, and a better reward."[28]

The Hebrew word for "regarded" in the phrase, "He *regarded* disgrace for the sake of Christ as of greater value than the treasures of Egypt," is a word that indicates careful thought and not a quick decision. Moses thought through his decision, weighing the pros and cons. "He weighed what Egypt had to offer against what God offered. When he reached a conclusion it was well-founded and certain. God's offer was infinitely superior in every way."[29]

Bible expositor E. Schuyler English suggests the following reconstruction of Moses' line of reasoning:

Jehovah has revealed future things to me, invisible things, but things of glory, heavenly things. I believe what He says. At the same time He has made known to me that I am His chosen instrument to deliver His people, my brethren according to the flesh, from bondage. But I am the adopted son of Pharaoh's daughter. To me the throne of Egypt has been promised, as heir through her. If I follow God's program for me, I must suffer reproach, the reproach of the Messiah, the Deliverer. If, on the other hand, I remain in the royal court, all the wealth of Egypt is mine—and how great is that wealth! If I take the course Jehovah has laid out for me, I must suffer affliction with my brethren, and I have seen how heavy their burdens are. Whereas if I am ready to be called Pharaoh's grandson, the pleasures of all that Egypt has to offer, the pleasures of sin, may be enjoyed. Each of these things—the affliction of the people of God, and the pleasures of sin—is temporal. I am looking to life after death. Then, he who has suffered within the will of God will be rewarded; but he who has followed the way of the flesh will be judged. What God has spoken is surely true. I make my choice. I refuse to be called the son of Pharaoh's daughter, preferring by choice to suffer affliction with God's people than to enjoy the pleasures of sin, accounting the reproach of the Messiah, with its present satisfaction and eventual reward, greater riches by far than the treasures of Egypt.[30]

Regarding the prospect of suffering for Christ, Moses would certainly have agreed with what the apostles wrote many centuries later. The apostle Peter said that "if you are insulted because of the name of Christ, you are blessed, for the Spirit of glory and of God rests on you" (1 Peter 4:14). The apostle Paul said, "For our light and momentary troubles are achieving for us an eternal glory that far outweighs them all. So we fix our eyes not on what is seen, but on what is unseen. For what is seen is temporary, but what is unseen is eternal" (2 Cor. 4:17–18).

Moses gave up temporal pleasure for the sake of his Savior, Jesus Christ. His priorities were as they should have been. And what joy Moses' commitment must have brought to the heart of God!

Abraham and the Savior

During his three-year ministry, Jesus often encountered hostile Jews who rejected what he said. On one such occasion, Jesus engaged in a dialogue with some Jews about Abraham (John 8:54–56). As a backdrop, keep in mind that the Jews felt that because they were the natural descendents of Abraham, they were in a privileged position before God. Jesus countered by pointing out that *true* spiritual descendants of Abraham do what Abraham did—that is, they believe and obey God. These Jews should have responded by faith in the one sent by God (Jesus) rather than merely trusting in their Abrahamic lineage.

Jesus then made an astonishing statement to this group of Jews. He said, "Your father Abraham rejoiced at the thought of seeing my day; he saw it and was glad" (John 8:56). *Jesus Christ was the one to whom Abraham looked forward.* And when

Abraham thought of seeing Christ's "day," he was filled with gladness.

It is fascinating that the Angel of the Lord—whom in chapter 5 was shown to be the preincarnate Christ—appeared to Abraham and said: "I will surely bless you and make your descendants as numerous as the stars in the sky and as the sand on the seashore. Your descendants will take possession of the cities of their enemies, and *through your offspring* [or *seed*] all nations on earth will be blessed, because you have obeyed me" (Gen. 22:17–18, insert mine, italics added).

The reference to "offspring" or "seed" in this verse is a messianic prophecy that *through Christ* (in the future incarnation) all the nations of the earth would be blessed. We know from Galatians 3:8–16 that this promise to Abraham had *one individual* in view—the incarnate Messiah, Jesus Christ.

Are you catching the significance of all of this? It was the Angel of the Lord (the *pre*incarnate Christ) who informed Abraham that through Abraham's future earthly offspring (the incarnate Christ, born of a woman) all the nations of the earth would be blessed. Clearly, Christ was intimately involved in the outworking of the eternal plan of salvation throughout both the Old and New Testaments. As we shall see next, further evidence for this is found in Psalm 2.

Refuge in the Son (Psalm 2)

In his excellent volume, *Christology of the Old Testament*, E. W. Hengstenberg soundly demonstrates that Psalm 2 is a messianic psalm—that is, it is a psalm that deals with the Messiah, Jesus Christ.[31] In this psalm, we find a reference to Christ's acting in the role of Savior. The psalmist writes: "Serve the LORD with fear and rejoice with trembling. *Kiss the Son*, lest he be angry and you be destroyed in your way, for his wrath can flare up in a moment. *Blessed are all who take refuge in him*" (Ps. 2:11–12, italics added). Hengstenberg provides convincing evidence that the "Son" in this verse is not a reference to an earthly king, as some have supposed, but is a reference to the second person of the Trinity, Jesus Christ.[32] A number of other scholars agree with Hengstenberg on this.[33]

The word *kiss* in this context is used in accordance with Oriental usages, for it was by a kiss that respect was indicated for one of superior rank. A kiss was "the ancient mode of doing homage or allegiance to a king."[34] The "kiss" in this verse indicates *believing* the Son, *obeying* the Son, *loving* the Son, and being *loyal* to the Son:

> *Kiss the Son,* not with a betraying kiss, as Judas kissed him, but with a believing kiss. With a kiss of affection and sincere love: "Kiss the Son; enter into a covenant of friendship with him, and let him be very dear and precious to you; love him above all, love him in sincerity, love him much, as she did to whom much was forgiven, and, in token of it, kissed his feet," Luke 7:38. With a kiss of allegiance and loyalty, submit to his government, take his yoke upon you.[35]

What is particularly significant in verses 11 and 12 is that the phrase "Blessed are all who take refuge in him" is a specific reference to the Son. To take refuge in the Son is to recognize that it is the Son who saves; *it is the Son who is the Savior.* Moreover, the very act of taking refuge in the Son is an implicit recognition of the deity of the Son. Indeed, "to the Son of God is attributed that same confidence and trust that is given to Jehovah."[36]

The Prophets and the "Spirit of Christ"

In 1 Peter 1:10–11, the apostle Peter speaks of the prophets and their words about salvation in Christ: "Concerning this salvation, the prophets, who spoke of the grace that was to come to you, searched intently and with the greatest care, trying to find out the time and circumstances to which the Spirit of Christ in them was pointing when he predicted the sufferings of Christ and the glories that would follow."

Scholars have debated over what may be meant by the phrase, "Spirit of Christ." Grammatically, the phrase may refer either to Christ himself (as the Spirit *of* Christ) or to the Holy Spirit (as the Spirit *from* Christ). The form of the word in the Greek is the same in either case *(Christou)*.[37]

A number of scholars have concluded that it was indeed *Christ's* spirit who was at work in the prophets.[38] Based on this verse, Clement of Alexandria suggested that Jesus was "the Prophet of prophets, and Lord of all the prophetical spirit."[39]

Along these same lines, theologian Millard Erickson summarizes:

> Christ's revealing work covers a wide span of time and forms. He first functioned in a revelatory fashion even before his incarnation. As the Logos [the divine Word], he is the light which has enlightened everyone coming into the world; thus, in a sense all truth has come from and through him (John 1:9). There are indications that Christ himself was at work in the revelations which came through the prophets who bore a message about him . . . (1 Peter 1:11). Although not personally incarnate, Christ was already making the truth known.[40]

R. C. H. Lenski comments that in 1 Peter 1:11, "the deity and the pre-existence of Christ are involved: Christ's Spirit testified in advance about Christ's sufferings and glories, that is, when as the incarnate Logos he would suffer in his humiliation and after that be crowned with glories in his exaltation."[41]

I am personally convinced that Christ himself was making truth known through the Old Testament prophets. But for those who are not sure, one further consideration bears mentioning. Even if the phrase "Spirit of Christ" refers not to Christ's spirit but to the Holy Spirit, we would have to conclude that the Holy Spirit *as* the "Spirit of Christ" was doing Christ's bidding in the prophets—pointing them to the future sufferings and glories of Jesus the Savior/Messiah.

The Book of Life

We shall examine one final verse that deals with the eternal plan of salvation. Revelation 13 focuses on the beast and the false prophet in the future tribulation period (that seven-year period preceding the second coming of Christ in which God will pour out his judgments on humankind). Verse 8 tells us: "All inhabitants of the earth will worship the beast—all whose names have not been written in the book of life belonging to the Lamb that was slain from the creation of the world."

The idea of a divine register containing names goes back as far as Moses' encounter with God on Mount Sinai (Exod. 32:32–33). The apostle Paul speaks of his fellow workers as those "whose names are in the book of life" (Phil. 4:3). In the Book of Revelation the "book of life" is mentioned six times (3:5; 13:8; 17:8; 20:12, 15; and 21:27), and contains the names of all those who belong to God. In Revelation 13:8 and 21:27, the book of life is said to belong to the Lamb of God, Jesus Christ.

More specifically, the book belongs to "the Lamb that was slain from the creation of the world" (Rev. 13:8). That Christ was "slain from the creation of the world" indicates that Christ's redemptive sacrifice was decreed in the counsels of eternity. Indeed, "as Jesus Christ was in the divine purpose appointed from the foundation of the world to redeem man by his blood, he therefore is, in a very eminent sense, the Lamb slain from the foundation of the world, that is, from the creation."[42]

Revelation 13:8 is in keeping with what we learn elsewhere of the sacrifice of the Lamb of God. 1 Peter 1:18–20 tells us: "For you know that it was not with perishable things such as silver or gold that you were redeemed from the empty way of life handed down to you from your forefathers, but with the precious blood of Christ, a lamb without blemish or defect. He was chosen before the creation of the world, but was revealed in these last times for your sake."

How thankful we should all be to our Savior who—from beginning to end, from the first to the last, from origination to consummation—has taken care of every aspect of our salvation. All that we have examined in this chapter—the eternal decree, God's eternal plan of salvation, Christ as the Savior of both Old and New Testaments, the first preaching of the gospel in Genesis 3:15, the early institution of blood sacrifices, Christ's interactions with Abraham and Moses, the Son of God as a refuge, and the Lamb's book of life—point to the central role of the Son in the outworking of the plan of salvation throughout human history.

Blessed be the Lamb!

8

Christ the Eternal *Logos*

Unlike the Synoptic Gospel writers (Matthew, Mark, and Luke), John begins his Gospel in eternity—"*In the beginning was the Word, and the Word was with God, and the Word was God*" (John 1:1, italics added). It is from this eternal perspective that John understands the true significance of the work of Christ.

We have already learned much from John's Gospel about the preexistence and eternality of Christ. For example:

- In the Introduction, we noted that Jesus implicitly claimed to be *Yahweh*—the eternal "I AM WHO I AM" (John 8:58; cf. Exod. 3:14). We also saw that prior to the creation, the Father, Son, and Holy Spirit enjoyed an eternal loving fellowship with each other (John 17:24).
- In chapter 1, we noted the full deity of Christ (John 20:28), as well as plurality within the Godhead (1:1).
- In chapter 2, we examined John the Baptist's testimony regarding the preexistence and eternality of Christ (John 1:15, 30; 3:31). We also examined the many verses in John's Gospel indicating that Jesus was "sent" from heaven to earth by the Father (3:13; 6:33, 38, 46, 51, 62;

8:23, 42) and will "return" or "go back" to the Father (13:3; 16:27–28). As well, we took a brief look at some of Christ's divine attributes, including: self-existence (1:4; 5:26), omnipresence (1:47–49), omniscience (2:25; 16:30; 21:17), omnipotence (1:3; 2:19; 11:1–44), and sovereignty (5:21–22, 27–29; 10:18).

- In chapter 3, we saw that Christ was the sovereign Creator of the universe (John 1:3).
- In chapter 5, we noted that no one has ever seen the Father's form (John 5:37), but Jesus came to earth to make the Father known to humankind (1:14, 18).
- In chapter 6, we considered evidences for Jesus' role as the divine Shepherd (Ps. 23; John 10).
- Then, in chapter 7, we saw that Jesus claimed that he—the divine Savior—was the theme of the Old Testament Scriptures (John 5:39–40).

Without doubt, John's Gospel is the richest book in the New Testament in regard to various evidences for Christ's preexistence and eternality. Among the most powerful of these evidences is John's affirmation that Christ is the divine "Word."

The Greek noun for "Word" in John 1:1 is *Logos,* a term that has been the subject of much debate down through the centuries since the time of Christ. Its importance lies in the fact that Christ the *Logos* is portrayed as a preexistent, eternal being. Indeed, John even says that the *Logos* is God. The *Logos* is also said to be the Creator of the universe, for "through him all things were made; without him nothing was made that has been made" (John 1:3).

The concept of "the Word" has a long history beginning in Old Testament times. In the Old Testament, the "Word of God" is metaphorically portrayed as having an active character and was viewed as an effective agent for accomplishing God's will.[1] For example, God is quoted in Isaiah as asserting: ". . . my word that goes out from my mouth: It will not return to me empty, but will accomplish what I desire and achieve the purpose for which I sent it" (55:11).

Another aspect of the Jewish understanding of "the Word" is evident in the Jewish Targums—simplified paraphrases of the Old Testament Scriptures. In the Targums, we learn that the Jews—out of reverence for God—sometimes substituted the phrase *the Word of God* in place of the word *God*. The Jews were fearful of breaking the third commandment: "You shall not misuse the name of the LORD your God, for the LORD will not hold anyone guiltless who misuses his name" (Exod. 20:7). New Testament scholar Leon Morris explains:

> The Targumists tried to give the sense of the passage being read, and not simply to translate mechanically. These Targums were produced at a time when, from motives of reverence and from a fear of breaking the third commandment, Jews had ceased to pronounce the divine name. When they came to this name in the original the readers and translators substituted some other expression they thought more reverent, such as "the Holy One" or "the Name." Sometimes they said "the Word *(Memra)*." For example, where our Bible says, "And Moses brought forth the people out of the camp to meet God" (Exod. 19:17), the Targum reads "to meet the Word of God."[2]

Around A.D. 25, a Jewish philosopher named Philo developed a different concept of the Word (or *Logos*) that was dualistic in nature. Philo taught that God (who is spirit) is good, but matter is evil. Because matter is evil, material things could not have been created by a holy God. For him to do so would have been sin. Since matter was not created by God, Philo reasoned, matter must be just as eternal as God. They must have co-existed for all eternity.

So holy is God, Philo said, that God could not even come into contact with the material universe. He would become defiled if he did. Because of this, God has always been completely separate from the physical universe. But, Philo suggested, there was a "mediating principle" through which God communicated and interacted with the material universe. This impersonal intermediary he called the *Logos*.[3]

When we come to John's Gospel, we find that John does not adopt either the Old Testament concept or Philo's philosophical concept when he refers to Jesus Christ as the *Logos*. For John, the "Word" is a divine *person* who has come into the world to reveal *another person* (the Father) to the world.

All things considered, it would seem that John chose the term "Word" (or *Logos*) because both Greeks and Jews would be somewhat familiar with the term, but he invested it with an entirely new meaning. He gave it a much higher connotation than it ever had before. Indeed, when John used *Logos* of Jesus Christ, he did so not with the intention of presenting Christ as a divine principle but as a living being who was the source of all life; not as a mere personification (as Philo had suggested in his writings), but as a person who was nothing less than God himself: ". . . the Word was *with* God, and the Word *was* God" (John 1:1, italics added).

We must stress the significance of John's making such an assertion in view of his monotheistic background. The belief in monotheism was not an optional doctrine for the Jews. It was a conviction to be clung to and defended with fierce tenacity. John's background was one that recognized with an unshakable certainty the existence of only one true God. It is against this backdrop that John unflinchingly asserted that Christ the *Logos* is God.

In the Beginning

The words "In the beginning" in John 1:1 translate the Greek words, *en arche*. It is highly significant that these are the very words that begin the Book of Genesis in the Septuagint, the Greek translation of the Hebrew Old Testament that predates the time of Christ. The obvious conclusion we must draw is that John's "beginning" is identical to the Genesis "beginning." (Further parallels between the two accounts are found in the fact that both refer to God, creation, light, and darkness.[4])

We noted in chapter 2 that church father and philosopher Augustine held that the universe was not created *in* time, but rather that time itself was created *along with* the universe.[5] Scriptural evidence was cited that supports this view (Heb. 1:2; 11:3). In light of this scriptural evidence, Reformed theologian Louis Berkhof concluded that "it would not be correct to assume that time was already in existence when God created the world, and that He at some point in that existing time, called 'the beginning,' brought forth the universe. The world was created *with* time rather than *in* time. Back of the beginning mentioned in Genesis 1:1 lied a beginningless eternity."[6] Hence, when John said, "In the beginning," he had specific reference to the beginning of time when the universe was created.

It is important to grasp this, because John tells us that "In the beginning [when time began] *was* the Word." The verb *was* in this verse is an imperfect tense in the Greek, indicating continued existence. When the time-space universe came into being, Christ the divine Word *was already existing* in a loving, intimate relationship with the Father and the Holy Spirit. The imperfect tense "reaches back indefinitely beyond the instant of the beginning."[7] Leon Morris notes that "the verb 'was' is most naturally understood of the eternal existence of the Word: 'the Word continually was.'"[8] Thus, the *Logos* did not come into being at a specific point in eternity past, but at that point at which all else began to be, he already was. No matter how far back we go in eternity past, we will never come to a point at which we could say of Christ the *Logos,* as Arius once did, that "there was a time when he was not."

Because Christ is the eternal *Logos,* all that can be said of God can be said of Jesus Christ. Indeed, in our passage "John is not merely saying that there is something divine about Jesus. He is affirming that He is God, and doing so emphatically."[9]

Unbroken, Intimate Fellowship

When heaven and earth came into being at the creation, there was Christ the *Logos,* already existing in the closest association with the Father. This close association is affirmed in John's Gospel: "the Word was with God" (1:1). Benjamin Warfield tells us that "it is not merely coexistence with God that is asserted, as two beings standing side by side, united in a local relation, or even in a common conception. What is suggested is an active relation of intercourse."[10] The Greek preposition for "with" is *pros,* and carries the idea of intimate, unbroken fellowship and communion. Christ the *Logos* spent eternity past in company with, and in intimate, unbroken fellowship with, the Father in an eternal loving relationship. "Both the Word and His relationship to the Eternal [the Father] are eternal. There was never part of His preexistence which found Him to be separated in any sense from the Godhead."[11]

It is important to recognize that in John 1:1–2, Christ the *Logos* is said to be *distinct from* and at the same time *equal with* God. He was *with* God (the Greek preposition *pros* implies two distinct persons) and at the same time is said to *be* God. Hence, the Father and the Word "are not the same, but they belong together. The fact that One may be said to be 'with' the Other clearly differentiates them. Yet, though they are distinct, there is no disharmony. John's expression points us to the perfect unity in which they are joined."[12] We see, then, that John 1:1–2 suggests trinitarian distinctions: "Now all is clear; we now see how this Word who is God 'was in the beginning,' and how this Word who is God was in eternal reciprocal relation with God. . . . The *Logos* is one of the three divine persons of the eternal Godhead."[13]

The Shekinah Glory

John's choice of words in describing the incarnation of the *Logos* is highly revealing. When John said that "the Word became flesh and made his dwelling among us" (John 1:14), he drew heavily from his knowledge of the Old Testament. The phrase, "made his dwelling among us," literally means "to pitch one's tent."[14] Bible scholar F. F. Bruce elaborates on the significance of this phrase:

> The statement that the incarnate Word "pitched his tabernacle (Greek: *eskenosen*) among us" harks back to the tabernacle (Greek: *skene*) of Israel's wilderness wanderings. The tabernacle was erected by God's command in order that his dwelling-place might be established with his people: "let them make me a sanctuary," he said, "that I may dwell in their midst" (Ex. 25:8). So, it is implied, as God formerly manifested his presence among his people in the tent which Moses pitched, now in a fuller sense he has taken up residence on earth in the Word made flesh.[15]

John's use of the Greek word *eskenosen* ("pitched his tabernacle") becomes even more significant when it is realized that the glory that resulted from the immediate presence of the Lord in the tabernacle came to be associated with "the *Shekinah*," a word that refers to "the radiance, glory, or presence of God dwelling in the midst of his people."[16] When the *Logos* became flesh (John 1:14), the glorious presence of God was fully embodied in him, for he is the true *Shekinah*.[17] Bible expositor J. Dwight Pentecost thus writes: "The same glory that Moses beheld in the tabernacle in Exodus 40:34–38 and that the priest saw in the temple in 1 Kings 8:10–11 was revealed in the person of Jesus Christ on the Mount of Transfiguration. Peter testified to this in 2 Peter 1:16–18."[18]

It is critical to recognize that the *Logos* did not cease to be the *Logos* when he "became flesh." Christ still had the fullness of the Shekinah glory in him, but that glory was veiled so he could function in the world of humanity. "The Word did not cease to be what it was before; but it became what it was not before—*flesh*. . . . *The Word* became flesh and remains in every sense *the Word* though now made flesh. This

Word, being God, could not possibly change into something else, for then God would cease to be God."[19] This is the mystery of the Incarnation: Christ the *Logos* was fully God and fully human. The Shekinah glory dwelt in the tabernacle of the flesh of Jesus.

The true temple of God was therefore not the edifice in Jerusalem, but the very body of Jesus. It was in him that the glory of God shone. As Benjamin Warfield put it, "the flesh of our Lord became . . . the Temple of God on earth (cf. Jn. 2:19), and the glory of the Lord filled the house of the Lord."[20] For this reason, John testified, "we have seen his glory" (John 1:14)—no doubt a reference to the transfiguration, in which Jesus, toward the end of his three-year ministry, pulled back the veil of his glory so that "His face shone like the sun, and his clothes became as white as the light" (Matt. 17:2).

It would be wise to make a qualification before proceeding further. While Jesus' human body was, in one sense, a "temple" in which the Shekinah glory dwelt, his body was not an *exact parallel* to the Old Testament tabernacle. For, in the Old Testament, God always remained *distinct from* the tabernacle, even though he dwelt *in* the tabernacle. In the New Testament, we learn that Jesus in the Incarnation permanently took upon himself a human nature. Hence, Jesus' human body was not a *mere* temple that embodied the Shekinah glory, but rather became a very real part of his being as the God-man.

The Incarnate *Logos*

It may seem out of place that a book on the life and times of the *pre*incarnate Christ would include a good amount of material on the incarnate Christ (in this chapter, and in chapters 9 through 12). However, there is good reason for this inclusion. First, all of Christ's preincarnate appearances in Old Testament times served to set the stage for his incarnation. All that Christ did among human beings *prior* to the Incarnation helped prepare the way for what he would accomplish *during* his incarnation. Second, as we shall see, Christ himself taught a great deal about his preincarnate state *after* he had become incarnate. For these reasons, then, we will examine what Scripture says of the incarnate Christ, but only insofar as it is related in some way to our broader study of the *pre*incarnate Christ.

Christ the Life and Light of Humankind

John's Gospel tells us that one of the purposes of the Incarnation was for Christ the eternal *Logos* to bring *life* and *light* to fallen humankind. Indeed, we read: "In him was life, and that life was the light of men. The light shines in the darkness, but the darkness has not understood it" (John 1:4–5).

It is noteworthy that John speaks of "life" thirty-six times in his Gospel—more than any other book in the New Testament. John even says that the purpose of his writing is "that by believing you may have life in his name" (John 20:31). Leon Morris comments:

> This Gospel constantly associates life with the Word. He came that men might have life and have it more abundantly (10:10). He died that men might have everlasting life (3:16). He gave His flesh for the life of the world (6:51). Only those who eat His flesh and drink His blood have life (6:53f.), and similarly only those who come to Him have life (5:40). When He gives life, men perish no more (10:28). He said that He had power to lay down His life and to take it up again (10:18), and He did just that. As Lord of life He raised Lazarus from the dead (cf. 11).[21]

Besides bringing "life," Christ the divine *Logos* also brought "light" to a humanity living in darkness. The prophet Isaiah had described the future (from his vantage point) coming of salvation in terms of people living in darkness seeing a great light (Isa. 9:2; cf. Matt. 4:16). This was fulfilled in the person of Jesus Christ.

The question that arises at this point is, In what way is Christ a light? "Light" in the Gospel of John is equated with a knowledge of God. It carries the idea of revelation that can lead human beings toward "life," *if they choose to follow that light*. This divine "light" thus places people under a solemn responsibility and brings them into judgment if they refuse or turn away from the light.

God had given all humanity "light" through the creation, for the creation reveals to all mankind that there is indeed a Creator (Ps. 19). However, as J. Dwight Pentecost notes, "willful rejection of the light or revelation through creation brought progressive darkness until men were ignorant of God. Jesus Christ came to dispel that ignorance. He who is God came in flesh so that men might see that revelation and come out of ignorance into knowledge."[22]

It is interesting that John called Jesus "the true light" (John 1:9). This brings to mind that Jesus called himself "the true bread" (6:32–33) and "the true vine" (15:1). Jesus is the true light in the sense that he is God's complete and full revelation of God to man. All that men may expect by way of divine revelation and salvation is to be seen in him and him alone.

Notice that John uses a present-tense verb when he says that "the light shines" (v. 5). This is significant, for it indicates that the light is *continually* in action. "Even as John writes it is shining. The light of the world, the light of men, never ceases to shine."[23]

As the *true* light that is continually shining, Jesus perpetually dispels spiritual darkness. Of course, the very nature of light is to dispel darkness, just as a candle in a dark room spreads light without being dimmed by the darkness. In the original creation, "darkness was upon the face of the deep" (Gen. 1:2 KJV) until God called light into being (v. 3); likewise, Christ the divine Word banishes the spiritual darkness by the light that he shines in the world.

The teaching that Christ is the light of men is quite reminiscent of the Israelite forefathers who—after their exodus from Egypt, and during their time in the dark wilderness—followed the pillar of light via the Angel of the Lord (Christ). Hendriksen notes that "those who had followed it and had not rebelled against its guidance had reached Canaan. The others had died in the desert. So it is here: the true followers not only will *not* walk in the darkness of moral and spiritual ignorance, of impurity, and of gloom, but will reach the land of light."[24] Indeed, those who follow the light are the possessors of the life Christ gives.

We might appropriately say that a "second exodus" is currently underway. Believers are leaving the darkness of this world and entering the light of God's kingdom. These are the ones who joyfully anticipate their "promised land."

Christ the Divine Revealer

In keeping with Jesus' function as the "Light" of humankind, John 1:18 tells us that Jesus is the *Revealer* of God: "No one has ever seen God, but God the One and Only [Jesus Christ], who is at the Father's side, has made him known" (insert mine). Just as human beings use words to express thoughts, so the Son—the divine Word *(Logos)*—came to fully reveal and manifest God the Father to humanity. In the *Logos*, we find the final and absolute revelation of God to humankind. Theologian Robert Lightner explains:

Christ revealed the Person of God as He had never been made known before. He declared the Father to man (cf. John 1:18; 14:8, 9; 1 Tim. 3:16). The glory of God was made known by Christ (John 1:14; 2 Cor. 4:6; Isa. 40:5). God's power was revealed by God's Son. He did this many times and in many different ways (John 3:2; 1 Cor. 1:24). The wisdom of God was made known in the Person of Christ (John 7:46; 1 Cor. 1:24). The life of God was also declared by Him (1 John 1:1–3). To be sure, God's boundless love was revealed and demonstrated by the Savior (John 3:16; Rom. 5:8; 1 John 3:16). The grace of God, the undeserved favor which He bestowed upon mankind, was also revealed by the Lord Jesus (Luke 2:40; John 1:17; 2 Thess. 1:12).[25]

Christ's role as the Revealer of the Father is the clear emphasis of many Scripture passages. Jesus told a group of Pharisees, for example, that "when a man believes in me, he does not believe in me only, but in the one who sent me. When he looks at me, he sees the one who sent me" (John 12:44–45). Some time later, Jesus told Philip that "anyone who has seen me has seen the Father" (John 14:9b). The Book of Hebrews tells us that "in the past God spoke to our forefathers through the prophets at many times and in various ways, but in these last days he has spoken to us by his Son, whom he appointed heir of all things, and through whom he made the universe" (Heb. 1:1–2).

The "Logos" Doctrine and the Eternality of Christ

To grasp the full import of the "Logos" doctrine and its relevance to the eternality of Christ, let us close by briefly reviewing what we have learned. We have seen that John views the true significance of the work of Christ from the perspective of eternity. He thus begins his Gospel by telling us that Jesus the divine Word has existed for all eternity *as* God and *with* God—that is, *as* God the Son and *with* God the Father. Indeed, prior to the beginning of time, Jesus enjoyed an eternal loving fellowship with the Father and with the Holy Spirit. Plurality within the Godhead is clearly evident in John's Gospel.

When Jesus stepped out of his glorious abode in heaven and became a man, his human body was, in a sense, a temple in which the Shekinah glory dwelt. This recalls how the Shekinah glory dwelt in the Tabernacle in Old Testament times.

As the incarnate *Logos*, with his glory veiled in human flesh, Christ brought life and light to a humanity dwelling in utter darkness. If it were not for him, humanity would *still* be engulfed in darkness, with no hope of salvation.

We have learned some interesting aspects of Christ's glory in this chapter—but we have only scratched the surface. We shall discuss the glory of Christ in greater detail in chapter 12, "Christ and His Eternal Glory."

9

Christ and His Divine Names

In the ancient world, a name was not a mere label as it is today. A name was considered as equivalent to whomever or whatever bore it. The sum total of a person's internal and external pattern of behavior was gathered up into his name. Indeed, knowing a person's name amounted to knowing his essence. This is illustrated for us in 1 Samuel 25:25a: "Nabal . . . is just like his name—his name is Fool, and folly goes with him."

We also see this illustrated in the names of major Bible characters. The name *Abraham*, for instance, means "father of a multitude," and was quite fitting since Abraham was the father of the Jewish nation. The name *David* means "beloved," and was fitting because David was a king specially loved by God. The name *Solomon* comes from a word meaning "peace," and is fitting because Solomon's reign was characterized by peace. In each case, we learn something about the individual from his name.

Though God reveals his attributes in many ways in Scripture, one of the most significant modes of the divine self-disclosure is the revelation inherent in the names of God. A survey of Scripture shows that the *name* and *being* of God often occur together in the form of a parallelism (a literary form indicating a close parallel relationship). The Psalms illustrate this for us (italics added): "Therefore I will praise *you* among the nations, O LORD; I will sing praises to *your name*" (Ps. 18:49); "Sing to *God*, sing praise to *his name*, extol *him* who rides on the clouds—his *name* is the LORD—and rejoice before him" (Ps. 68:4); "Remember how the enemy has mocked *you*, O LORD, how foolish people have reviled *your name*" (Ps. 74:18); "I will praise *you*, O LORD *my God*, with all my heart; I will glorify *your name* forever" (Ps. 86:12). Clearly, Scripture portrays God and his name as inseparable. To know one is to know the other.

Since this is true, we can learn much about Christ and his eternal nature from the names and titles ascribed to him in both the Old and New Testaments. Just as Christ was called the Son of Mary in reference to his *humanity*, so he is called *Yahweh, Elohim, Adonai, Theos,* and *Kurios,* all in reference to his *deity*. It is noteworthy that the divine titles of Christ are far more numerous in Scripture than the human (see Appendix A).

In this chapter, we will look at some of the divine names or titles that best reveal Christ's eternal nature and deity. An understanding of these names will help us to better perceive the true majesty, glory, and power of Christ as he appeared to saints in Old Testament times, as well as in New Testament times as God in the flesh.

Jesus Christ as *Yahweh*

Jesus implicitly ascribed the divine name *Yahweh* to himself during a confrontation he had with a group of hostile Jews. Someone in the group had said to him: ". . . Abraham died and so did the prophets, yet you say that if anyone keeps your word, he will never taste death. Are you greater than our father Abraham?" (John 8:52–53). Jesus responded: "Your father Abraham rejoiced at the thought of seeing my day; he saw it and was glad" (v. 56). The Jews mockingly replied: "You are not yet fifty years old, and you have seen Abraham!" (v. 57).

To which Jesus replied, "I tell you the truth, before Abraham was born, I am!" (v. 58).

The Jews immediately picked up stones with the intention of killing Jesus, for they recognized that he was identifying himself as *Yahweh*.[1] The Jews were acting on the prescribed penalty for blasphemy in Old Testament law: death by stoning (Lev. 24:16).

The name *Yahweh*, which occurs over 5,300 times in the Old Testament, is connected with the Hebrew verb "to be." We first learn of this name in Exodus 3 where Moses asked God by what name he should be called. God replied to him, "I AM WHO I AM. . . . This is what you are to say to the Israelites, 'I AM has sent me to you'" (v. 14).

"I AM" may seem like an odd name to the modern ear. But Moses understood in some measure what God was saying to him. The name clearly conveys the idea of eternal self-existence.[2] *Yahweh* never came into being at a point in time, for he has always existed. He was never born; he will never die. He does not grow older, for he is beyond the realm of time. To know *Yahweh* is to know the eternal one.

All of this adds significance to Jesus' encounter with the Jews. Knowing how much they venerated Abraham, Jesus deliberately contrasted the created origin of Abraham with his own eternal, uncreated nature (John 8:58). "It was not simply that he was older than Abraham, although his statement says that much, too, but that his existence is of a different kind than Abraham's—that Abraham's existence was created and finite, beginning at a point in time, while Christ's existence never began, is uncreated and infinite, and therefore eternal."[3] In Jesus, therefore, "we see the timeless God, who was the God of Abraham and of Isaac and of Jacob, who was before time and who will be after time, who always *is*."[4]

We noted in chapter 8 that because the name *Yahweh* was considered the most ineffable name of God, the ancient Jews had a superstitious dread of pronouncing it. In fact, whenever they came across this name in public readings of Scripture, they always substituted another name in its place—most often, the name *Adonai* (meaning "Lord"). This veneration of *Yahweh's* name is illustrated for us by two ancient writers. Philo, a first-century Hellenistic Jew, tells us: "The four letters [*Yhwh*] may be mentioned or heard only by holy men whose ears and tongues are purified by wisdom, and by no others in any place whatsoever."[5] Josephus, the first-century Jewish historian, similarly writes: "Moses besought God to impart to him the knowledge of His name and its pronunciation so that he might be able to invoke Him by name at the sacred acts, whereupon God communicated His name, hitherto unknown to any man; and it would be a sin for me to mention it."[6]

In view of this, it is understandable why the Jews of the first century tried to stone Jesus for blasphemy when he implicitly identified himself as *Yahweh*. In their thinking, there was no greater crime a person could commit. They were dumbfounded that someone in their midst was claiming to be the eternal self-existent one.

It is noteworthy that in John 8:58 Jesus began his assertion of deity with the words, *"I tell you the truth,* before Abraham was born, I am!" (italics added). In the King James Version, the phrase "I tell you the truth" is rendered "verily, verily." Jesus used such language only when he was making an important and emphatic statement. It represents the strongest possible oath and claim.[7] We might paraphrase it, "I assure you, most solemnly I tell you." Jesus did not want there to be any confusion over the fact that he was claiming to be eternal God. He was claiming in the strongest possible terms that he had independent, continuous existence from before time.

Further support for Jesus' identity as *Yahweh* is found in his crucifixion. In Zechariah 12:10b, *Yahweh* is speaking prophetically: "They will look on me, the one they have pierced. . . ." Though *Yahweh* is speaking, this is obviously a reference to Christ's future crucifixion.[8] We know that "the one they have pierced" is Jesus, for he is described this same way by the apostle John in Revelation 1:7.

The Septuagint provides us with additional insights on Christ's identity as *Yahweh*. The Septuagint is a Greek translation of the Hebrew Old Testament that dates prior to the birth of Christ. It renders the Hebrew phrase for "I AM" in Exodus 3:14 as *ego eimi*.[9] On a number of occasions in the Greek New Testament, Jesus used this term as a way of identifying himself as God.[10] For example, Jesus declared: "Unless you believe that I am *[ego eimi]* He, you shall die in your sins" (John 8:24 NASB). The original Greek for this verse does not have the word *he*. The verse is literally: "If you do not believe that I am, you shall die in your sins."

Then, according to verse 28, Jesus told the Jews: "When you lift up the Son of Man, then you will know that I am *[ego eimi]* He . . ." (NASB). Again, the original Greek reads: "When you lift up the Son of Man, then you will know that I am" (there is no *he*). Jesus purposefully used the phrase as a means of identifying himself as *Yahweh*.[11]

It is also highly revealing that Old Testament passages about *Yahweh* were directly applied to Jesus in the New Testament. For instance, Isaiah 40:3 says: "A voice of one calling: 'In the desert prepare the way for the LORD *[Yahweh]*; make straight in the wilderness a highway for our God.'" Mark's Gospel tells us that Isaiah's words were fulfilled in the ministry of John the Baptist preparing the way for Jesus Christ (Mark 1:2–4).

Joel 2:32 is another example: "And everyone who calls on the name of the LORD *[Yahweh]* will be saved. . . ." The apostle Paul quotes this passage in the context of calling upon Jesus Christ for salvation (Rom. 10:13). "Calling upon *Yahweh*" and "calling upon Jesus Christ" are here equated.

Still another illustration is Isaiah 6:1–5, where the prophet recounts his vision of *Yahweh* "seated on a throne, high and exalted" (v. 1). As Isaiah beheld this heavenly scene, he witnessed seraphs (heavenly angels) saying to one another: "Holy, holy, holy is the LORD *[Yahweh]* Almighty; the whole earth is full of his glory" (v. 3). Isaiah later quotes *Yahweh* as

saying: "I am the LORD; that is my name! I will not give my glory to another . . ." (42:8). About eight centuries after this, the
apostle John—under the inspiration of the Holy Spirit—wrote
that Isaiah "saw Jesus' glory" (John 12:41). *Yahweh's* glory and
Jesus' glory are equated.

Christ's deity is further confirmed for us in that many of the
actions of *Yahweh* in the Old Testament are performed by
Christ in the New Testament. For example, in Psalm 119 we
are told about a dozen times that it is *Yahweh* who gives and
preserves life. But in the New Testament, Jesus claims this
power for himself: "For just as the Father raises the dead and
gives them life, even so the Son gives life to whom he is
pleased to give it" (John 5:21). Later in John's Gospel, when
speaking to Lazarus' sister Martha, Jesus says: "I am the resurrection and the life. He who believes in me will live, even
though he dies; and whoever lives and believes in me will never die . . ." (John 11:25).

In the Old Testament, the voice of *Yahweh* was said to be
"like the roar of rushing waters" (Ezek. 43:2). Likewise, we
read of the glorified Jesus in heaven: "His feet were like
bronze glowing in a furnace, and his voice was like the sound
of rushing waters" (Rev. 1:15). What was true of *Yahweh* was
just as true of Jesus.

It is also significant that in the Old Testament, *Yahweh* is described as "an everlasting light," one that would make the sun,
moon, and stars obsolete: "The sun will no more be your light
by day, nor will the brightness of the moon shine on you, for
the LORD will be your everlasting light, and your God will be
your glory. Your sun will never set again, and your moon will
wane no more; the LORD will be your everlasting light, and
your days of sorrow will end" (Isa. 60:19–20). But Jesus will do
the same for the future eternal city in which the saints will
dwell forever: "The city does not need the sun or the moon to
shine on it, for the glory of God gives it light, and the Lamb is
its lamp" (Rev. 21:23).

David F. Wells, in his book *The Person of Christ*, points us to even further parallels between Christ and *Yahweh:*

> If *Yahweh* is our sanctifier (Exod. 31:13), is omnipresent (Ps. 139:7–10), is our peace (Judg. 6:24), is our righteousness (Jer. 23:6), is our victory (Exod. 17:8–16), and is our healer (Exod. 15:26), then so is Christ all of these things (1 Cor. 1:30; Col. 1:27; Eph. 2:14). If the gospel is God's (1 Thess. 2:2, 6–9; Gal. 3:8), then that same gospel is also Christ's (1 Thess. 3:2; Gal. 1:7). If the church is God's (Gal. 1:13; 1 Cor. 15:9), then that same church is also Christ's (Rom. 16:16). God's Kingdom (1 Thess. 2:12) is Christ's (Eph. 5:5); God's love (Eph. 1:3–5) is Christ's (Rom. 8:35); God's Word (Col. 1:25; 1 Thess. 2:13) is Christ's (1 Thess. 1:8; 4:15); God's Spirit (1 Thess. 4:8) is Christ's (Phil. 1:19); God's peace (Gal. 5:22; Phil. 4:9) is Christ's (Col. 3:15; cf. Col. 1:2; Phil. 1:2; 4:7); God's "Day" of judgment (Isa. 13:6) is Christ's "Day" of judgment (Phil. 1:6, 10; 2:16; 1 Cor. 1:8); God's grace (Eph. 2:8, 9; Col. 1:6; Gal. 1:15) is Christ's grace (1 Thess. 5:28; Gal. 1:6; 6:18); God's salvation (Col. 1:13) is Christ's salvation (1 Thess. 1:10); and God's will (Eph. 1:11; 1 Thess. 4:3; Gal. 1:4) is Christ's will (Eph. 5:17; cf. 1 Thess. 5:18). So it is no surprise to hear Paul say that he is both God's slave (Rom. 1:9) and Christ's (Rom. 1:1; Gal. 1:10), that he lives for that glory which is both God's (Rom. 5:2; Gal. 1:24) and Christ's (2 Cor. 8:19, 23; cf. 2 Cor. 4:6), that his faith is in God (1 Thess. 1:8, 9; Rom. 4:1–5) and in Christ Jesus (Gal. 3:22), and that to know God, which is salvation (Gal. 4:8; 1 Thess. 4:5), is to know Christ (2 Cor. 4:6).[12]

We conclude, then, that Jesus as *Yahweh* is eternally self-existent, co-equal and co-eternal with God the Father and God the Holy Spirit. Before time began, Christ was "I AM." He was before all things. Like the Father and the Holy Spirit, he is everlastingly the living one.

Jesus Christ as *Kurios*

The New Testament equivalent of *Yahweh* is *Kurios*. Like *Yahweh*, *Kurios* means "Lord" and usually carries the idea of a sovereign being who exercises absolute authority. (The word *can* be used of a human being, as in Col. 3:22 where it means "master.") On occasions where the word is used of Christ in the New Testament, it is clearly intended to be taken in an absolute sense as a parallel to the name *Yahweh* in the Old Testament.

Indeed, *The Interpreter's Dictionary of the Bible* tells us that "to an early Christian accustomed to reading the Old Testament, the word 'Lord,' when used of Jesus, would suggest His identification with the God of the Old Testament."[13] Theologian William G. T. Shedd likewise suggests that "any Jew who publicly confessed that Jesus of Nazareth was 'Lord,' would be understood to ascribe the divine nature and attributes to Him."[14] Hence, the statement that "Jesus is Lord" *(Kurios)* constitutes a clear affirmation that Jesus is *Yahweh* (see Rom. 10:9; 1 Cor. 12:3; Phil. 2:11).

The apostle Paul points us to the close relationship between *Yahweh* and *Kurios* in Philippians 2. He tells us that Christ was given a name "above every name, that at the name of Jesus every knee should bow, in heaven and on earth and under the earth, and every tongue confess that Jesus Christ is Lord *[Kurios]* . . ." (vv. 9–11). Paul, an Old Testament scholar *par excellence,* is alluding to Isaiah 45:22–24: ". . . I am God, and there is no other. By myself I have sworn, my mouth has uttered in all integrity a word that will not be revoked: Before me every knee will bow; by me every tongue will swear." Paul was drawing on his vast knowledge of the Old Testament to make the point that Jesus Christ is *Yahweh,* the Lord of all mankind.

Jesus specifically referred to himself as *Kurios* when he identified himself as "Lord of the Sabbath" to some of his Jewish critics. Matthew 12:1 tells us that Jesus' disciples had become hungry and began to pick some heads of grain in a field for food. The Pharisees saw this and objected: "Look! Your disciples are doing what is unlawful on the Sabbath" (v. 2). Jesus justified the disciples' behavior by pointing to 1 Samuel 21:6, where David, whom the Pharisees held in great respect, is seen eating consecrated bread. Jesus then made a startling claim to the Pharisees: "For the Son of Man is Lord [*Kurios*] of the Sabbath" (Matt. 12:8).

This is particularly significant because the Jews knew that God himself was both the author and Lord of the Sabbath (Exod. 31:13, 17). The Pharisees recognized in Jesus' words a claim to deity and "went out and plotted how they might kill Jesus" (Matt. 12:14). They were again acting on the knowledge that the penalty for blasphemy was death (Lev. 24:16).

As Lord and Master over all mankind, there are several occasions in the New Testament in which prayer is offered to Jesus after he had ascended into heaven. This is especially significant in view of the Jewish emphasis that prayer can be offered to God only. To pray to any other being would be sacrilegious to the utmost degree.

An example of prayer offered to Jesus as *Kurios* is found in the account of Stephen's stoning. Stephen had given a speech before the Sanhedrin, and he closed his speech with these cutting words: "Was there ever a prophet your fathers did not persecute? They even killed those who predicted the coming of the Righteous One. And now you have betrayed and murdered him—you who have received the law that was put into effect through angels but have not obeyed it" (Acts 7:52–53). Upon hearing this, the Jews became furious and dragged Stephen out of the city, and began to stone him (v. 57). While they were stoning him, Stephen prayed, "Lord [*Kurios*] Jesus, receive my spirit" (v. 59). As a pious Hellenistic Jew, Stephen would never have prayed to anyone less than God.

The apostle Paul also mentioned prayer to Christ on several occasions. In 1 Corinthians, he addressed his readers: "To the church of God in Corinth, to those sanctified in Christ Jesus and called to be holy, together with all those everywhere who call on the name of our Lord Jesus Christ—their Lord [*Kurios*] and ours" (1 Cor. 1:2).

On another occasion, Paul—after having a vision of heaven—said: "To keep me from becoming conceited because of these surpassingly great revelations, there was given me a thorn in my flesh, a messenger of Satan, to torment me. Three times I pleaded with the Lord *[Kurios]* to take it away from me. But he said to me, 'My grace is sufficient for you, for my power is made perfect in weakness' . . ." (2 Cor. 12:7–9).

To sum up, then, we have seen from our survey of Scripture that every knee will one day bow before Jesus the Lord *(Kurios);* that as Lord of the Sabbath, Jesus is sovereign over the Sabbath; and that as the Lord and Master of humankind, Jesus hears the prayers of his people. And since *Kurios* is the expository equivalent of *Yahweh*, references to Christ as Lord *(Kurios)* in the New Testament clearly point to his identity as the eternal *Yahweh* of the Old Testament.

Jesus Christ as *Elohim*

Elohim, a common name for God in the Old Testament (used about 2,570 times), literally means "strong one," and its plural ending (*im* in Hebrew) indicates fullness of power.[15] *Elohim* is portrayed in the Old Testament as the powerful and sovereign governor of the universe, ruling over the affairs of humankind. As related to God's sovereignty, the word *Elohim* is used to describe him as "God of all the earth" (Isa. 54:5), "God of all mankind" (Jer. 32:27), "God of heaven" (Neh. 2:4), and "God of gods and Lord of lords" (Deut. 10:17).

We have already noted that Jesus is called *Yahweh* in Isaiah 40:3, but he is also called *Elohim* in the same verse: "In the desert prepare the way for the LORD *[Yahweh];* make straight in the wilderness a highway for our God *[Elohim]*." This verse was written in reference to the future ministry of Christ (see John 1:23), and represents one of the strongest affirmations of Christ's deity in the Old Testament. In referring to "our God," Isaiah was affirming that Jesus Christ was the God of both the Old and New Testaments. This is further confirmed in Isaiah 9:6 where we read of Christ: "And he will be called Wonderful Counselor, Mighty God *[Elohim]*, Everlasting Father, Prince of Peace."

Christ's identity as God is consistently and emphatically set forth in the New Testament. As a backdrop, it is significant that when Paul and Barnabas were in Lystra and miraculously healed a man by God's mighty power, those in the crowd shouted, "The gods have come down to us in human form!" (Acts 14:11). When Paul and Barnabas perceived that the people were preparing to worship them, "they tore their clothes and rushed out into the crowd, shouting: 'Men, why are you doing this? We too are only men, human like you'" (v. 15a). As soon as they perceived what was happening, they immediately corrected the gross misconception that they were gods.

By contrast, it is highly revealing that Jesus never sought to correct his followers, or "set them straight," when they called him God. Nor did he ever try to correct them when they worshiped him. Of course, we wouldn't expect Jesus to try to correct them if he truly was God in the flesh.

The New Testament word for God, *Theos*, is the corresponding parallel to the Old Testament *Elohim*.[16] A well known example of Christ's being addressed as God *(Theos)* is found in the story of "doubting Thomas" in John 20. Jesus had been brutally crucified on the cross, but he had also gloriously risen from the dead. Thomas had not been with the disciples when the risen Christ first appeared to them. Some people, in times of desolating grief, find comfort in one another's company. Others prefer being alone with their sorrow. Thomas belonged to this latter group.

The disciples had told Thomas all about Christ's appearance to them. But Thomas refused to believe. He demanded not only the sight of Christ's wounds, but the actual touching of them as a condition of believing that Christ had risen from the dead: "Unless I see the nail marks in his hands and put my finger where the nails were, and put my hand into his side, I will not believe it" (John 20:25).

When the risen Jesus appeared the following week, he had a special word for Thomas, inviting him to exploit his sense of touch as well as sight—thereby revealing that he knew what

Thomas had said to the others the previous week. The evidence of eye and ear was sufficient, and Thomas felt no further need to satisfy himself with probing fingers (John 20:26–27).

Thomas may have been slower in coming to believe in Christ's resurrection, but when he did so, his faith was touchingly expressed by the affirmation: "My Lord and my God [*Theos*]!" (John 20:28). Certainly this represents a climax in John's Gospel. Christ had earlier given many indications of his deity. He ascribed names of deity to himself (John 8:58); he claimed holiness (John 8:46); he displayed omniscience (John 11:11–14); he raised people from the dead (John 5:28–30); and he claimed to be the Judge of all men (John 5:22, 27). At long last, the deity of Christ had "sunk in" for Thomas! He recognized that Christ indeed was God.

The significant thing about all this is that Christ did not try to correct Thomas after the disciple had called him God. Why? Because, in fact, Jesus is God. Jesus never conceived of himself as anything less.

Jesus continues to be called *Theos* throughout the rest of the New Testament. Take, for instance, the account of the jailer's conversion in Acts 16. The jailer had asked Paul and Silas how to be saved. They responded: "Believe in the Lord Jesus, and you will be saved—you and your household" (v. 31). Then, after the jailer believed and became saved, we are told that the jailer "was filled with joy because he had come to believe in God [*Theos*]—he and his whole family" (v. 34). Believing in Christ and believing in God are seen as identical acts.

The apostle Paul was a staunch defender of the deity of Christ. In his brief letter to Titus, he exhorted his young convert to live a self-controlled life "while we wait for the blessed hope—the glorious appearing of our great God [*Theos*] and Savior, Jesus Christ" (Titus 2:13).[17] Paul, who had been trained in the strictest form of Judaism (its main tenet being *monotheism*), boldly proclaimed that Jesus Christ is himself God. This is an astonishing assertion for a former Jew who was at one time antagonistic toward Christianity.

We now look to Hebrews 1:8 for the Father's testimony regarding Christ's identity. In this passage, the Father (the first person of the Trinity) is seen addressing the Son (the second person of the Trinity). The Father says to him: "Your throne, O God *[Theos]*, will last for ever and ever, and righteousness will be the scepter of your kingdom." This is a quote from Psalm 45:6–7, where "God" is seen addressing "God" [using the Hebrew word *Elohim*]. Though the concept of the Trinity is inscrutable to finite minds, this and other passages show us that the Father and the Son are co-equal and co-eternal. Neither is greater or lesser than the other. Neither has existed longer than the other. Equal yet distinct. And, of course, the same is true of the Holy Spirit.

The evidence continues to mount as we look to the words of Peter in his second epistle: "To those who through the righteousness of our God *[Theos]* and Savior Jesus Christ have received a faith as precious as ours" (1:1). In the Greek, the phrase "Jesus Christ" acts as an *appositive* to the phrase "God and Savior." An appositive is a noun or a noun-phrase that is used as an explanatory equivalent of another noun. Peter is unquestionably affirming that Jesus Christ is God.

The fact that both *Theos* and *Elohim* are ascribed to Jesus gives added significance to the words recorded for us in Matthew's Gospel: "'The virgin will be with child and will give birth to a son, and they will call him *Immanuel'*—which means, *'God with us'*" (Matt. 1:23, italics added). Truly, Jesus Christ was "God with us" in the fullest possible sense. He is the everlasting God who stepped out of eternity and into time to redeem humanity.

Jesus Christ as the Alpha and Omega, the First and the Last

In Revelation 22:12–13, Christ the divine King says: "Behold, I am coming soon! My reward is with me, and I will give to everyone according to what he has done. I am the Alpha and the Omega, the First and the Last, the Beginning and the End" (also see Rev. 1:8).

These final words in the Book of Revelation were intended to be a comfort and encouragement to Christians as they await the coming of their King. Christ assures his followers that he is coming soon and that he will bring rewards with him.

To the modern ear, the claim to be the Alpha and the Omega may seem strange. But, for the ancient Jew, Christ was describing himself in a way they would have readily understood. Though the letters *Alpha* and *Omega* are the first and last letters of the Greek alphabet, John recorded the Book of Revelation for Jewish readers, who were also familiar with the Hebrew language and alphabet. And therein lies the significance of Christ's claim. In Jewish thinking, a reference to the first and last letters of an alphabet (*aleph* and *tau* in Hebrew) was regarded as including all the intermediate letters, and came to represent totality or entirety.[18]

It is with this idea in mind that the Jews in their ancient commentaries on the Old Testament said that Adam transgressed the whole law from *aleph* to *tau*. Abraham, by contrast, observed the whole law from *aleph* to *tau*. The Jews also believed that when God brings blessing upon Israel, he does so abundantly, from *aleph* to *tau*.

When used of God (or Christ), the first and last letters express eternality and omnipotence. Christ's claim to be the Alpha and the Omega is an affirmation that he is the all-powerful one of eternity past and eternity future. "In describing Himself as 'the first and the last' Christ is relating Himself to time and eternity. He is the eternal God who has always existed in the past and who will always exist in the future."[19] For any created being, however exalted, to claim to be the Alpha and the Omega as these terms are used of Jesus Christ would be utter blasphemy.

The qualifying phrase "the First and the Last" is used of God in the Old Testament. Isaiah 44:6, for example, records God as saying: "I am the first and I am the last; apart from me there is no God." Again, in Isaiah 48:12, God says: "I am he; I am the first and I am the last," and God says this right after his pronouncement that "I will not yield my glory to another" (v. 11b). Christ's use of this title was undoubtedly intended to be taken as a claim to equality with God. And it is precisely this that was to bring comfort and encouragement to Christ's followers. Christ wanted them to be absolutely assured that he is the all-powerful sovereign who will be victorious.

What's in a Name?

We have seen that the ancients viewed a person's name as an expression of his nature and character. The names used of Christ in the Old and New Testaments give us a stirring glimpse of his true identity as eternal God. These names help us to better understand the true majesty, glory, and power of Christ as he appeared to saints in Old Testament times.

To recap:

1. Jesus is *Yahweh*. We learn from this that Jesus is eternally self-existent. He never came into being at a point in time, for he has always existed. To know *Yahweh* is to know the eternal one.
2. Jesus is *Kurios*. This New Testament name, when used of Christ, is intended to be taken as a parallel of the name *Yahweh* in the Old Testament. The name conveys Christ's absolute authority over man.
3. Jesus is *Elohim*. This is the Old Testament name for God. It means "strong one," and its plural ending indicates fullness of power. It pictures Christ as the powerful and sovereign governor of the universe, ruling over the affairs of humanity.
4. Jesus is *Theos*. This is the New Testament name for God. Every verse pointing to Christ as *Theos* in turn points to his identity as *Elohim* in the Old Testament.

5. Jesus is the *Alpha and the Omega* and the *First and the Last*. These names indicate that Christ is the all-powerful one of eternity past and eternity future.

The evidence for Christ's deity and eternality from a study of these names seems mountainous. When it is realized that there are *still more* names we could look at—with evidence piled on top of more evidence—it is clear that the Christ of Scripture, as our eternal God and Savior, is completely worthy of our worship and adoration. He is the exalted one. His name is above every other name. Truly Jesus—with the Father and the Holy Spirit—is worthy to be praised, from age to age.

10

The Virgin Birth

Why a chapter on the virgin birth in a book on the life and times of the preincarnate Christ? There are several reasons. First, we find in the Gospel accounts of the virgin birth fascinating evidences for Christ's preexistence and eternality, as well as his identity as Lord *(Yahweh/Kurios)* in both Old and New Testament times.[1] Moreover, it is enthralling to observe in the Gospel accounts the reactions of people as they became aware that the babe Jesus was actually eternal God in human flesh. What an awesome privilege these people had.

We saw in chapter 8 that all of Christ's preincarnate appearances in Old Testament times served to set the stage in some way for his incarnation. All that Christ did among human beings *prior* to the Incarnation helped prepare the way for what he would accomplish *during* his incarnation. Recall, for example, that it was the preincarnate Christ as the Angel of the Lord who informed Abraham that through Abraham's *future earthly offspring* (that is, through the *incarnate* Christ—born of a woman) all the nations of the earth would be blessed (Gen. 22:17–18; see also Gal. 3:8, 16).

We also noted earlier that the Incarnation was a key component in God's eternal plan of salvation. The Incarnation was purposed by God from the very beginning. Christ *had* to become a man so he could *die* in man's place. Truly, then, the virgin birth was a supreme moment in the outworking of this eternal plan. We shall therefore focus our attention in this chapter on the eternal Son's miraculous entry into humanity and the events surrounding his birth.

Preparing the Way

Early in John's Gospel we are told that God specifically sent a man called John the Baptist for the purpose of preparing the way for the approaching birth of the Messiah. This man would be the fulfillment of several Old Testament prophecies (Isa. 40:3; Mal. 3:1).

John the Baptist testified concerning the one for whom he prepared the way, saying, "This was he of whom I said, 'He who comes after me has surpassed me because he was before me'" (John 1:15). The Baptist used these same words when, at the beginning of Jesus' earthly ministry, he beheld Jesus coming toward him as he was baptizing people in the Jordan river: "Look, the Lamb of God, who takes away the sin of the world! This is the one I meant when I said, 'A man who comes after me has surpassed me because *he was before me.*' I myself did not know him, but the reason I came baptizing with water was that he might be revealed to Israel" (John 1:29–31, italics added).

As we noted in chapter 2, this statement is highly revealing of Christ's eternality. Though Jesus was born six months *later* than John the Baptist, John acknowledges that by virtue of Christ's preexistence, Christ was "before" him. The Baptist's affirmation makes perfect sense when interpreted in light of the prologue of the Gospel of John: "In the beginning was the Word, and the Word was with God, and the Word was God" (John 1:1). Jesus had eternally existed *as* God and *with* God the Father.[2] Jesus was "before" John because he was eternal. Theologian Robert Reymond suggests that the Baptist was saying this: "He who comes *after* me was *before* me (in His active involvement as the Angel of the Lord, indeed, as Yahweh Himself in Old Testament times), and the reason I can say this of Him is because He was *eternally before* me as the eternal God."[3]

Some time later, a Jew questioned John the Baptist as to why everyone was now flocking to Jesus and away from him. John pointed out that "the one who comes from above is above all; the one who is from the earth belongs to the earth, and speaks as one from the earth. The one who comes from heaven is above all" (John 3:31).

As excellent as the Baptist's witness was, it was subject to limitation because of his humanness. While he was in fact "sent from God," the crucial point to bear in mind is that John did not come down from heaven as Jesus had. "Jesus' own witness is of supreme validity because, when he speaks of heavenly things, he bears witness to what he has seen and heard in the heavenly sphere."[4]

A teacher can draw only from the sphere of his own experience in his teaching. The superiority of Jesus' teaching and witness stems from the fact of his experience in heaven for eternity past. Jesus was superior to any earthly revealer because he came from heaven, and his testimony concerning the Father and the truth he revealed about him were not *indirect* but *direct*. Indeed, "He testifies to what he has seen and heard . . ." (John 3:32). Christ and his testimony are absolutely preeminent because of who he is—that is, God.

The Annunciation to Mary

In the first chapter of Luke's Gospel we read: "In the sixth month, God sent the angel Gabriel to Nazareth, a town in Galilee, to a virgin pledged to be married to a man named Joseph, a descendant of David. The virgin's name was Mary. The angel went to her and said, 'Greetings, you who are highly favored! The Lord is with you'" (Luke 1:26–28).

Earlier in man's history, the angel Gabriel had given special revelations from God regarding the coming Messiah to the prophet Daniel (Dan. 8:16; 9:21). Now, over five hundred years later, this same angel appeared to Mary with the news that the prophesied Messiah would be born by her, a virgin. This is in fulfillment of Isaiah 7:14, which prophesied that the Messiah would be born of a virgin.

Mary's humble status is evident in that she was a resident of Nazareth in Galilee. Galileans in general were looked down on by the Jews in Jerusalem as an inferior people. They were considered second-class citizens. Nazareth was especially a place of vice in biblical times. "Nazareth had become a military camp town with which all manner of sin and corruption were associated. The Nazarenes were particularly despised by the rest of the Jews."[5]

Mary was a simple country woman in this less-than-desirable city, and she was betrothed to Joseph, a humble carpenter. Betrothal in ancient times—which usually lasted one year—was much stronger than marital engagements are today. In fact, a betrothed couple was considered husband and wife except that they did not live together until after the wedding.[6] So strong was the betrothal relationship that the betrothed woman was considered a widow if her fiancé died.[7]

This serves as a very important backdrop for our study of the virgin birth, for it was in the context of a betrothed relationship that Mary would soon be found pregnant due to the supernatural work of the Holy Spirit. She no doubt mused over what her fiancé, Joseph, would think when she was found to be pregnant.

Following Gabriel's greeting to Mary, she was "greatly troubled at his words and wondered what kind of greeting this might be" (Luke 1:29). Apparently, in her modesty and humility, Mary did not understand why a heavenly angel greeted her in such exalted terms and told her that the Lord was with her.

Gabriel then said, "Do not be afraid, Mary, you have found favor with God. You will be with child and give birth to a son, and you are to give him the name Jesus. He will be great and will be called the Son of the Most High. The Lord God will give him the throne of his father David, and he will reign over the house of Jacob forever; his kingdom will never end" (Luke 1:30–33).

The angel's pronouncement that the child would be called Jesus is full of meaning. The name "Jesus" means "*Yahweh* saves" or "*Yahweh* is salvation." This name is the counterpart of the Old Testament name, "Joshua." Just as Joshua in the Old Testament led Israel out of the wilderness experience into a new land and a new life, so Jesus would lead people out of a spiritual wilderness experience into a new sphere of existence and a new life.

Robert Reymond has suggested that the meaning of Jesus' name, "*Yahweh* saves," is an evidence for his deity. He qualifies what he means by noting that the name meaning "*Yahweh* saves" in itself "does not *need* to mean that the one who bears this name is identical with *Yahweh*; others [such as Joshua] bore the name under the Old Testament economy to symbolize the fact that *Yahweh* was at work in the salvation of his people. But I suggest that in Jesus' case we should understand that it connotes more than a mere symbol, inasmuch as some intimation of the identity between Jehovah [*Yahweh*] and the Messiah seems to be contained in the words of the angel (Matt. 1:21)'"[8] Moreover, Reymond suggests,

> when one adds to this compelling data first the fact that *Yahweh* again and again in the Old Testament declares that He alone is Israel's "Savior" (Isa. 43:3, 11; 45:21; 49:26; 60:16; Hos. 13:4; cf. 1 Sam. 10:19; 14:39; 2 Sam. 22:3; Pss. 7:10; 17:7; 106:21; Isa. 45:15; 63:8; Jer. 14:8) and then the fact that Jesus is often declared (along with God the Father) to be "the Savior" in the New Testament (Luke 2:11; John 4:42; Acts 5:31; 13:23; Eph. 5:23; Phil. 3:20; 1 Tim. 4:10; 2 Tim. 1:10; Titus 1:4; 2:13; 3:6; 2 Pet. 1:1, 11; 2:20; 3:2, 18; 1 John 4:14), it is difficult to avoid the conclusion that when Jesus was named "*Yahweh* saves," the name connoted more than merely that He stood as one more in the long line of "saviors" [human deliverers] (cf. Judg. 3:9, 15; 6:36; 2 Kings 13:5; Neh. 9:27). Rather His name meant that in Him, as Him-

self *Yahweh* incarnate, the line of "saviors" had now been con-
summated in a transcendent manner.[9]

In any event, besides informing Mary of the Savior's name,
Gabriel also informed her that Jesus would be called *great;* he
would be called *the Son of the Most High;* and he would *reign on
the throne of his father David.* Each of these three descriptions is
highly revealing of Jesus' true identity. The term "great" is a
title which, when unqualified, is usually reserved for God
alone.[10] Being called *the Son of the Most High* is significant, for
Most High is a title often used of God in both the Old and New
Testaments (see, for example, Gen. 14:19; 2 Sam. 22:14; Ps.
7:10). Bible expositor John A. Martin suggests that "Mary
could not have missed the significance of that terminology.
The fact that her Baby was to be called the 'Son of the Most
High' pointed to His equality with *Yahweh.* In Semitic thought
a son was a 'carbon copy' of his father, and the phrase 'son of'
was often used to refer to one who possessed his 'father's'
qualities."[11]

This "great" one—eternal God in human flesh—would
rule, according to Gabriel, on the throne of David. Jesus, who
in his humanity was a direct descendent of David (Matt. 1:1),
will rule from David's throne during the future millennial
kingdom in which there will be perfect righteousness and jus-
tice (2 Sam. 7:16; Ps. 89:3–4, 28–39). This kingdom will be inaugurated immediately following the second coming of Christ
(Rev. 19).

To describe this future rule of Christ, three significant
words are used in Luke 1:32–33: *throne, house,* and *kingdom*
("The Lord God will give him the *throne* of his father David,
and he will reign over the *house* of Jacob forever; his *kingdom*
will never end"). It is significant that each of these words is
found in the covenant God made with David in which God
promised that one from David's line would rule forever
(2 Sam. 7:16). Gabriel's words must have immediately
brought these Old Testament promises to mind for Mary, a
devout young Jew. Indeed, Gabriel's words constituted "an

announcement as clear as it was possible to make it that Mary's Son would come into this world to fulfill the promise given to David that one of David's sons would sit on David's throne and rule over David's kingdom."[12] Jesus would come not only to be the *Savior* but to be the *Sovereign*.

Mary then responded to Gabriel's announcement by inquiring, "How will this be, since I am a virgin?" (Luke 1:34). The angel answered, "The Holy Spirit will come upon you, and the power of the Most High will overshadow you. So the holy one to be born will be called the Son of God. Even Elizabeth your relative is going to have a child in her old age, and she who was said to be barren is in her sixth month. For nothing is impossible with God" (vv. 35–37).

The Holy Spirit's ministry in this miraculous conception was necessary because of Christ's preexistence (see Isa. 7:14; 9:6; Gal. 4:4). The Holy Spirit's supernatural work in Mary's body enabled Christ—eternal God—to take on a human nature. "From the production of the egg out of Mary's ovary to the actual birth, the fetal state in Mary's womb was entirely under the controlling, sanctifying ministry of the Holy Spirit."[13] And, as noted earlier, through this incarnation a key aspect of the eternal plan of salvation came to fruition. Our eternal Savior became flesh with the specific purpose of dying on our behalf so that those who trusted in him would be saved and dwell with God forever.

Through the miracle of the virgin birth, the eternal Son reached out and took to himself a true and complete humanity without diminishing his essential deity. He united deity and humanity inseparably and eternally in one person.

As noted in chapter 1, a fact that is often overlooked in theological discussions is that all three persons of the Trinity were involved in the Incarnation. Though the Holy Spirit played the central role and was the agent through whom the Incarnation was brought about (Luke 1:35), we are told in Hebrews 10:5 that it was the Father who prepared a human body for Christ. Moreover, the preexistent, eternal Christ is said to have taken upon himself flesh and blood, as if it were an act of his own individual will (Heb. 2:14). Clearly, all three persons of the Trinity were sovereignly involved in bringing about the Incarnation.

How overwhelming the announcement of the Incarnation must have been to young Mary. It is impossible to know the kinds of emotions she felt at the moment of Gabriel's revelation that eternal God would be in her womb. But Mary responded to the announcement in a humble manner: "I am the Lord's servant," she said. "May it be to me as you have said" (Luke 1:38).

In simple faith and submission, Mary presented herself to the Lord, to do with her according to his sovereign will. She submitted to God, despite the possible disgrace, slander, ill repute, or even death she knew she might have to suffer. After all, unfaithfulness in a betrothed person was punishable by death. If she was found to be pregnant during this betrothal period, most people would assume only one thing—unfaithfulness. But Mary's faith in God was such that she unquestioningly submitted to her Lord.

The Annunciation to Joseph

When Joseph discovered that Mary was pregnant, he had two options available to him, neither of which was marriage. (As a righteous man, it was inconceivable to him that he would marry one who was carrying what he then presumed to be another man's child.) One option was that he could accuse her publicly of immorality and have her stoned to death (Deut. 22:13–21). Her death would then have served to break the marriage contract. A second alternative open to him was to divorce her. Because Joseph was a righteous man and did not want to expose Mary to public disgrace, he decided to quietly divorce her (Matt. 1:19).

But then an angel appeared to Joseph in a dream and informed him that what was in Mary's womb was of the Holy Spirit (Matt. 1:20).[14] This was no earthly conception or pregnancy, he was told. What had been planned in eternity past was now being fulfilled in his wife-to-be. The angel told him: "She will give birth to a son, and you are to give him the name Jesus, because he will save his people from their sins" (Matt. 1:21). In the original Greek, the last part of this verse is especially emphatic: "It is He and no other who will save His people from their sins."

The angel's revelation to Joseph was necessary because Mary was in a humanly impossible situation. She knew she had been faithful to Joseph, yet she also knew that she had submitted to God's will in being the human mother of the divine-human Messiah. There is no way she could have adequately explained to Joseph what had happened. This is why God sent an angel to Joseph to explain what was going on. The angel's announcement to Joseph served to defend Mary's moral integrity so that Joseph could marry her in good conscience.

When Joseph awoke from the dream, he did as the angel had commanded him and "took Mary home as his wife" (Matt. 1:24). Joseph violated all Jewish custom by immediately taking her into his home rather than waiting until the one-year betrothal period had passed. However, as our text tells us, "he had no union with her until she gave birth to a son. And he gave him the name Jesus" (v. 25). That Joseph "had no union" with Mary until Jesus was born emphasizes that "there was no human causation involved in the fathering of Jesus."[15]

Like Mary, Joseph must have been truly overwhelmed at the revelation he had received from the angel. The Messiah would be born from his wife's womb. "The eternal Son of the eternal God had existed as One with the Father from all eternity. The One who by his power had created the universe would come in human flesh through Mary's womb. Jesus Christ, the eternal One, reached out through his birth and took to himself a true and complete humanity. He united true humanity and true deity in one person forever. Such was the revelation given to Joseph."[16]

Angels Abounding

In dire contrast to Jesus' intrinsic glory and majesty, he was born in lowly conditions and placed in a manger. But his majesty was acknowledged in other ways. Following his birth, a glorious angel appeared to some shepherds living out in the fields nearby to make an announcement of monumental importance—the Messiah had been born.

It is hard to imagine what it must have been like as the darkness of the night was suddenly dissipated by the glorious appearance of this angel. Understandably, the shepherds were "terrified" at what they beheld (Luke 2:9b).

The angel immediately comforted them and told them not to be afraid. After all, the angel had come not as a minister of death but as one who came to announce life to "all the people" (Luke 2:10). This recalls Genesis 12:3, in which we are prophetically told that "all peoples on earth" would be blessed through the coming of the Messiah.

The angel then made an astonishing announcement: "Today in the town of David [Bethlehem] a Savior has been born to you; he is Christ the Lord" (Luke 2:11, insert mine). We noted earlier that according to the Old Testament, God and only God is the Savior of his people. God said, "I, even I, am the LORD, and apart from me there is no savior" (Isa. 43:11). And now, Christ the babe is called Savior. This is a powerful testimony to Christ's identity as God.

Note that the angel informed the shepherds that "Christ *the* Lord" had been born, not "Christ *your* Lord." Christ is the Sovereign, in other words, not just of men but of angels as well.[17] Christ is the Lord *(Kurios)* in an unqualified sense over all creation.

As the angel continued speaking with the shepherds, suddenly and without warning "a great company of the heavenly host appeared with the angel, praising God and saying, 'Glory to God in the highest, and on earth peace to men on whom his favor rests'" (Luke 2:13–14). These angels had known and served Christ in his preexistent state. And, now, following the virgin birth, they praised God because the one they had known and served for so long had now been born as a human being—a tiny babe in Bethlehem.

When the angels departed into heaven, the shepherds said to one another, "Let's go to Bethlehem and see this thing that has happened . . ." (Luke 2:15). It is not easy to convey in English the sense of urgency that is present in the original Greek in this verse. We might paraphrase it, "Come on, let us quickly go and see."[18] The shepherds were excited about what they had been told, no doubt partly due to the heavy messianic expectations in first-century Judaism. They knew a Messiah was coming, but now they were told he *had come*.

After the shepherds saw the divine babe, "they spread the word concerning what had been told them about this child, and all who heard it were amazed at what the shepherds said to them" (Luke 2:17–18). The Greek word for *amaze* means "to wonder," "to be astonished." The word conveys the idea that when people heard the testimony of the shepherds, they got "goose-pimples" down their spines. The prophesied Messiah had now come—eternal God in human flesh.

Adoration of the Babe

Shortly after the birth of Jesus, he was extolled and worshiped by a select few individuals who recognized the true significance of his birth. How uniquely wonderful it must have been to behold the one who, since creating humankind, had appeared and interacted among human beings as the Angel of the Lord in Old Testament times, but had now been born as a human babe.

Simeon and Anna

Simeon was a righteous and devout man who lived in Jerusalem. God had revealed to him that he would not die until he had seen the Christ—the promised Messiah to whom the entire Old Testament pointed. Moved by the Holy Spirit one day, Simeon went into the temple courts, where Jesus' parents soon followed. When Simeon beheld Jesus, he took him into his arms and prayed to God: "Sovereign Lord, as you have promised, you now dismiss your servant in peace. For my eyes have seen your salvation, which you have prepared in the sight of all people, a light for revelation to the Gentiles and for glory to your people Israel" (Luke 2:29–32).

Simeon recognized the babe as the one who would bring salvation to the world. This little babe was God the Savior. Though it would still be thirty years before Jesus began his public ministry, Simeon knew that this was the Christ, the Messiah, who was before him. And now that he had seen the coming of God's salvation, Simeon said he was ready to die peacefully.

Mary, Joseph, Jesus, and Simeon were then approached by the prophetess Anna. This aged widow (eighty-four years old) had given herself to continuous worship and fasting and prayer in the temple (Luke 2:36–38). As a prophetess, she was well aware of the many messianic passages pointing to the birth of Christ (e.g., Gen. 3:15; Isa. 7:14; Mic. 5:2). She was apparently spending her many years awaiting the coming of this Messiah. When she heard Simeon speak, her spirit must have rejoiced because the one for whom she had been waiting had finally come. She therefore gave thanks to God, for she knew she was in the presence of the promised one.

Wise Men from the East

Besides being praised by local people such as the shepherds, Simeon, and Anna, Jesus was visited by Magi from the east (Matt. 2:1–12). The Magi were wise men who were experts in studying the movements of the stars. They were not magicians or astrologers in any evil sense. These specialists in astronomy had seen Jesus' "star" in the east and came to worship him.

Scholars have long debated whether this "star" was a genuine star in the stellar heavens, or was perhaps a supernatural manifestation of God's glory. Bible scholar Louis A. Barbieri asks: "Could it be that 'the star' which the Magi saw and which led them to a specific house was the Shekinah glory of God? That same glory had led the children of Israel through the wilderness for 40 years as a pillar of fire and cloud. Perhaps this was what they saw in the East, and for want of a better term they called it a 'star.' All other efforts to explain this star are inadequate."[19]

J. Dwight Pentecost is another who sees this star as a manifestation of the glory of God:

> This was not a natural phenomenon but a supernatural one. If these men were astronomers, they would have been familiar with such a phenomenon and would have explained it naturally. It would have required more than a natural phenomenon to send them on such a journey. This star is better explained as a manifestation of the shining glory of God that He reveals to those who are recipients of revelation. There seems to be a parallel in the case of Abraham, a wise, powerful man from the East to whom God appeared and revealed His glory (Acts 7:2). This revelation of God's glory moved Abraham out of his home and country. Separated from his kindred, Abraham followed the God who had revealed Himself in glory. Similarly the star evidently was the shining of God's glory; by it God sovereignly revealed to these men that a King had been born in Israel.[20]

The likelihood of the "star" being the Shekinah glory of God is further supported by the fact that it would have been impossible for a single star in the stellar heavens to single out an individual dwelling in the village of Bethlehem. Only if the light of the "star" were similar to the pillar of fire that led Israel in the desert could the house be positively identified.

Upon entering the house specified by the "star," the wise men saw the child with his mother Mary. When they beheld Jesus, they "bowed down and worshiped him. Then they opened their treasures and presented him with gifts of gold and of incense and of myrrh" (Matt. 2:11). These were gifts that were typically given to a king in biblical times. These wise men recognized that the babe was royalty and was destined to reign as king.

Eternal God in Human Flesh

In the Introduction, we noted that some people, when reflecting on the birth of Christ, see in their mind's eye the nativity scenes so popular at Christmas time. Jesus is portrayed as a baby wrapped in swaddling clothes in a lowly manger. Those unfamiliar with the biblical account often conclude that this scene represents the actual beginnings of Jesus Christ.

We have seen, however, that Scripture is resoundingly clear that in the virgin birth, eternal God was born as a human through Mary. And Christ in his human body died on the cross for us, paying the ultimate penalty for the sins of humankind.

All of this—Jesus' incarnation and subsequent death on the cross—was part of the outworking of God's colossal plan of salvation that was conceived in eternity past. Christ's birth as a babe therefore had cosmic dimensions, far beyond what any human being could have ever conceived. Because he became human and died for us, we who believe in him shall dwell with him forever. Praise be to our great God and Savior, Jesus Christ!

11

Eternal God in Human Flesh

In the Incarnation, the incomprehensible came to pass. The glorious Son of God forsook the splendor of heaven and became as genuinely human as we ourselves are. Surrendering his glorious estate, he voluntarily entered into human relationships within the time-space world. "Leaving the free, unconditioned, world-ruling absoluteness of the divine form, the Son entered the limits of time and space of the creature."[1] Jesus became a man, was crucified on the cross, rose from the dead as the glorified God-man, and ascended back into his original glory. And all of this, he did for our sake.

The Incarnation is not an easy doctrine. When pondering the great truth that Christ as eternal God took on a human nature, we are immediately faced with a deluge of mind-boggling questions. For example, how could Christ be both fully human and fully divine at the same time? What is the relationship between the human and divine natures in Christ? Do the two natures merge to form a third compound nature or do they remain forever distinct? Did Christ in his two natures have two wills or just one will? Did Christ have conflicting desires—some human and some divine? Did Christ give up any of his divine attributes during his incarnate state? Was Christ *still* human following his death and resurrection?

These are difficult questions. But they are questions that the Scriptures address in varying degrees of detail. In this chapter, we shall focus our attention on these and other issues related to Christ in his incarnate state.

This is an important topic to deal with, even in a book on the preincarnate Christ, because all that Christ did among human beings in his *preincarnate* state prepared in some way for what he would accomplish in his *incarnate* state. To fully appreciate the person of Christ in all of his grandeur, both "states" must be considered together.

Most of this book has dealt with Christ *before* the manger. In the previous chapter, we focused on Christ *in* the manger (the virgin birth). In this present chapter, we shall look at Christ *after* the manger. In so doing, we shall discover the lengths to which the eternal Son was willing to go to secure the salvation of humankind. We begin with a brief look at what Scripture says about the perfect humanity of the incarnate Christ.

The Humanity of Christ

To deny either the undiminished deity *or* the perfect humanity of Christ in the Incarnation is to put oneself outside the pale of orthodoxy.[2] 1 John 4:2–3 tells us: "This is how you can recognize the Spirit of God: Every spirit that acknowledges that Jesus Christ has come in the flesh is from God, but every spirit that does not acknowledge Jesus is not from God. This is the spirit of the antichrist, which you have heard is coming and even now is already in the world."

Innumerable passages in the New Testament confirm Christ's full humanity in the Incarnation. Hebrews 2:14 tells us, for example, that since his children "have flesh and blood, he too shared in their humanity so that by his death he might destroy him who holds the power of death—that is, the devil." 1 Timothy 3:16 affirms that Jesus "appeared in a body, was vindicated by the Spirit, was seen by angels, was preached among the nations, was believed on in the world, was taken up in glory." Romans 8:3 says that God sent Jesus "in the likeness of sinful man to be a sin offering."

Normal Fetal Growth and Birth

While remaining fully God within the womb, as a human being Jesus experienced a normal fetal state, had an umbilical cord through which he received sustenance to his human body from his mother Mary, developed for nine months in the womb, and experienced a natural human birth. "Apart from the virgin conception and overshadowing ministry of the Holy Spirit, Mary's pregnancy was no different than that of any other human mother."[3]

It is important to grasp that it was the *conception* of Jesus in Mary's womb that was supernatural, not his *birth* (see Isa. 7:14; Luke 1:35; 2:6–7). The miraculous conception that resulted from the overshadowing ministry of the Holy Spirit (Luke 1:35) made it possible for the preexistent, eternal Son to take on a human nature through Mary.

Normal Human Development

Scripture is clear that even though Jesus never for a moment surrendered any aspect of his deity, he experienced normal human development through infancy, childhood, adolescence, and into adulthood. According to Luke 2:40, Jesus "grew," "became strong," and "was filled with wisdom." These are things that could never be said of Jesus' divine nature. It was in his humanity that he grew, became strong, and became filled with wisdom.

Likewise, Luke 2:52 tells us that "Jesus grew in wisdom and stature." Again, Jesus' growth in wisdom and stature is something that can only be said of his humanity. Many scholars have noted that Jesus' expert use of the Old Testament Scriptures during his three-year ministry was due to his "growth in wisdom" as he studied the Old Testament while growing up. Theologian Robert Gromacki notes: "His knowledge and application of Old Testament texts to real situations stemmed not from his divine omniscience, but from His keen intellect and His desire to learn."[4] Likewise, Bible scholar Edgar J. Goodspeed comments:

> No wonder Jesus could use [the writings of the Hebrew prophets] with such power in his brief ministry; he had studied and pondered them for many years, as no one has ever done, before or since. It is customary to dismiss his mastery of what was basic in them as simply effortless revelation, as though he just knew all about their meaning all the time, because he was himself; but that is not the picture of the gospels. He had to grow, as Luke is careful to say, in wisdom as well as stature.[5]

Christ's development as a human being was normal in every respect, with two major exceptions: (1) Christ always did the will of God, and (2) he never sinned. As Hebrews 4:15 tells us, in Christ "we do not have a high priest who is unable to sympathize with our weaknesses, but we have one who has been tempted in every way, just as we are—yet was without sin." Indeed, Christ is "holy," "blameless," and "pure" (Heb. 7:26). Hence, though Christ was utterly sinless, his human nature was exactly the same as ours in every other respect.[6]

Jesus' full humanity is plainly evident in the fact that he consistently displayed human characteristics. Besides growing as a normal child (Luke 2:40, 52), Jesus had a physical body of flesh and bones (Luke 24:39), experienced weariness (John 4:6), hunger (Luke 4:2), sorrow (Matt. 26:37), weeping (John 11:35), and needed sleep (Luke 8:23).

Scripture is also clear that Christ possessed a fully human spirit and soul. For example, John 11:33 describes the emotion that Jesus felt in his human *spirit* when his friend Lazarus died. At the prospect of his impending crucifixion, Jesus was troubled in his *soul* (John 12:27) and in his *spirit* (John 13:21). When he died on the cross, he gave up his *spirit* to the Father (John 19:30). In view of these Scriptures, "it is evident that Christ possessed a true humanity not only in its material aspects as indicated in his human body, but in the immaterial aspect specified in Scripture as being his soul and spirit. It is therefore not sufficient to recognize that Jesus Christ as the Son of God possessed a human body, but is necessary to view Him as having a complete human nature including body, soul, and spirit."[7]

Jesus Affirmed His Humanity

On a number of occasions, Jesus referred to his humanity in very clear terms. For example, recall that when Jesus was tempted by Satan, Jesus responded with the words: "Man does not live on bread alone, but on every word that comes from the mouth of God" (Matt. 4:4). Jesus was here applying to himself Deuteronomy 8:3, a passage that in its original context was written regarding *man's* relationship to God. On another occasion, Jesus told some angry Jews who were trying to kill him: "You are determined to kill me, a man who has told you the truth that I heard from God . . ." (John 8:40).[8]

Jesus' human nature was certainly recognized by others. One example of this is found in Acts 2:22 where we find Peter preaching his Pentecost sermon. In this sermon, Peter said: "Men of Israel, listen to this: Jesus of Nazareth was a *man* [emphasis added] accredited by God to you by miracles, wonders and signs, which God did among you through him, as you yourselves know." The apostle Paul provides another example in his assertion that "there is one God and one mediator between God and men, the man Christ Jesus, who gave himself as a ransom for all men . . ." (1 Tim. 2:5).

Hence, though Jesus was (is) fully and eternally God, he took on a fully human nature in the Incarnation. "We are neither more nor less human than He was. When His hands, feet, and side were pierced, blood came out of the wounds. It would have been the same for us."[9]

Condescension and Exaltation: Philippians 2:6–9

If Jesus Christ is in fact God, then how does his deity relate to his humanity? This question is dealt with in Philippians 2:6–

9. Paul, speaking of the Incarnation, says that Christ, "being in very nature God, did not consider equality with God something to be grasped, but made himself nothing, taking the very nature of a servant, being made in human likeness" (vv. 6–7).

Paul's affirmation that Christ was "in very nature God" is extremely significant. Christ in his essential being *is* and *always has been* eternal God—just as much as the Father and the Holy Spirit. Theologian Charles Ryrie notes that the word *nature* in the Greek connotes "that which is intrinsic and essential to the thing. Thus here it means that our Lord in His preincarnate state possessed essential deity."[10] Reformed theologian Benjamin Warfield comments that the word *nature* "is a term which expresses the sum of those characterizing qualities which make a thing the precise thing that it is."[11] Used of God, the word refers to "the sum of the characteristics which make the being we call 'God,' specifically God, rather than some other being—an angel, say, or a man."[12]

It is noteworthy that the word *being* (in the phrase, "being in very nature God") is a present-tense participle and carries the idea of *continued existence* as God.[13] Here the thought is that "Christ always has been in the form of God with the implication that He still is."[14] Robert Reymond notes that "when we take into account the force of the present participle, which conveys the idea of 'continually [beforehand] subsisting' (which in turn excludes any intimation that this mode of subsistence came to an end when He assumed the form of servant), we have here as bold and unqualified an assertion of both the preexistence and the full and unabridged deity of Jesus Christ as one could ever hope to find in the pages of the New Testament."[15] Thus, this verse indicates that Jesus Christ, in eternity past, continually and forever existed in the form of God, outwardly manifesting his divine attributes. *This* is the one who was born from the womb of Mary as a human being, all the while retaining his full deity.

Having said all this about Christ's essential deity, a key question remains: In what way did Christ "make himself nothing" when he became incarnate (Phil. 2:7)? This question has been debated down through the centuries, and the debate will no doubt continue until the Second Coming. Space limitations do not allow for an in-depth study of this issue. The following brief summary is sufficient for our purposes.

The Veiling of Christ's Preincarnate Glory

Paul's statement that Christ made himself "nothing" in the Incarnation involves three basic issues: the veiling of his preincarnate glory, a voluntary nonuse of some of his divine attributes, and the condescension involved in taking on the likeness of men.

However, one thing is certain. This does *not* mean that Jesus gave up his deity. Indeed, this is impossible, since God cannot cease to be God. Regarding the veiling of Christ's preincarnate glory, Scripture indicates that it was necessary for Christ to give up the *outer appearance* of God in order to take upon himself the form of man. Of course, Christ never actually *surrendered* his divine glory. Recall that on the Mount of Transfiguration (prior to his crucifixion), Jesus allowed his intrinsic glory to shine forth for a brief time, illuminating the whole mountainside (see Matt. 17:1–13). Nevertheless, it was necessary for Jesus to *veil* his preincarnate glory in order to dwell among mortal men.

Had Christ *not* veiled his preincarnate glory, mankind would not have been able to behold him. It would have been the same as when the apostle John, over fifty years after Christ's resurrection, beheld Christ in his glory and said: "I fell at his feet as though dead" (Rev. 1:17); or, as when Isaiah beheld the glory of Christ in his vision in the temple and said, "Woe to me! I am ruined!" (Isa. 6:5a; see John 12:41).

Christ's Voluntary Nonuse of Some Divine Attributes

A second issue involved in Christ making himself "nothing" in the Incarnation had to do with submission to a *voluntary nonuse of some of his divine attributes* in order for him to accomplish his objectives. Christ could never have actually *surrendered* any of his attributes, for then he would have ceased to be God.[16] But he could (and did) voluntarily cease using some of them during his time on earth (approximately 4 B.C. to A.D. 29) in order to live among men and their limitations.

Though Christ sometimes chose not to use his divine attributes, at other times he *did* use them. For example, on different occasions during his three-year ministry, Jesus exercised the divine attributes of *omniscience* (that is, all-knowingness—John 2:24; cf. 16:30), *omnipresence* (being everywhere-present—John 1:48), and *omnipotence* (being all-powerful, as evidenced by his many miracles—John 11). Hence, whatever limitations Christ may have suffered when he "made himself nothing" (Phil. 2:7), he did not subtract a single divine attribute or in any sense make himself less than God.

One of the divine attributes is known in theological circles as "immutability," which refers to the fact that God cannot change in his nature or essence. This attribute is expressly affirmed of Christ in Hebrews 13:8. As such, it is clear that Christ, as God, cannot change in his essential being, and hence he could never give up any of his divine attributes. Indeed, "God cannot change His nature by act of His will any more than any other being. Attributes inherent in a personal essence cannot be dismissed."[17] All of Christ's divine attributes are his *eternal* possession and continued in the incarnate state.[18]

The question that arises at this point is: Why did Jesus choose on occasion *not* to use some of his divine attributes? It would seem that Christ submitted to a voluntary nonuse of some of his attributes in keeping with his purpose of living among human beings and their limitations. He does not seem to have ever used his divine attributes on his own behalf, though certainly his attributes were gloriously displayed in the many miracles he performed for others.

To be more specific, the scriptural testimony indicates that Christ never used his omniscience to make his own life *as a human being* easier. "He suffered all the inconveniences of His day even though in His divine omniscience He had full knowledge of every human device ever conceived for human comfort."[19]

Nor did Christ use his omnipotence or omnipresence to make his life as a human easier. Though Jesus as God could have, in his omnipotence, just willed himself from Bethany to Jerusalem and he would have been instantly there, he instead traveled by foot like every other human and experienced fatigue in the process. Of course, as God, Christ in his divine nature (with his attribute of omnipresence) was in both Bethany and Jerusalem at the same time. But he voluntarily chose not to use this attribute on those occasions during his three-year ministry that would have made his life as a human being easier. "In a word, He restricted the benefits of His attributes as they pertained to His walk on earth and voluntarily chose not to use His powers to lift Himself above ordinary human limitations."[20]

Christ's Condescension

A third issue involved in Christ's making himself "nothing" in the Incarnation had to do with his condescending by taking on the *likeness* (literally "form" or "appearance") of men, and taking on the *form* ("essence" or "nature") of a bondservant.[21] Christ was thus truly human. This humanity was one that was subject to temptation, distress, weakness, pain, sorrow, and limitation.[22] Yet, at the same time, it must be noted that the word *likeness* suggests *similarity but difference*. As theologian Robert Lightner explains, "though His humanity was genuine, He was different from all other humans in that He was sinless."[23] Nevertheless, Christ's taking on the likeness of men represented a great *condescension* on the part of the second person of the Trinity.

Theologians have been careful to point out that the Incarnation involved a gaining of *human* attributes and not a giving up of *divine* attributes. That this is meant by Paul is clear in his affirmation that in the Incarnation Christ was "taking the very nature of a servant," "being made in human likeness," and "being found in appearance as a man" (Phil. 2:7–8). As J. I. Packer puts it, "He was no less God then [in the Incarnation] than before; but He had begun to be man. He was not now God *minus* some elements of His deity, but God *plus* all that He had made His own by taking manhood to Himself. He who *made* man was now learning what it felt like to *be* man."[24] In other words, it was not the subtraction of deity but the addition of humanity.

To sum up, then, in order to dwell among human beings, Christ made himself "nothing" in the sense that he veiled his preincarnate glory, he submitted to a voluntary nonuse (without a surrendering) of some of his divine attributes, and he condescended by taking on a human nature. Having done this, Christ as the God-man was obedient to the point of death, "even death on a cross" (Phil. 2:8).

The Union of the Human and Divine Natures in Christ

How infinite God and finite humanity can be united in one single person is one of the most difficult of all theological problems. It ranks in complexity with the Trinity and the paradox of divine sovereignty versus human free will. The secret of Christ's self-humbling is forever unfathomable. It transcends human reason.[25] Nevertheless, Scripture provides us with some intriguing facts about this inscrutable union. The remainder of this chapter will summarize these facts.

What Is a Nature?

Crucial to a proper understanding of the Incarnation is grasping what is meant by the word *nature*. This word is commonly used to designate the divine or human elements in the person of Christ. In other words, "nature" when used of Christ's divinity refers to all that belongs to deity, including all the attributes of deity. "Nature" when used of Christ's humanity refers to all that belongs to humanity, including all the attributes of humanity. Another way to describe *nature* is that it refers to "the sum-total of all the essential qualities of a thing, that which makes it what it is."[26]

The Incarnate Christ: One Person

Though the incarnate Christ had both a human and a divine nature, he was only one person—as indicated by his consistent use of "I," "me," and "mine" in reference to himself. Jesus never used the words "us," "we," or "ours" in reference to his human-divine person. Nor did the divine nature of Christ ever carry on a verbal conversation with his human nature.

This is completely unlike the doctrine of the Trinity. The persons in the Godhead use personal pronouns of each other—that is, the Father says "you" to the Son, and the Son says "you" to the Father. And when God created man, he said "Let *us* make man in *our* image" (Gen. 1:26a, italics added). This is because there are three persons within the Godhead. However, as Robert Gromacki notes, "there is no direct analogy between the trinitarian oneness of God and the theanthropic [God-Man] person of Christ. In the former, there are three persons but only one nature, divine; in the latter there is only one person with two natures, human and divine."[27]

Hence, the eternal Son of God—who, prior to the Incarnation, was one in person *and* nature (wholly divine)—became, in the Incarnation, two in nature (divine and human) while remaining one person. The Son, who had already been a person for all eternity past, joined himself not with a human person but with a human nature at the Incarnation.[28]

An Inscrutable Mystery

One of the most complex aspects of the relationship of Christ's two natures is that, while the attributes of one nature are never attributed to the other, the attributes of both natures are properly attributed to his one person. Thus Christ at the same moment in time had what seem to be contradictory qualities. He was finite and yet infinite, weak and yet omnipotent, increasing in knowledge and yet omniscient, limited to being in one place at one time and yet omnipresent. In the Incarnation, the person of Christ is the partaker of the attributes of both natures, so that whatever may be affirmed of either nature—human or divine—may be affirmed of the one person.

Though Christ sometimes operated in the sphere of his humanity and in other cases in the sphere of his deity, in all cases what he did and what he was could be attributed to his one person. Thus, though Christ in his human nature knew hunger (Luke 4:2), weariness (John 4:6), and the need for sleep (Luke 8:23), just as Christ in his divine nature was omniscient (John 2:24), omnipresent (John 1:48), and omnipotent (John 11), *all of this was experienced by the one person of Jesus Christ.*

With this backdrop in mind, it is significant to note that both human and divine characteristics and deeds may be attributed to Christ's person under *any of his names*—whether they be divine or human titles.[29] Indeed, "regardless of the designation Scripture employs, the *person* of the Son, and not one of His natures, is always the subject of the statement."[30] Robert Gromacki explains:

> It is proper to say that Jesus was the Redeemer even though no human could save another. It is also correct to state that the Son of God thirsted although God doesn't have to drink to sustain Himself. Human attributes were ascribed to Him under a divine title: Emmanuel, the Son of God, was born (Matt. 1:23; Luke 1:35) and the Lord of glory was crucified (1 Cor. 2:8). On the opposite side, divine attributes were ascribed to Him under a human title: the Son of man ascended to heaven where He was before (John 6:62) and the slain Lamb was worthy to receive power, riches, wisdom, strength, honor, glory, and blessing (Rev. 5:12).[31]

The Human-Divine Union Lasts Forever

When Christ became a man in the Incarnation, he did not enter into a temporary union of the human and divine natures that ended at his death and resurrection. Rather, Scripture is clear that Christ's human nature continues forever.

Christ was raised immortal in the very same human body in which he died (Luke 24:37–39; Acts 2:31; 1 John 4:2; 2 John 7). When Christ ascended into heaven, he ascended in the same physical human body, as witnessed by several of his disciples (Acts 1:11). When Christ returns, he will return as the "Son of Man"—a messianic title that points to his humanity (Matt. 26:64). At the same time, even though Jesus has fully retained his humanity and will return as the glorified God-man, the glory that he now has in heaven is no less than the resplendent glory that has been his for all eternity past (see John 17:5).

The Death of the God-Man

If Christ forever retained his humanity following the crucifixion, then what precisely occurred when Christ the God-man died on the cross? To answer this question, we must note that the Greek word for death *(thanatos)* conveys the idea of separation. When a person physically dies, his immaterial nature (soul and spirit) separates from his physical body. When Jesus died on the cross, the divine person with his divine nature *and* with his human immaterial nature (soul and spirit) departed from his human body. *There was no separation of the divine nature from the human nature in the person of Jesus when he died.* Christ was just as much a human being *after* his death and resurrection as he was before.

Addressing this subject, Robert Gromacki affirms that Christ "was no less human after His death than any normal individual is after his death. Human death occurs when the immaterial self, consisting of soul and spirit, is separated from the material body. Although the body may be in the ground, he as a human person is either in heaven or in hell."[32] At the resurrection, Christ's real self, including his divine nature and his immaterial human nature, were joined to the same physical body in which he died, now immortal and incorruptible.

At the Incarnation, then, the person of Christ became eternally wedded to a human nature. He did not discard any part of his humanity at his death, resurrection, or ascension.

The Relation of the Human and Divine Natures

How could two different natures—one infinite and one finite—exist within one person? Or, as Gromacki asks, "Would not one nature be dominated by the other? Would not each nature have to surrender some of its qualities in order for each to coexist beside each other? Could Jesus Christ be truly God and truly man at the same time?"[33]

In the early history of the church, there was much confusion regarding how such incompatible natures could be joined in one person without one or the other losing some of its essential characteristics. The discussion that resulted from this confusion, however, led to the orthodox statement that the two natures are united without mixture and without loss of any essential attributes, and that the two natures maintain their separate identities without transfer of any property or attribute of one nature to the other.[34] As theologian Robert Lightner puts it,

> In the union of the human and divine in Christ each of the natures retained its own attributes. Deity did not permeate humanity, nor did humanity become absorbed into deity. The two natures retain their complete identity even though they have been joined together in a personal union. Christ is thus *theanthropic* (God-man) in person. Embracing perfect humanity made him no less God, and retaining his undiminished deity did not make him less human.[35]

In the joining of the human and divine natures in one person, it is critical to recognize that there was no mixture to form a third compound nature. The human nature always remained human, and the divine nature always remained divine. "To rob the divine nature of God of a single attribute would destroy His deity, and to rob man of a single human attribute would result in destruction of a true humanity. It is for this reason that the two natures of Christ cannot lose or transfer a single attribute."[36]

Along these lines, the Chalcedonian Creed (see Appendix F) affirms that the two natures were united *without mixture, without change, without division,* and *without separation.*[37] Hence, the union of the two natures in Christ should not be thought of as deity possessing humanity, for this would deny true humanity its rightful place. On the other hand, the Incarnation was not merely humanity indwelt by deity. "Christ did not differ from other men simply in degree of divine influence as sometimes advanced by modern liberals. In His unique personality He possessed two natures, one eternal and divine, the other human and generated in time."[38]

Christ must be seen as a "theanthropic" person. We noted earlier that "theanthropic" means "God-man." This word is actually a compound word that combines two Greek words: *theos* (meaning "God") and *anthropos* (meaning "man"). Jesus is the *Theos-anthropos,* the God-man.

Christ, however, did not have a theanthropic nature that resulted from a merging of the divine and human natures in Christ. We must stress that Christ in the Incarnation was neither a divine man nor a human God. He is the God-man, *fully God* and *fully man.* He is no less God because of his humanity and no less human because of his deity.[39]

The Relation of the Two Natures to the Self-Consciousness of Christ

As God, Jesus during his incarnate state was always aware of his deity. His divine self-consciousness was as fully operative when he was a babe in Mary's arms in Bethlehem as it was in his most mature experience as an adult.

But what about a human self-consciousness? In his book *Jesus Christ Our Lord,* John F. Walvoord notes that there is evidence that "the human nature developed and with it a human self-consciousness came into play. . . . It seems possible to conclude that He had both a divine and a human self-consciousness, that these were never in conflict, and that Christ sometimes thought, spoke, and acted from the divine self-consciousness and at other times from the human."[40]

It seems legitimate to conclude, then, that Jesus in the Incarnation was *one* person with *two* different kinds of consciousness—a divine consciousness and a human consciousness. In his divine consciousness he could say, "I and the Father are one" (John 10:30), "Before Abraham was born, I am!" (John 8:58), and "I am the way and the truth and the life. No one comes to the Father except through me" (John 14:6). In his human consciousness Jesus could make such statements as, "I am thirsty" (John 19:28).

The Relation of the Two Natures to the Will(s) of Christ

If Christ had two kinds of consciousness, did he also have two wills? The Council of Chalcedon said that Christ had two natures united in one person, thus implying two wills. An examination of the Gospels indicates that every single decision and action of Christ stemmed from either his divine nature or from his human nature—or, in some cases, a blending of both. In view of this, it may be proper to think of Christ as having two wills. Theologian William G. T. Shedd says that "each nature, in order to be whole and entire, must have all of its essential elements. A human nature without voluntariness would be as defective as it would be without rationality."[41] However, since both actions stem from one person (will-er), it is correct to speak of one will in Christ. In short, Christ's will was one in *source* (he was one person) but two in *manifestation* (through his two natures).

Two Spheres of Activity—Human and Divine

The Gospel accounts are clear that Christ operated at different times under the major influence of one or the other of his two natures. Indeed, Christ operated in the human sphere to the extent that it was necessary for him to accomplish his earthly purpose as determined in the eternal plan of salvation.

At the same time, he operated in the divine sphere to the extent that it was possible in the period of his humiliation.

It is interesting that both of Christ's natures come into play in many events recorded in the Gospels. For example, Christ's initial approach to the fig tree to pick and eat a fig to relieve his hunger reflected the natural ignorance of the human mind (Matt. 21:19a). (That is, in his humanity he did not know from a distance that there was no fruit on that particular tree.) But then he immediately revealed his omnipotence by causing the tree to wither (v. 19b).

On another occasion, Jesus in his omniscience knew that his friend Lazarus had died and set off for Bethany (John 11:11). When Jesus arrived in Bethany, he asked (in his humanness, without exercising omniscience) where Lazarus had been laid (v. 34). Robert Reymond notes that "as the God-man, [Jesus] is simultaneously omniscient as God (in company with the other persons of the Godhead) and ignorant of some things as man (in company with the other persons of the human race)."[42]

Important Results of the Human-Divine Union

One could write an entire book on the important results of the human-divine union in the person of Christ. We will offer only a brief summary here, focusing on Christ as Redeemer and High Priest.

Christ Our Redeemer

Humankind's redemption was completely dependent upon the human-divine union in Christ. If Christ the Redeemer had been *only* God, he could not have died, since God by his very nature cannot die. It was only as a man that Christ could represent humanity and die as a man. As God, however, Christ's death had infinite value sufficient to provide redemption for the sins of all mankind. Clearly, then, Christ had to be both God and man to secure man's salvation (1 Tim. 2:5).

This is related to the Old Testament concept of the kinsman-redeemer. In Old Testament times, the phrase *kinsman-redeem-*

er was always used of one who was related by blood to someone he was seeking to redeem from bondage. If someone was
sold into slavery, for example, it was the duty of a blood relative—the "next of kin"—to act as that person's "kinsman-redeemer" and buy him out of slavery (Lev. 25:47–48).

Jesus is the Kinsman-Redeemer for sin-enslaved humanity. For Jesus to become a kinsman-redeemer, however, he
had to become related by blood to the human race. This indicates the necessity of the Incarnation. Jesus became a man in
order to redeem man (Heb. 2:14–16). And because Jesus was
also fully God, his sacrificial death had infinite value (Heb.
9:11–28).

Christ Our Priest

Christ's human-divine union also enabled Christ to become
our eternal High Priest. By the Incarnation, Christ became a
man and hence could act as a human priest. As God, Christ's
priesthood could be everlasting and perfect in every way.

Because the divine Christ became a man in the Incarnation,
he as our Priest is able to intercede in prayer for us. Since Jesus
was truly one of us, experiencing all of the temptations and trials of human existence, he is fully able to understand and em-
pathize with us in our struggles as human beings. Hebrews
4:15–16 tells us that "we do not have a high priest who is unable to sympathize with our weaknesses, but we have one
who has been tempted in every way, just as we are—yet was
without sin. Let us then approach the throne of grace with
confidence, so that we may receive mercy and find grace to
help us in our time of need."

If Christ was *not* human, or only *incompletely* human, then
he would not have been able to make the kind of intercession
a priest must make on behalf of those whom he represents. Because Christ is fully human and fully God, "he is able to save
completely those who come to God through him, because he
always lives to intercede for them" (Heb. 7:25).

Even now, Christ—the glorified God-man in his heavenly abode—is interceding on our behalf on an individual, personal basis. He knows each of us intimately, including all our weaknesses, temptations, and human failings. How reassuring it is that Christ, who is completely familiar with what it is like to be a human, prays for us specifically according to our need. Praise be to our eternal God, Savior, Redeemer, and High Priest, Jesus Christ!

12

Christ and His Eternal Glory

A common thread that runs through the whole of Christ's eternal existence—in eternity past before the creation, during Old Testament times as the Angel of the Lord, during New Testament times as God-incarnate, in the heavenly abode following the resurrection, at the Second Coming, and in the future eternal state—is that he manifests the fullness of the divine glory. Christ is the God of glory both *before* and *after* the manger. It is therefore appropriate that the final chapter in this book be on Christ and his eternal glory.

The apostle Paul informs us that God dwells "in unapproachable light" (1 Tim. 6:16). So brilliant and glorious is this light that no mortal can survive in its midst (see Rev. 1:17). The light in which God dwells is superior to all things visible. "It is something other than the radiance of all suns and stars. It is not to be beheld by earthly eyes; it is far removed from all things this side (2 Cor. 12:4). Only the angels in heaven can behold it (Matt. 18:10); only the spirits of the perfected in the eternal light (Matt. 5:8; 1 John 3:2; Rev. 22:4); only the pure and holy, even as He Himself is pure (1 John 3:2, 3)."[1]

As we consider the eternal glory of Christ, it is important that we begin with the recognition that the word *glory*, when used of God, refers to the luminous manifestation of God's person, his glorious revelation of himself to man.[2] This definition is borne out by the many ways the word is used in Scripture. For example, *brilliant light* consistently accompanies the divine manifestation in his glory (Matt. 17:2–3; 1 Tim. 6:16; Rev. 1:16). Moreover, the word *glory* is often linked with verbs of *seeing* (Exod. 16:7; 33:18; Isa. 40:5) and verbs of *appearing* (Exod. 16:10; Deut. 5:24), both of which emphasize the visible nature of God's glory.

God's glory not only involves brilliant light, but also the presence of *smoke* (Isa. 6:4) and a *cloud* (Num. 16:42). Illustrations of the presence of a cloud during divine appearances are numerous in Scripture:

• Recall that "while Aaron was speaking to the whole Israelite community, they looked toward the desert, and there was the glory of the Lord appearing in the cloud" (Exod. 16:10).

• When the tabernacle in the wilderness was completed, the glory cloud settled upon it, preventing human entrance: "Then the cloud covered the Tent of Meeting, and the glory of the Lord filled the tabernacle. Moses could not enter the Tent of Meeting because the cloud had settled upon it, and the glory of the Lord filled the tabernacle" (Exod. 40:34–35).

• God's glory was also seen in a cloud when Solomon's temple was dedicated: "When the priests withdrew from the Holy Place, the cloud filled the temple of the Lord. And the priests could not perform their service because of the cloud, for the glory of the Lord filled his temple" (1 Kings 8:10–11).

The fact that Jesus manifests the fullness of the divine glory is highly revealing of his true identity. Indeed, in the Old Testament, God said that "I am the Lord; that is my name! I will not give my glory to another or my praise to idols" (Isa. 42:8). Yet, Jesus, too, manifested the divine glory (see Matt. 17:1–23). This can mean only one thing: Jesus is God.

The Shekinah Glory and the Angel of the Lord

Christ's intrinsic glory is as eternal as God is. There has never been a time in which Christ lacked any degree of divine glory. Even as the Angel of the Lord—the form in which Christ made many preincarnate appearances in Old Testament times—Christ manifested his intrinsic glory.

Recall that the divine Angel was *visibly present* to the Israelites in their wilderness wanderings. It was at the edge of the wilderness that God (that is, *Christ*) as the Angel of the Lord first went before his people as a pillar of cloud by day to lead them, and a pillar of fire by night (Exod. 13:21). This way the Israelites could travel during the day *and* the night. The fire and the cloud were both manifestations of the Angel's Shekinah glory.

We know this was no ordinary angel by a comparison of chapters 13 and 14 in Exodus. Exodus 13:21 speaks of *God* going before Israel, and later the statement was recorded that "the *angel* of God, who had been traveling in front of Israel's army, withdrew and went behind them . . ." (14:19, italics added). Clearly, the Angel and God are equated. And, as I demonstrated in chapter 5, this Angel could only have been the preincarnate Christ, not the Father or the Holy Spirit.

The divine Angel personally intervened when Egypt attempted to attack the Israelites from behind. Exodus 14:19–20 tells us that "the angel of God, who had been traveling in front of Israel's army, withdrew and went behind them. The pillar of cloud also moved from in front and stood behind them, coming between the armies of Egypt and Israel. Throughout the night the cloud brought darkness to the one side and light to the other side; so neither went near the other all night long."

"Then Moses stretched out his hand over the sea, and all that night the LORD drove the sea back with a strong east wind and turned it into dry land. The waters were divided," enabling the Israelites to cross "the sea on dry ground." But suddenly the Egyptians began to pursue them, "and all of

Pharaoh's horses and chariots and horsemen followed them into the sea" (Exod. 14:21–23).

Then, according to the Exodus account, the divine Angel completed his deliverance of Israel from Egypt:

> During the last watch of the night the LORD looked down from the pillar of fire and cloud at the Egyptian army and threw it into confusion. He made the wheels of their chariots come off so that they had difficulty driving. And the Egyptians said, "Let's get away from the Israelites! The LORD is fighting for them against Egypt."
>
> Then the LORD said to Moses, "Stretch out your hand over the sea so that the waters may flow back over the Egyptians and their chariots and horsemen." Moses stretched out his hand over the sea, and at daybreak the sea went back to its place. The Egyptians were fleeing toward it, and the LORD swept them into the sea. The water flowed back and covered the chariots and horsemen—the entire army of Pharaoh that had followed the Israelites into the sea. Not one of them survived.
>
> But the Israelites went through the sea on dry ground, with a wall of water on their right and on their left. That day the LORD saved Israel from the hands of the Egyptians, and Israel saw the Egyptians lying dead on the shore. And when the Israelites saw the great power the LORD displayed against the Egyptians, the people feared the LORD and put their trust in him and in Moses his servant (Exod. 14:24–31).

Moses and the Divine Glory

Some time after the exodus, humble and meek Moses made one of the boldest requests ever made before God: "Now show me your glory" (Exod. 33:18). God responded to this request by telling Moses, "You cannot see my face, for no one may see me and live" (v. 20). But then the Lord said to Moses, "There is a place near me where you may stand on a rock. When my glory passes by, I will put you in a cleft in the rock and cover you with my hand until I have passed by. Then I will remove my hand and you will see my back; but my face must not be seen" (vv. 21–23).

In view of the fact that no human being can see God in his full glory and live, what Moses requested of God was more than the Lord would grant for Moses' own good. Nevertheless, God did place Moses in a cleft in a rock, apparently a cavelike crevice, and then caused his glory to pass by. Old Testament scholar Walter Kaiser tells us that in our passage, "the glory of God refers first and foremost to the sheer weight or the reality of his presence. The presence of God would come near Moses in spatial terms."[3] But God's glory would also involve indescribable illumination—too brilliant for a mere mortal to witness.

What, then, actually occurred during this encounter Moses had with God? Kaiser explains that

> Moses would not be able to endure the spectacular purity, luminosity, and reality of staring at the raw glory of God himself. Instead, God would protect Moses from accidental (and apparently, fatal) sight of that glory. Therefore, in a striking anthropomorphism (a description of the reality of God in terms or analogies understandable to mortals), God would protect Moses from the full effects of looking directly at the glory of God by placing his hand over Moses's face until all God's glory had passed by.[4]

It was only after God's glory had passed by Moses that God removed his gracious, protecting hand. Then Moses would view what God permitted—that is, God's "back." But what does this mean? We know from other passages that God is Spirit and is formless (John 4:24). Just as the word *hand* is an anthropomorphism, so the word *back* is an anthropomorphism. With this in mind, Kaiser notes that the Hebrew word for "back" carries the idea of *aftereffects*.[5] "This would fit the context as well as the range of meanings for the Hebrew word used. Moses did not see the glory of God directly, but once it had gone past, God did allow him to view the results, the afterglow, that his presence had produced."[6]

Isaiah Saw Jesus' Glory

Moses was not the only one who encountered God's glory. Isaiah had a vision in the temple in which he found himself in the presence of God's glory:

> In the year that King Uzziah died, I saw the Lord seated on a throne, high and exalted, and the train of his robe filled the temple. Above him were seraphs, each with six wings: With two wings they covered their faces, with two they covered their feet, and with two they were flying. And they were calling to one another:
>
> "Holy, holy, holy is the LORD Almighty;
>   the whole earth is full of his glory."
>
> At the sound of their voices the doorposts and thresholds shook and the temple was filled with smoke.
> "Woe to me!" I cried. "I am ruined! For I am a man of unclean lips, and I live among a people of unclean lips, and my eyes have seen the King, the LORD Almighty" (Isa. 6:1–5).

This passage is rich in meaning. Isaiah 6 finds the prophet in the temple in 740 B.C., perhaps mourning the death of godly King Uzziah. He may have gone there to pray in his grief.

While in the temple, God granted Isaiah a glorious vision that would give him strength for the duration of his ministry. Isaiah saw the Lord seated on a throne, "high and exalted" (Isa. 6:1). God's long and flowing robe points to his kingly majesty. Though an earthly king had died, the true King of the universe still reigned supreme from on high.

Isaiah saw "seraphs" above God's throne (Isa. 6:2–3). These were magnificent angels who proclaimed God's holiness and glory. The word *seraph* comes from a root meaning "to burn," emphasizing the purity and brightness of these angelic beings.

These angels covered their faces with their wings in God's presence. Despite their own brightness and purity, they apparently could not look at the greater brightness and purity of God, who—as we have seen—dwells "in unapproachable light" (1 Tim. 6:16).

The angels proclaimed, "Holy, holy, holy is the LORD Almighty . . ." (Isa. 6:3). The triple reference points to the fullness or completeness of God's holiness. Triple repetition is often used in Scripture to emphasize a truth.

At the sound of the angels' voices, the doorposts and the thresholds in the temple shook and "the temple was filled with smoke" (Isa. 6:4). We noted earlier that human encounters with God often involved the presence of smoke (Exod. 20:18–19). This smoke was no doubt the cloud of glory that Isaiah's ancestors had seen in the wilderness (Exod. 13:21; 16:10) and which the priests in Solomon's day had viewed in the temple upon its dedication (1 Kings 8:10–13).

All this becomes extremely significant when we go to John's Gospel and read that what Isaiah actually saw was *Jesus'* glory. The words of Isaiah 6:3 refer to the glory of "the LORD Almighty" (or, more literally, the "*Yahweh* of hosts"), but John says that these words were in reference to Jesus Christ (John 12:41). Jesus and *Yahweh* are here equated.

How awesome this must have been for Isaiah. Seven hundred years before the Messiah was born in Bethlehem, Isaiah saw the glory of the preincarnate Christ in a vision. And the one whom Isaiah had personally encountered in this vision is the same one whose birth as a human he prophesied (Isa. 4:2; 7:14; 9:6–7; 11:1–5, 10; 32:1; 42:1–4; 49:1–7; 52:13–53:12; 61:1–3).

Christ and His Transfiguration

We noted in chapter 8 that when Christ the *Logos* became flesh (John 1:14), the glorious presence of God was fully embodied in him, for he is the true *Shekinah*. I do not wish to repeat the material from chapter 8 here. But I do want to reiterate that the same Shekinah glory that Moses beheld in the tabernacle (Exod. 40:34–38) and that the priest saw in the temple (1 Kings 8:10–11) was revealed in the person of Jesus Christ on the Mount of Transfiguration.

In the transfiguration (which occurred prior to Jesus' crucifixion), Jesus "pulled back the veil" (so to speak) and allowed his intrinsic glory to shine forth in all of its splendor. According to the three Synoptic Gospels (Matthew, Mark, and Luke), while Jesus was praying, "the appearance of his face changed" (Luke 9:29). "His face shone like the sun," and his clothing was also changed so that it "became as white as the light" (Matt. 17:2), or "as bright as a flash of lightning" (Luke 9:29). His clothing was "dazzling white, whiter than anyone in the world could bleach them" (Mark 9:3). If this magnificent transformation took place at night, as Luke's account suggests (9:32, 37), the scene unfolding before the disciples must have been all the more awesome, beyond the capacity of words to describe.[7]

To fully grasp the significance of what occurred on the Mount, let us examine the details of the transfiguration as recorded in Matthew's Gospel:

> After six days Jesus took with him Peter, James and John the brother of James, and led them up a high mountain by themselves. There he was transfigured before them. His face shone like the sun, and his clothes became as white as the light. Just then there appeared before them Moses and Elijah, talking with Jesus.
>
> Peter said to Jesus, "Lord, it is good for us to be here. If you wish, I will put up three shelters—one for you, one for Moses and one for Elijah."
>
> While he was still speaking, a bright cloud enveloped them, and a voice from the cloud said, "This is my Son, whom I love; with him I am well pleased. Listen to him!"
>
> When the disciples heard this, they fell facedown to the ground, terrified. But Jesus came and touched them. "Get up," he said. "Don't be afraid." When they looked up, they saw no one except Jesus (Matt. 17:1–8).

Metamorphosis on a High Mountain

The mention of the "high mountain" recalls Old Testament theophanies (appearances of God) on the "mountain of God" or Mount Sinai (Exod. 24; 1 Kings 19), in which Moses and Elijah received visions of the glory of God. It is fascinating that these two Old Testament saints, who had received visions of God's glory in Old Testament times, now appear to Christ on a high mountain as Christ is transfigured.

The word *transfigured* (Matt. 17:2) is rich with meaning. The verb, which comes from the Greek word *metamorphoo*, does not refer to a superficial change of outward appearance. Rather, it denotes a transformation of Christ's essential form, proceeding from within. "We get the word metamorphosis from this Greek word. It means 'to be changed into another form,' not merely a change in outward appearance. . . . For a brief time Jesus' human body was transformed (glorified) and the disciples saw Him as He will be when He returns visibly in power and glory to establish His kingdom on earth (see Acts 15:14–18; 1 Cor. 15:20–28; Rev. 1:14–15; 19:15; 20:4–6)."[8]

J. Dwight Pentecost offers us some helpful insights on how Christ's human body acted as a veil to his intrinsic glory, a veil that was "pulled back" during the transfiguration:

> Christ was not transfigured by means of an external light focused on Him so that He reflected the glory of God. Rather, this was the outshining of the essential glory that belongs to Jesus Christ. . . . It was necessary that Christ's glory be veiled when He came into this world. Christ's glory was not surrendered at the time of the Incarnation but was veiled, lest the people whom He had come to redeem should be consumed by its brightness.
>
> In revealing plans for the tabernacle to Moses, God instructed him to erect a curtain between the Holy of Holies, where God purposed to dwell, and His people. That veil was not so much designed to teach Israel that they were unworthy to enter the presence of God—which in truth it did—as much as to protect Israel from being consumed by the brightness of God's glo-

ry. The veil, then, was a gracious provision by a holy God to
make it possible for Him to dwell in the midst of an unholy
people. The writer to the Hebrews said that the body of Jesus
Christ was to Him what the veil was in the tabernacle (Heb.
10:19–20).[9]

At the transfiguration, the one who had hidden his glory
beneath the form of a servant (Phil. 2:6–8) allowed his intrinsic
glory to break through the veil of his flesh and shine out until
his very clothing kindled to the dazzling brightness of the
light. What a magnificent sight it must have been!

Moses and Elijah

After Jesus was transfigured before the disciples, Moses
and Elijah appeared on the mountain with Jesus. Moses was
the greatest lawgiver of the Old Testament and Elijah was
the first of the great prophets. Together, Moses and Elijah
point to the hour of fulfillment of all that the Old Testament
foreshadowed.

I picture in my mind's eye Christ with Moses on one side
and Elijah on the other. They spoke together of Christ's coming
crucifixion, resurrection, and glory. "Both Law and Prophets
speak of His suffering and of His glory as well. He, the one in
the middle, is the fulfillment of the Law and the Prophets."[10]

Luke's Gospel is the only account of the transfiguration that
specifically tells us the topic of Jesus' discussion with Moses
and Elijah: "They spoke about [Jesus'] departure, which he
was about to bring to fulfillment at Jerusalem" (Luke 9:31).
The Greek word translated *departure* literally means "exodus."
This casts an interesting light on Jesus' attitude toward his approaching death:

> The Old Testament Exodus liberated a people from the bond-
> age they had endured and brought them into liberty and free-
> dom. When Christ came into the world, He came as a Servant
> (Phil. 2:6–8). Christ viewed His death not only as the act of a
> Servant obedient to His Father's will but also as an act that

would liberate Him from this period of bondage to which He
had subjected Himself by the Incarnation. He anticipated the
glorious liberty from bondage into which He would be brought
by the Resurrection.[11]

The Appearance of a Cloud

While Christ was speaking with Moses and Elijah, "a bright
cloud enveloped them, and a voice from the cloud said, 'This
is my Son, whom I love; with him I am well pleased. Listen to
him!'" (Matt. 17:5). Peter, James, and John—as devout stu-
dents of the Old Testament—knew well what the appearance
of the cloud meant. It was the cloud that spoke of *Yahweh's*
physical presence (see Exod. 13:21–22; 40:38; Num. 9:15; Ps.
99:7; Isa. 4:5; 2 Chron. 7:1). In a sense, the cloud is God's tabernacle, a pavilion that both reveals *and* conceals his glory.

The words "listen to him," which the Father uttered from
within the cloud, are extremely significant. As good Jews, the
disciples would have been awestruck at being in the presence
of Moses and Elijah, two of the greatest figures in the Old Testament. But Jesus had succeeded Moses and Elijah, who suddenly disappeared, leaving no one except Jesus (Matt. 17:8).
Moses and Elijah had completed their work and were now superseded. Jesus, not Moses or Elijah, was now God's authorized ruler and spokesman.

All this brings to mind Deuteronomy 18:15, which contains
a messianic prediction of a prophet greater than Moses, to
whom the people were to listen. Christ is truly the greater
prophet.

A Learning Experience

While one purpose of the transfiguration was to encourage
Jesus in view of his coming death, we must conclude that another purpose was to encourage the disciples in the trials that
they would soon face. In view of Christ's frequent references
to his impending death, the disciples probably needed far
more encouragement than Jesus did. The disciples never fully
grasped the importance of Jesus' death, and it was difficult for

them to fit this death into their concept of the Lord's future program.

Clearly, the transfiguration left an indelible mark upon the disciples. When John wrote his Gospel some fifty to sixty years later (A.D. 85–90), he said: "The Word became flesh and made his dwelling among us. We have seen his glory, the glory of the One and Only, who came from the Father, full of grace and truth" (John 1:14). When Peter wrote his second epistle (A.D. 66), he said: "We did not follow cleverly invented stories when we told you about the power and coming of our Lord Jesus Christ, but we were eyewitnesses of his majesty. For he received honor and glory from God the Father when the voice came to him from the Majestic Glory, saying, 'This is my Son, whom I love; with him I am well pleased.' We ourselves heard this voice that came from heaven when we were with him on the sacred mountain" (2 Peter 1:16–18). Clearly, the transfiguration was a dramatic and reassuring experience that indicated to the disciples that no matter what happened in the immediate future with Christ (that is, the crucifixion), the glory of the kingdom was still ahead.

Jesus' Prayer to the Father

The hour of Jesus' crucifixion was drawing painfully near. Just prior to his arrest, Jesus uttered an extended prayer to the Father (John 17:1–26). Most of the prayer constituted an intercession on Jesus' part for his disciples. But Jesus also prayed for himself. At one point in the prayer, Jesus said to the Father: "I have brought you glory on earth by completing the work you gave me to do. And now, Father, glorify me in your presence with the glory I had with you before the world began" (vv. 4–5).

A number of scholars have noted that Christ's request, "glorify me in your presence with the glory I had with you before the world began," must be interpreted in light of the Incarnation. These scholars have noted that in the Incarnation, *Christ never gave up any glory;* rather, his glory was *veiled* in human flesh. However, Christ in his human nature possessed no intrinsic glory. R. C. H. Lenski thus concludes:

> "Now glorify thou me" means, "in my human nature"; "with the glory which I had with thee before the world was" means, "with the glory of my divine nature." The Logos did not empty himself of his divine glory when the world began nor at a point in time. In the Incarnation he veiled this glory and did not use it according to his human nature during his humiliation because of his work among men. But now that the work is completed he requests to be glorified according to his human nature with the glory that was his before the world began.[12]

Hence, Christ was not here praying as God but as the God-man. As the second person of the Trinity, Jesus could not receive either power or glory not already essentially his own. The Godhead corporately and each member of the Godhead individually is incapable of any increase or decrease of glory. But, as the God-man, Christ prays *as man* to be taken up personally in that human nature he descended from heaven to assume, and to be reinstated in the essential glory that, as the eternal Son of God, he had with the Father before the world was.

Roman Soldiers Brought to Their Knees

When Jesus had finished praying, an interesting event occurred. We read in John's Gospel:

> When he had finished praying, Jesus left with his disciples and crossed the Kidron Valley. On the other side there was an olive grove, and he and his disciples went into it.
>
> Now Judas, who betrayed him, knew the place, because Jesus had often met there with his disciples. So Judas came to the grove, guiding a detachment of soldiers and some officials from the chief priests and Pharisees. They were carrying torches, lanterns and weapons.
>
> Jesus, knowing all that was going to happen to him, went out and asked them, "Who is it you want?"

"Jesus of Nazareth," they replied.

"I am he," Jesus said. (And Judas the traitor was standing there with them.) When Jesus said, "I am he," *they drew back and fell to the ground* (John 18:1–6, italics added).

Scholars have pondered why these strong Roman soldiers drew back and fell to the ground. One scholar has lamely suggested that these powerful soldiers fell over each other in confusion at Jesus' calm response to being arrested.[13] Other scholars see a manifestation of the supernatural in this event. John F. Walvoord correctly suggests that "it may be implied that there was . . . a flash of glory when in the Garden of Gethsemane Christ said, 'I am he,' and those who beheld Him 'went backward and fell to the ground' (John 18:6)."[14]

The soldiers' response would have been similar to that of many others who fell down due to an encounter with the divine. For example, the apostle John, upon seeing Christ in his glory, "fell at his feet as though dead" (Rev. 1:17). When Abraham beheld the Almighty, he "fell facedown" (Gen. 17:3). When Manoah and his wife saw the Angel of the Lord, they "fell with their faces to the ground" (Judg. 13:20). Ezekiel, upon seeing the glory of God, "fell facedown" (Ezek. 3:23; 43:3; 44:4). The soldiers would therefore have been in good company if they fell back as a result of seeing the glory of Christ.

Crucifixion, Burial, and Resurrection

Shortly after his arrest by the Roman soldiers, Jesus suffered a degrading death upon the cross. Before entering into the glorious abode of heaven with the Father (as Jesus prayed for in John 17:5), Jesus had to pass through the darkness of death.

After Jesus had died on the cross, his body was buried in accordance with Jewish burial customs. He was wrapped in a linen cloth, and about a hundred pounds of aromatic spices—mixed together to form a gummy substance—were applied to the wrappings of cloth around his body.

After his body was placed in a solid rock tomb, an extremely large stone was rolled by means of levers against the entrance. This stone would have weighed somewhere around two tons (4,000 pounds). It is not a stone that would have been easily moved by human beings.

Roman guards were then stationed at the tomb. These strictly disciplined men were highly motivated to succeed in all they were assigned by the Roman government. Fear of cruel punishment produced flawless attention to duty, especially in the night watches. These Roman guards would have affixed the Roman seal on the tomb, a stamp representing Rome's sovereign power and authority.

All this makes the situation at the tomb following Christ's resurrection highly significant. The Roman seal had been broken, an offense that carried an automatic penalty of crucifixion upside down for the person who did it. Moreover, the large stone was moved a substantial distance from the entrance, as if it had been picked up like a pebble and plucked out of the way. The Roman guards had also fled. Since the penalty in Rome for a guard leaving his position was death, we can assume they must have had a substantial reason for fleeing! What an awesome and glorious sight it must have been to behold the risen Christ exiting the tomb of death.

Jesus in His Post-Ascension Glory

Patmos is a mountainous, desert island located on the Aegean Sea, about sixty square miles in size. On this desolate island, people were exiled for crimes committed on mainland Rome. The aged apostle John, as a punishment for sharing the good news of Jesus Christ with everyone he met, was exiled here by Domitian, the emperor of Rome. John was sent here to die of either old age or starvation.

Little did John know what God had in store for him on the seclusion of this tiny island. Somewhere around A.D. 90—some 60 years after Jesus had resurrected from the dead and ascended into heaven—John had the most sweeping and pan-

oramic vision ever received by a saint of God. John was
uniquely privileged to behold Christ in his glory. John heard
the glorified Lord speaking to him:

> I turned around to see the voice that was speaking to me.
> And when I turned I saw seven golden lampstands, and
> among the lampstands was someone "like a son of man,"
> dressed in a robe reaching down to his feet and with a golden
> sash around his chest. His head and hair were white like wool,
> as white as snow, and his eyes were like blazing fire. His feet
> were like bronze glowing in a furnace, and his voice was like
> the sound of rushing waters. In his right hand he held seven
> stars, and out of his mouth came a sharp double-edged sword.
> His face was like the sun shining in all its brilliance.
>
> When I saw him, I fell at his feet as though dead. Then he
> placed his right hand on me and said: "Do not be afraid. I am
> the First and the Last. I am the Living One; I was dead, and be-
> hold I am alive for ever and ever! And I hold the keys of death
> and Hades" (Rev. 1:12–18).

It is no wonder that John fell before Christ as a dead man—
what with Christ's head and hair being brilliantly white, his
eyes appearing like blazing fire, and his face shining like the
sun. This is not unlike the description of Christ on the Mount
of Transfiguration (Matt. 17:2), which, upon seeing, the disciples "fell facedown to the ground terrified" (v. 6).

During Jesus' earthly ministry, John had enjoyed periods of
intimate fellowship with Jesus and had even laid his head on
Jesus' breast in the Upper Room. But now we find John falling
at Christ's feet, knocked cold by his resplendent glory. John
now found himself in the presence of the glorified Son of God
whose power, majesty, and glory are no longer veiled as was
true during Jesus' earthly ministry. John responds the only
way he can: falling in helpless abandon to the ground in the
presence of the Almighty.

In compassion for the disciple whom he loved, Jesus
touched John and told him not to be afraid (Rev. 1:17). Follow-

ing this, John was given a detailed revelation of things future, culminating in the glorious second coming of Christ.

Christ's Coming in Glory

Christ has long been despised, scorned, and rejected of men (the crown of thorns was just the beginning). But some day in the near future, Christ will come again as a sovereign King, and he will be vindicated before all the universe. Every eye will see him, and every knee shall bow and every tongue confess that this glorious one is none other than the meek and lowly Jesus, who at his first coming came as the Lamb of God to take away the sins of the world, but now—at the Second Coming—comes as King of kings and Lord of Lords (Rev. 19).

Christ's second coming will be a truly glorious event. Jesus said, "At that time the sign of the Son of Man will appear in the sky, and all the nations of the earth will mourn. They will see the Son of Man coming on the clouds of the sky, with power and great glory" (Matt. 24:30). We as Christians joyfully await "the blessed hope—the glorious appearing of our great God and Savior, Jesus Christ" (Titus 2:13).

Revelation: A Book of Christ's Glory

From the beginning to the end of the Book of Revelation, we find Christ's magnificent glory being manifest. I can do no better than to quote Isbon T. Beckwith, who, in his commentary on Revelation, has summarized:

> Nowhere else are found these wonderful scenes revealing to the eye and ear the majesty of Christ's ascended state, and these numerous utterances expressing in terms applicable to God alone the truth of his divine nature and power. He is seen in the first vision in a form having the semblance of a man, yet glorified with attributes by which the Old Testament writers have sought to portray the glory of God; his hair is white as snow, his face shines with the dazzling light of the sun, his

eyes are a flame of fire, his voice as the thunder of many waters; he announces himself as eternal, as the one who though
he died is the essentially living One, having all power over
death (1:13–18). He appears in the court of heaven as coequal
with God in the adoration offered by the highest hosts of heav-
en and by all the world (5:6–14). He is seen coming forth on the
clouds as the judge and arbiter of the world (14:14–16). Wear-
ing crowns and insignia which make him as King of kings and
Lord of lords, he leads out the armies of heaven to the great
battle with Antichrist (19:11–21). In keeping with these scenes,
attributes and prerogatives understood to belong to God only
are assigned to him either alone or as joined with God; he is
the Alpha and Omega, the first and the last, the beginning and
the end (22:13, 1:17, 2:8)—a designation which God also utters
of himself (1:8, cf. Isa. 44:6, 48:12); worship is offered to him in
common with God (7:10, 5:13)—a worship which angelic beings are forbidden to receive (19:10); doxologies are raised to
him as to God (1:6); the throne of God is his throne, the priests
of God are his priests (3:21, 22:1, 20:6); life belongs essentially
to him as to God (1:18, 4:9, 10).[15]

The City of Glory

In Revelation 21 we find a description of the eternal city in
which the saints of all ages will dwell for all eternity. This is a
city of great glory which, I believe, is what Jesus was referring
to during his earthly ministry when he told the disciples: "In
my Father's house are many rooms; if it were not so, I would
have told you. I am going there to prepare a place for you. And
if I go and prepare a place for you, I will come back and take
you to be with me that you also may be where I am" (John
14:2–3). This glorious abode has been personally prepared by
Christ for his followers.

This is the city that those saints listed in the "Faith Hall of
Fame" in Hebrews 11 looked forward to: "They were longing
for a better country—a heavenly one. Therefore God is not
ashamed to be called their God, for he has prepared a city for
them" (Heb. 11:16).

Theologian Millard Erickson comments on the glorious splendor of this city: "Images suggesting immense size or brilliant light depict heaven as a place of unimaginable splendor, greatness, excellence, and beauty.... It is likely that while John's vision employs as metaphors those items which we think of as being most valuable and beautiful, the actual splendor of heaven far exceeds anything that we have yet experienced."[16] Truly, as the apostle Paul said, "No eye has seen, no ear has heard, no mind has conceived what God has prepared for those who love him" (1 Cor. 2:9).

What is of great significance is the statement in Revelation 21:23 that "the city does not need the sun or the moon to shine on it, for the glory of God gives it light, and the Lamb is its lamp." This is in keeping with the prophecy in Isaiah 60:19: "The sun will no more be your light by day, nor will the brightness of the moon shine on you, for the LORD will be your everlasting light, and your God will be your glory."

Dr. Lehman Strauss's comments on the Lamb's glory are worthy of meditation: "In that city which Christ has prepared for His own there will be no created light, simply because Christ Himself, who is the uncreated light (John 8:12), will be there.... The created lights of God and of men are as darkness when compared with our Blessed Lord. The light He defuses throughout eternity is the unclouded, undimmed glory of His own Holy presence. In consequence of the fullness of that light, there shall be no night."[17]

In view of the incredible intrinsic glory of the Lamb, a glory that will light up the eternal city, this adds all the more significance to the Incarnation. "Think what power must have been required to condense this glory into the humanity of Jesus and to keep it veiled for the thirty-three years He lived on earth! That's the marvel of the Incarnation!"[18]

> *To him*
> *who loves us*
> *and has freed us from our sins by his blood,*

and has made us to be a kingdom and priests
to serve his God and Father—
to him be glory and power
for ever and ever!
Amen.
(Rev. 1:5b–6).

Appendix A

A Glossary of Names, Titles, and Attributes of Christ

A strong argument for the deity of Christ is the fact that many of the names, titles, and attributes ascribed to *Yahweh* are also ascribed to Jesus Christ. Below is a brief summary:

Table A.1
A Comparison of *Yahweh* and Jesus[1]

Description	As Used of *Yahweh*	As Used of Jesus
Yahweh ("I AM")	Exodus 3:14 Deuteronomy 32:39 Isaiah 43:10	John 8:24 John 8:58 John 18:4–6
God	Genesis 1:1 Deuteronomy 6:4 Psalm 45:6–7	Isaiah 7:14; 9:6 John 1:1, 14 John 20:28 Titus 2:13 Hebrews 1:8 2 Peter 1:1
Alpha and Omega (First and Last)	Isaiah 41:4 Isaiah 48:12 Revelation 1:8	Revelation 1:17–18 Revelation 2:8 Revelation 22:12–16
Lord	Isaiah 45:23	Matthew 12:8 Acts 7:59–60 Acts 10:36 Romans 10:12 1 Corinthians 2:8 1 Corinthians 12:3 Philippians 2:10–11

Savior	Isaiah 43:3	Matthew 1:21
	Isaiah 43:11	Luke 2:11
	Isaiah 63:8	John 1:29
	Luke 1:47	John 4:42
	1 Timothy 4:10	Titus 2:13
		Hebrews 5:9
King	Psalm 95:3	Revelation 17:14
	Isaiah 43:15	Revelation 19:16
	1 Timothy 6:14–16	
Judge	Genesis 18:25	John 5:22
	Psalm 50:4, 6	2 Corinthians 5:10
	Psalm 96:13	2 Timothy 4:1
	Romans 14:10	
Light	2 Samuel 22:29	John 1:4, 9
	Psalm 27:1	John 3:19
	Isaiah 42:6	John 8:12
		John 9:5
Rock	Deuteronomy 32:3–4	Romans 9:33
	2 Samuel 22:32	1 Corinthians 10:3–4
	Psalm 89:26	1 Peter 2:4–8
Redeemer	Psalm 130:7–8	Acts 20:28
	Isaiah 48:17	Ephesians 1:7
	Isaiah 54:5	Hebrews 9:12
	Isaiah 63:9	
Our Righteousness	Isaiah 45:24	Jeremiah 23:6
		Romans 3:21–22
Husband	Isaiah 54:5	Matthew 25:1
	Hosea 2:16	Mark 2:18–19
		2 Corinthians 11:2
		Ephesians 5:25–32
		Revelation 21:2, 9
Shepherd	Genesis 49:24	John 10:11, 16
	Psalm 23:1	Hebrews 13:20
	Psalm 80:1	1 Peter 2:25
		1 Peter 5:4
Creator	Genesis 1:1	John 1:2–3, 10
	Job 33:4	Colossians 1:15–18
	Psalm 95:5–6	Hebrews 1:1–3, 10
	Psalm 102:25–26	
	Isaiah 40:28	

Giver of Life	Genesis 2:7 Deuteronomy 32:39 1 Samuel 2:6 Psalm 36:9	John 5:21 John 10:28 John 11:25
Forgiver of Sin	Exodus 34:6–7 Nehemiah 9:17 Daniel 9:9 Jonah 4:2	Mark 2:1–12 Acts 26:18 Colossians 2:13 Colossians 3:13
Lord Our Healer	Exodus 15:26	Acts 9:34
Omnipresent	Psalm 139:7–12 Proverbs 15:3	Matthew 18:20 Matthew 28:20 Ephesians 3:17; 4:10
Omniscient	1 Kings 8:39 Jeremiah 17:9–10, 16	Matthew 11:27 Luke 5:4–6 John 2:25 John 16:30 John 21:17 Acts 1:24
Omnipotent	Isaiah 40:10–31 Isaiah 45:5–13	Matthew 28:18 Mark 1:29–34 John 10:18 Jude 24
Preexistent	Genesis 1:1	John 1:15, 30 John 3:13, 31–32 John 6:62 John 16:28 John 17:5
Eternal	Psalm 102:26–27 Habakkuk 3:6	Isaiah 9:6 Micah 5:2 John 8:58
Immutable	Malachi 3:6 James 1:17	Hebrews 13:8
Receiver of Worship	Matthew 4:10 John 4:24 Revelation 5:14 Revelation 7:11 Revelation 11:16	Matthew 14:33 Matthew 28:9 John 9:38 Philippians 2:10–11 Hebrews 1:6
Speaker with Divine Authority	"Thus saith the Lord . . .," used hundreds of times.	Matthew 23:34–37 John 7:46 "Truly, truly, I say . . ."

Appendix B

Messianic Prophecies Fulfilled in Christ

From the Book of Genesis to the Book of Malachi, the Old Testament abounds with anticipations of the coming Messiah. Numerous predictions—fulfilled to the "crossing of the t" and the "dotting of the i" in the New Testament—relate to his birth, life, ministry, death, resurrection, and glory.

Some liberal scholars have attempted to argue that these prophecies were made *after* Jesus lived, not before. They have suggested that the books of the Old Testament were written close to the time of Christ and that the messianic prophecies were merely Christian inventions. But to make this type of claim is to completely ignore the historical evidence. Indeed, Norman Geisler and Ron Brooks point out:

> Even the most liberal critics admit that the prophetic books were completed some 400 years before Christ, and the Book of Daniel by about 167 B.C. Though there is good evidence to date most of these books much earlier (some of the psalms and earlier prophets were in the eighth and ninth centuries B.C.), what difference would it make? It is just as hard to predict an event 200 years in the future as it is to predict one that is 800 years in the future. Both feats would require nothing less than divine knowledge.[1]

God's ability to foretell future events is one thing that separates him from all the false gods. Addressing the polytheism of Isaiah's time, God said:

- "Who then is like me? Let him proclaim it. Let him declare and lay out before me what has happened since I established my ancient people, and what is yet to come—yes, let him foretell what will come" (Isa. 44:7).
- "Do not tremble, do not be afraid. Did I not proclaim this and foretell it long ago? You are my witnesses. Is there any God besides me? No, there is no other Rock; I know not one" (Isa. 44:8).
- ". . . Who foretold this long ago, who declared it from the distant past? Was it not I, the LORD? And there is no God apart from me . . . " (Isa. 45:21).
- "I foretold the former things long ago, my mouth announced them and I made them known; then suddenly I acted, and they came to pass. . . . Therefore I told you these things long ago; before they happened I announced them to you so that you could not say, 'My idols did them; my wooden image and metal god ordained them'" (Isa. 48:3, 5).

Of course, anyone can *make* predictions—that is easy. But having them *fulfilled* is another story altogether. "The more statements you make about the future and the greater the detail, the better the chances are that you will be proven wrong."[2] *But God was never wrong;* all the messianic prophecies in the Old Testament were fulfilled specifically and precisely in the person of Jesus Christ.

Jesus often indicated to listeners that he was the specific fulfillment of messianic prophecy. For example, he made the following comments on different occasions:

- "Do not think that I have come to abolish the Law or the Prophets; I have not come to abolish them but to fulfill them" (Matt. 5:17).
- "But this has all taken place that the writings of the prophets might be fulfilled" (Matt. 26:56).
- "This is what I told you while I was still with you: Everything must be fulfilled that is written about me in the Law of Moses, the Prophets and the Psalms" (Luke 24:44).
- "You diligently study the Scriptures because you think that by them you possess eternal life. These are the Scriptures that testify about me, yet you refuse to come to me to have life" (John 5:39–40).
- "If you believed Moses, you would believe me, for he wrote about me. But since you do not believe what he wrote, how are you going to believe what I say?" (John 5:46–47).

An in-depth study of the messianic prophecies in the Old Testament is beyond the scope of this appendix. However, the chart below lists some of the more important messianic prophecies that were directly fulfilled by Jesus Christ.

Table B.1
Messianic Prophecies Fulfilled by Jesus Christ

Topic	Old Testament Prophecy	New Testament Fulfillment in Christ
Seed of woman	Genesis 3:15	Galatians 4:4
Line of Abraham	Genesis 12:2	Matthew 1:1
Line of Jacob	Numbers 24:17	Luke 3:23, 34
Line of Judah	Genesis 49:10	Matthew 1:2
Line of Jesse	Isaiah 11:1	Luke 3:23, 32
Line of David	2 Samuel 7:12–16	Matthew 1:1
Virgin Birth	Isaiah 7:14	Matthew 1:23
Birthplace: Bethlehem	Micah 5:2	Matthew 2:6
Forerunner: John	Isaiah 40:3; Malachi 3:1	Matthew 3:3
Escape into Egypt	Hosea 11:1	Matthew 2:14
Herod Kills Children	Jeremiah 31:15	Matthew 2:16–18
King	Psalm 2:6	Matthew 21:5
Prophet	Deuteronomy 18:15–18	Acts 3:22–23
Priest	Psalm 110:4	Hebrews 5:6–10
Judge	Isaiah 33:22	John 5:30
Called "Lord"	Psalm 110:1	Luke 2:11
Called "Immanuel"	Isaiah 7:14	Matthew 1:23
Anointed by Holy Spirit	Isaiah 11:2	Matthew 3:16–17
Zeal for God	Psalm 69:9	John 2:15–17
Ministry in Galilee	Isaiah 9:1–2	Matthew 4:12–16
Ministry of Miracles	Isaiah 35:5–6	Matthew 9:35
Bore World's Sins	Psalm 22:1	Matthew 27:46
Ridiculed	Psalm 22:7–8	Matthew 27:39, 43
Stumbling Stone to Jew	Psalm 118:22	1 Peter 2:7
Rejected by Own People	Isaiah 53:3	John 7:5, 48
Light to Gentiles	Isaiah 60:3	Acts 13:47–48
Taught Parables	Psalm 78:2	Matthew 13:34
Cleansed the Temple	Malachi 3:1	Matthew 21:12
Sold for 30 Shekels	Zechariah 11:12	Matthew 26:15

Forsaken by Disciples	Zechariah 13:7	Mark 14:50
Silent Before Accusers	Isaiah 53:7	Matthew 27:12–14
Hands and Feet Pierced	Psalm 22:16	John 20:25
Heart Broken	Psalm 22:14	John 19:34
Crucified with Thieves	Isaiah 53:12	Matthew 27:38
No Bones Broken	Psalm 34:20	John 19:33–36
Soldiers Gambled	Psalm 22:18	John 19:24
Suffered Thirst on Cross	Psalm 69:21	John 19:28
Vinegar Offered	Psalm 69:21	Matthew 27:34
Christ's Prayer	Psalm 22:24	Matthew 26:39
Disfigured	Isaiah 52:14	John 19:1
Scourging and Death	Isaiah 53:5	John 19:1, 18
His "Forsaken" Cry	Psalm 22:1	Matthew 27:46
Committed Self to God	Psalm 31:5	Luke 23:46
Rich Man's Tomb	Isaiah 53:9	Matthew 27:57–60
Resurrection	Psalm 16:10	Matthew 28:6
Ascension	Psalm 68:18	Luke 24:50–53
Right Hand of God	Psalm 110:1	Hebrews 1:3

Any reasonable person who examines these Old Testament prophecies in an objective manner must conclude that Jesus was the promised Messiah. "If these Messianic prophecies were written hundreds of years before they occurred, and if they could never have been foreseen and depended upon factors outside human control for their fulfillment, and if *all* of these prophecies perfectly fit the Person and life of Jesus Christ, then Jesus had to be the Messiah."[3]

Indeed, Christ on three different occasions directly claimed in so many words to be the "Christ." (Note that the word *Christ* is the Greek equivalent of the Hebrew word *Messiah*.) For example, in John 4:25, Jesus encountered a Samaritan woman who said to him: "I know that Messiah" (called Christ) "is coming. . . ." To which Jesus replied, "I who speak to you am he" (v. 26). Later, Jesus referred to himself in the third person, in his high priestly prayer to the Father, as "Jesus Christ, whom you have sent" (John 17:3). In Mark 14:61–62, we find the high priest asking Jesus, "Are you the Christ, the Son of the Blessed One?"—to which Jesus declared unequivocally, "I am. . . ."

Others also recognized that Jesus was the prophesied Messiah. In response to Jesus' inquiry concerning his disciples' understanding of him, Peter confessed: "You are the Christ . . ." (Matt. 16:16). When Jesus said to Martha, "I am the resurrection and the life. He who believes in me will live, even though he dies; and whoever lives and believes in me will never die. Do you believe this?" Martha answered, "Yes, Lord. . . . I believe that you are the Christ . . ." (John 11:25–27).

Some may ask why Jesus didn't explicitly claim more often to be the prophesied Messiah. Robert L. Reymond offers us some keen insights in answering this question:

> Jews of the first century regarded the Messiah primarily as Israel's national deliverer from the yoke of Gentile oppression. . . . Had Jesus employed uncritically the current popular term as a description of Himself and His mission before divesting it of its one-sided associations and infusing it with its richer, full-orbed Old Testament meaning, which included the work of the Messiah as the Suffering Servant of Isaiah, His mission would have been gravely misunderstood and His efforts to instruct the people even more difficult. Consequently, the evidence suggests that He acknowledged He was the 'Christ' only where there was little or no danger of His claim being politicized—as in the case of the Samaritan woman, in private conversation with His disciples (at the same time, demanding that they tell no one that He was the Messiah), in semi-private prayer, or before the Sanhedrin when silence no longer mattered or served His purpose.[4]

Even if Jesus had never verbally claimed to be the prophesied Messiah, the very fact that he was the precise fulfillment of virtually hundreds of messianic prophecies cannot be dismissed, as some liberal critics have attempted. The odds against one person fulfilling all these prophecies is astronomical; indeed, it is impossible to calculate. But fulfill these prophecies, *Jesus did*—and then he added proof upon proof regarding his identity by the many astounding miracles he performed. Truly, Jesus is the Messiah.

Appendix C

Types of Christ in the Old Testament

A type may be defined as "a figure or representation of something to come."[1] Theologian Donald K. Campbell says that a type is "an Old Testament institution, event, person, object, or ceremony which has reality and purpose in biblical history, but which also by divine design foreshadows something yet to be revealed."[2] Types are therefore prophetic in nature, and many of the types we find in the Old Testament speak prophetically of Christ in some way. "A study of Christological typology includes about fifty important types of Christ—about half of the recognized total in the entire field of typology."[3]

It is important, however, to distinguish types and prophecies in their respective forms. Paul Lee Tan explains that "a *type* prefigures coming reality; a *prophecy* verbally delineates the future. One is expressed in events, persons, and acts; the other is couched in words and statements. One is passive in form, the other active."[4]

Two extremes are to be avoided in the study of typology. There are some interpreters who see too much as being typical in the Old Testament. Directly opposite to this group are those who see all alleged types as a case of forced exegesis. Both of these extremes are unbalanced and should be avoided. For those interested in a balanced approach to interpreting types, a number of good sources are available.[5]

Legitimate types in the Old Testament are types not because man has said so but because God is sovereign in the revelatory process. The reason some Old Testament persons or things foreshadowed someone or something in the New Testament is that God planned it that way.[6]

Scholars have long noted that the study of typology is concerned with typical persons, typical events, typical things, typical institutions, and typical ceremonies.[7] We can do little more than skim the surface of the various types in this brief appendix. We begin with a look at Old Testament persons who are typical of Christ in some way. The following chart is based largely on John F. Walvoord's research on types as contained in his book *Jesus Christ Our Lord*.

Table C.1
Typical Persons

Person	Typological Significance
Aaron	As a priest, Aaron was "appointed to his sacred office (Heb. 5:4) as was Christ to His priesthood (Heb. 5:5–6). Aaron was appointed to minister in the earthly sphere as Christ was appointed to the heavenly (Heb. 8:1–5). Aaron administered the old Mosaic covenant while Christ ministered the new covenant (Heb. 8:6). Aaron was appointed to offer sacrifices daily while Christ offered Himself once for all (Heb. 7:27). The Aaronic type reveals Christ in His true humanity and in His priestly work."[8]
Abel	As Abel offered an acceptable sacrifice, so Christ offered an acceptable sacrifice. As Abel was slain, so Christ was slain.
Adam	Adam is the head of the old creation; Christ is the head of the new creation. "Both Adam and Christ entered the world through a special act of God. Both entered the world sinless; both acted on behalf of those whom God considered in them representatively. The sin of Adam is contrasted to the act of obedience of Christ. . . . Adam as the husband of Eve is also a type of the Bridegroom in relation to the church as the bride."[9]
Benjamin	Benjamin was a type of Christ because of his two names. "With her dying breath, Rachel names her newborn son Ben-oni, meaning 'son of sorrow.' Jacob, however, names him Benjamin, meaning 'son of my right hand.' As Ben-oni, Christ was the Son of sorrow to His mother (Luke 2:35) and the One who knew suffering as the Man of sorrows and death. As Benjamin, Christ is 'the son of my right hand' to God the Father, victorious in the battle with sin as Benjamin was victorious as the warrior tribe."[10]

David   David is a type of Christ in that he was both a shepherd and a king. As a shepherd, he led and cared for his sheep. As a king, he ruled in power and sovereignty over his people.

Isaac   Isaac's birth was anticipated and involved in the promises of God long before it occurred, just like Christ's birth. Both were beloved by their fathers. In Genesis 22, Isaac on the sacrificial altar on Mount Moriah foreshadows the death of Christ. The story in Genesis 24 of a bride being secured for Isaac foreshadows the securing of the bride of Christ (the church) for Christ.

Joseph   Joseph is the most complete type of Christ in the Old Testament. "Both Joseph and Christ were born by special intervention of God (Gen. 30:22–24; Luke 1:35). Both were objects of special love by their fathers (Gen. 37:3; Matt. 3:17; John 3:35); both were hated by brethren (Gen. 37:4; John 15:24–25); both were rejected as rulers over their brethren (Gen. 37:8; Matt. 21:37–39; John 15:24–25); both were robbed of their robes (Gen. 37:23; Matt. 27:35); both were conspired against and placed in the pit of death (Gen. 37:18, 24; Matt. 26:3–4; 27:35–37); both were sold for silver (Gen. 37:28; Matt. 26:14–15); both became servants (Gen. 39:4; Phil. 2:7); both were condemned though innocent (Gen. 39:11–20; Isa. 53:9; Matt. 27:19, 24). As Joseph is a type of Christ in humiliation, so he is also in exaltation. Both were raised from humiliation to glory by the power of God. . . . Both exalt their brethren to places of honor and safety (Gen. 45:16–18; Isa. 65:17–25)."[11]

Joshua   Joshua, a Hebrew name, means "Jehovah saves," just as the Greek name *Jesus* does. As a type of Christ, "Joshua is significant first because he is the successor of Moses just as Christ succeeded Moses and the law (John 1:17; Rom. 8:2–4; Heb. 7:18–19; Gal. 3:23–25). Joshua like Christ won a victory where Moses had failed (Rom. 8:3–4). In the time of conflict and defeat both Joshua and Christ interceded for their own (Josh. 7:5–9; Luke 22:32; 1 John 2:1)."[12]

Kinsman-   In Old Testament times, the phrase *kinsman-redeemer* was
Redeemer   always used of one who was related by blood to someone he was seeking to redeem from bondage. Jesus is the Kinsman-Redeemer for sin-enslaved humanity. For Jesus to become a kinsman-redeemer, however, he had to become related by blood to the human race. This indicates the necessity of the Incarnation. Jesus became a man in order to redeem man (Heb. 2:14–16).

Melchizedek	Melchizedek's name is made up of two words meaning "king" and "righteous." Melchizedek was also a priest. Thus, Melchizedek foreshadows Christ as a righteous king/priest. Melchizedek was the king of "Salem," a word that means peace. This points forward to Christ as the King of peace. (See Appendix D.)
Moses	Moses prefigured Christ in many ways. "Like Christ, Moses as a child was in danger of death, being born in a period during which Israel was under oppression. By sovereign choice of God, both were chosen to be saviors and deliverers (Exod. 3:7–10; Acts 7:25). Both were rejected by their brethren (Exod. 2:11–15; John 1:11; Acts 7:23–28; 18:5–6."[13] Like Christ, Moses was a prophet (Num. 34:1–2; John 12:29; Matt. 13:57; 21:11; Acts 3:22–23), an intercessor (Exod. 17:1–6; Heb. 7:25), and king or ruler (Deut. 33:4–5; John 1:49).

Typical "Things"

A good example of a typical "thing" is the tabernacle in the Old Testament. The tabernacle was expressly designed by God "to provide not only a temporary place of worship for the children of Israel in their wanderings but also to prefigure the person and work of Christ to an extent not provided by any other thing."[14] The tabernacle prefigures Christ in his person, his sacrifice, his intercession, and his role as Savior.

Table C.2
Christ Fulfills the Tabernacle Types[15]

Tabernacle Type	Christ's Claim
The One Door	"I am the door; if anyone enters through Me, he shall be saved, and shall go in and out and find pasture" (John 10:9 NASB).
Brazen Altar (sacrifices)	"For even the Son of Man did not come to be served, but to serve, and to give his life as a ransom for many" (Mark 10:45).
Laver (for cleansing)	"'No,' said Peter, 'you shall never wash my feet.' Jesus answered, 'Unless I wash you, you have no part with me'" (John 13:8).

Lamps	"When Jesus spoke again to the people, he said, 'I am the light of the world. Whoever follows me will never walk in darkness, but will have the light of life'" (John 8:12).
Bread	"I am the bread of life" (John 6:48).
Incense (symbolic of prayer)	"I pray for them. I am not praying for the world, but for those you have given me, for they are yours" (John 17:9).
Mercy Seat	"I lay down my life for the sheep" (John 10:15b).

Typical Institutions and Ceremonies

Among the typical institutions and ceremonies in the Old Testament are the Levitical offerings, the feasts, and the priesthood—each of which foreshadow Christ and his work in some significant way. The following three charts summarize some of these types. Again, indebtedness to Walvoord's research is acknowledged.

Table C.3
Christ Fulfills the Levitical Offerings[10]

The Offering	Typical Significance
Burnt Offering	Prefigures how Christ offered himself spotless to God (Heb. 9:11–14; 10:5–7). The ox, sheep, and dove portray the yieldedness and innocence of Christ in death (see Isa. 53:7; John 1:29; Phil. 2:5–8).
Meal Offering	Prefigures Christ's sinless humanity (fine flour). The baking that took place during this offering speaks of Christ's testing and sufferings.
Peace Offering	Prefigures how Christ's atonement procured peace. Through Christ, God was propitiated and sinners were reconciled to God (Eph. 2:14, 17; Col. 1:20; Rom. 5:1).
Sin Offering	Prefigures how Christ bore the sins of his people (2 Cor. 5:21), thus vindicating the claims of the Law through substitutionary atonement.
Trespass Offering	Prefigures how Christ atoned for sins committed against God.

Table C.4
Christ Fulfills the Levitical Feasts

The Feast (Leviticus 23)	The Fulfillment in Christ
Passover (April)	Foreshadows the death of Christ on the cross. "The lamb which was sacrificed clearly was a type of Christ. In the New Testament Christ is declared to fulfill the spiritual meaning of the Passover and those who come into the safety of His shed blood are called to a holy life (1 Cor. 5:7; 1 Pet. 1:15–19)."[17]
Unleavened Bread (April)	This type speaks of Christ "as the Bread of life, the holy walk of the believer after redemption, and the communion with Christ. The absence of leaven typically represents the sinlessness of Christ and the believer's fellowship in that holiness. The prohibition of work during the feast brings out the fact that the holy walk of the believer, like his redemption, is not a result of human effort, but is a divine provision."[18]
Firstfruits (April)	Foreshadows the resurrection of Christ. First Corinthians 15:20 tells us that "Christ has indeed been raised from the dead, the firstfruits of those who have fallen asleep." Like the Feast of Firstfruits, "the resurrection of Christ anticipates the harvest which is to follow, the resurrection of the saints."[19]
Pentecost (June)	Foreshadows the outpouring of the Holy Spirit (or the Spirit of Christ) on the day of Pentecost (Acts 1:5; 2:4). "It does not have special Christological significance, however, except as a result of the work of Christ."[20]
Trumpets (September)	Foreshadows Israel's future regathering to the land by Christ (Matt. 24:31).
Atonement (September)	Foreshadows cleansing by Christ (Rom. 11:26). "The whole transaction speaks of Christ as our Substitute, dying and cleansing by shed blood, and putting away our sins from before God, as represented by the scapegoat. . . . The goat of the sin offering was carried outside the camp and burned, even as Christ was sacrificed outside Jerusalem (Heb. 13:11–13)."[21]
Tabernacles (September)	Foreshadows the rest and reunion believers can enjoy with Christ (Zech. 14:16–19).

Table C.5
The Priesthood and Christ's Mediation[22]

Person	Symbolism
High Priest	Foreshadows Christ as *the* High Priest effecting redemption, thereby opening communion with God. Two features distinguish the High Priest from ordinary priests. (1) He was anointed before the consecration sacrifices were slain, thus picturing the sinlessness of Christ. (2) Only upon him was the anointing oil poured, picturing Christ as the anointed one (John 3:34; Heb. 1:9).
Ordinary Priests	Foreshadows the Christian's *relationship to* Christ rather than Christ himself. Ordinary priests were first washed (symbolizing regeneration—Titus 3:5; Exod. 29:1–4; Lev. 8:6), for they were sinners. Then they were clothed (symbolizing Christ's righteousness). Next they were anointed with oil (symbolizing the Spirit). All believers are priests with direct access to God because of their relation to Christ, as Aaron's sons were related to Aaron.

As the above survey indicates, the Old Testament is rich in types pointing to the future person and work of Jesus Christ. In the revelatory process, God in his sovereignty so arranged the outworking of history so that certain individuals, things, events, ceremonies, and institutions foreshadowed Christ in some way. As beautiful as each of these types are, they are all exceeded by the *Antitype*—that is, the one to whom the types point, Jesus Christ.

Appendix D

Was Melchizedek a Preincarnate Appearance of Christ?

There is much conjecture today about Melchizedek. Some say he was an angel who took on human form during the time of Abraham. (This seems not to be the case, however, because the priesthood was a *human* function, not an *angelic* function; see Heb. 5:1.) Others say Melchizedek was a preincarnate appearance of Christ. (But Melchizedek is described as being *like* the Son of God, not as *being* the Son of God himself; Heb. 7:3.) It seems best to view Melchizedek as an actual historical person—a mere human being—who was a *type* of Christ.

Those who argue that Melchizedek was not just a type of Christ but was actually a preincarnate appearance of Christ usually cite Hebrews 7:3 in support of this view: "Without father or mother, without genealogy, without beginning of days or end of life, like the Son of God he remains a priest forever." No human being, it is argued, can be without father or mother, without genealogy, or without beginning of days or end of life. In response, many scholars believe that this verse simply means that the Old Testament Scriptures have no *record* of these events. F. F. Bruce provides us with some helpful insights here:

> When Melchizedek is described as being "without father, without mother, without genealogy, having neither beginning of days nor end of life," it is not suggested that he was a biological anomaly, or an angel in human guise. Historically Melchizedek appears to have be-

longed to a dynasty of priest-kings in which he had both predecessors and successors. If this point had been put to [the author of Hebrews], he would have agreed at once, no doubt; but this consideration was foreign to his purpose. The important consideration was the account given of Melchizedek in holy writ; to him the silences of [Old Testament] Scripture were as much due to divine inspiration as were its statements. In the only record which Scripture provides of Melchizedek—Gen. 14:18–20—nothing is said of his parentage, nothing is said of his ancestry or progeny, nothing is said of his birth, nothing is said of his death. He appears as a living man, king of Salem and priest of God Most High; and as such he disappears. In all this—in the silences as well as in the statements—he is a fitting type of Christ.[1]

Old Testament scholar Gleason Archer agrees with Bruce, noting that "the context makes clear that Melchizedek was brought on the scene as a type of the Messiah, the Lord Jesus. In order to bring out this typical character of Melchizedek, the biblical record purposely omits all mention of his birth, parentage, or ancestors."[2] This is not to say that Melchizedek *had* no father or mother. Rather, "this verse simply means that none of those items of information was included in the Genesis 14 account and that they were purposely omitted in order to lay the stress on the divine nature and imperishability of the Messiah, the Antitype."[3]

It should be noted that Melchizedek was a type of Christ in other ways besides his imperishability. Melchizedek's name is made up of two words meaning "king" and "righteous." Melchizedek was also a priest. Thus, Melchizedek foreshadows Christ as a righteous king/priest. We are also told that Melchizedek was the king of "Salem," a word that means *peace*. This points forward to Christ as the King of peace.

Appendix E

Rightly Dividing the Word:
Interpreting Difficult Passages

Questions are sometimes raised by people regarding certain Bible passages that seem to teach that Jesus is less than God the Father, or is in some sense inferior to the Father. In every case, this faulty conclusion is based on a misunderstanding of the passage under discussion. Some of the more common passages in this category are briefly addressed below.[1]

God the Father "Greater" than Christ? (John 14:28)

In the Upper Room Discourse, Jesus said to the disciples: "You heard me say, 'I am going away and I am coming back to you.' If you loved me, you would be glad that I am going to the Father, for the Father is greater than I" (John 14:28).

It is critical to recognize that Jesus is not speaking in this verse about his nature or his essential being (Christ earlier said "I and the Father are one" in this regard—John 10:30), but is rather speaking of his lowly position in the Incarnation.[2] As Christian apologist Robert Bowman notes, "Christ's human nature was not itself divine; the manhood of Christ was created, and therefore Christ as man had to honor the Father as his God. Thus, the Athanasian Creed states that Christ is 'equal to the Father as touching his Godhead and inferior to the Father as touching his manhood.' There is no question from a trinitarian perspective that, as man, Christ was in submission to the Father."[3]

In his commentary *Exposition of the Gospel of John*, Arthur W. Pink relates this verse to the great humiliation Christ suffered in becoming a man:

> In becoming incarnate and tabernacling among men, [Christ] had greatly humiliated Himself, by choosing to descend into shame and suffering in their acutest forms. . . . In view of this, Christ was now contrasting His situation with that of the Father in the heavenly Sanctuary. The Father was seated upon the throne of highest majesty; the brightness of His glory was uneclipsed; He was surrounded by hosts of holy beings, who worshiped Him with uninterrupted praise. Far different was it with His incarnate Son—despised and rejected of men, surrounded by implacable enemies, soon to be nailed to a criminal's cross.[4]

Benjamin B. Warfield agrees with Pink: "Obviously [this passage] means that there was a sense in which [Jesus] had ceased to be equal with the Father, because of the humiliation of His present condition, and in so far as this humiliation involved entrance into a status lower than that which belonged to Him by nature."[5]

"My God and Your God" (John 20:17)

After Jesus had resurrected from the dead and appeared to Mary, she clung on to him. Jesus then said to her, "Do not hold on to me, for I have not yet returned to the Father. Go instead to my brothers and tell them, 'I am returning to my Father and your Father, to my God and your God'" (John 20:17). Why did Jesus call the Father "my God"? Does this imply that Jesus himself is *not* God?

By no means! Prior to the Incarnation, Christ, the second person of the Trinity, had only a divine nature. But, in the Incarnation, Christ took on a human nature. It is thus in his humanity that Christ acknowledged the Father as "my God." Jesus in his divine nature could never refer to the Father as "my God," for Jesus was fully equal to the Father in every way regarding his divine nature.

Notice that Jesus said he was ascending "to my God and your God" (John 20:17). Why didn't Jesus just say, "I am ascending to *our* Father and *our* God"? Bowman, echoing the words of New Testament scholar R. H. Lightfoot,[6] answers:

> In fact, Jesus never spoke of the Father as "our Father," including himself along with his disciples. (In Matt. 6:9 Jesus told the disciples that

they should pray, "Our Father . . ." but did not include himself in that prayer.) Jesus was careful to distinguish the two relationships, because he was God's Son *by nature*, whereas Christians are God's "sons" *by adoption*. Similarly, the Father was Jesus' God because Jesus humbled himself to become a man (Phil. 2:7), whereas the Father is our God because we are by nature creatures.[7]

God the Father the "Head" of Christ? (1 Corinthians 11:3)

In 1 Corinthians 11:3 the apostle Paul writes, "Now I want you to realize that the head of every man is Christ, and the head of the woman is man, and the head of Christ is God." A close examination of this verse shows that it has nothing to do with inferiority or superiority of one person over another; rather, it has to do with *patterns of authority*.

Notice that Paul says the man is the head of the woman, even though men and women are utterly equal in their essential being. The Bible is very clear that men and women are equal in terms of nature. They are both *human* and both are *created in God's image* (Gen. 1:26–28). As well, they are said to be *one* in Christ (Gal. 3:28). These verses, taken with 1 Corinthians 11:3, show us that *equality of being* and *social hierarchy* are not mutually exclusive.

In the same way, Christ and the Father are utterly equal in their essential being, though Jesus is under the Father's headship. There is no contradiction in affirming both an *equality of being* and a *functional subordination* among the persons in the Godhead. Christ in his divine nature is fully equal to the Father, though *relationally* (or *functionally*) he is subordinate or submissive to the Father, especially since becoming a man. This verse in no way implies that Jesus is less than God.

Christ "Subject" to the Father? (1 Corinthians 15:28)

In 1 Corinthians 15:28 the apostle Paul said that Jesus "will be made subject to him who put everything under him, so that God may be all in all." Again, we must emphasize that the word *subject* has nothing to do with Christ's essential nature or being. Rather, the word points *functionally* to Christ's subjection to God the Father as the God-man in the outworking of the plan of salvation. "As the perfect man, Christ had to be obedient to God and thus fulfill God's plan to redeem humanity. Jesus voluntarily submitted to that plan, to

God the Father, in order to save humanity from eternal separation from God."[8]

Even today, Christ exists as the glorified God-man, still in full retention of his human nature (see Luke 24). In this sense, then, Christ is *still* in submission to the Father. Indeed, as Bowman notes, "if Jesus was raised as a human being—albeit a glorified, exalted, immortal human being—he would continue to submit to the Father as his God by virtue of his being a man. . . . The doctrine of the Trinity maintains that the three persons are equal to one another in essence or nature, and it leaves open the question of how the three persons relate to one another within the Trinity. Thus, while trinitarians insist that Christ is just as much God as the Father, they do not deny that the Son is in some sense submissive to the Father even after his ascension."[9]

Christ the "Only Begotten" Son (John 3:16)

John 3:16 tells us, "For God so loved the world, that He gave His only begotten Son, that whoever believes in Him should not perish, but have eternal life" (NASB). The words *only begotten* do not mean that Christ was created (as the heretic Arius taught), but rather means "unique," "specially blessed," or "favored."

The Greek word for "begotten" is *monogenes* and is formed from two separate words: *monos* (meaning "single," "only," "sole," or "lone") and *genes* (meaning "offspring," "progeny"). Together, the compound word *monogenes* means "unique, one of a kind." John F. Walvoord notes that "the thought is clearly that Christ is the Begotten of God in the sense that no other is."[10] Warfield comments: "The adjective 'only begotten' conveys the idea, not of derivation and subordination, but of uniqueness and consubstantiality: Jesus is all that God is, and He alone is this."[11]

Christ the "Firstborn of Creation"? (Colossians 1:15)

The apostle Paul in Colossians 1:15 says of Christ: "He is the image of the invisible God, the firstborn over all creation."

Some have wrongly understood this to mean that there was a time when Christ was not, and that he came into being at a point in time. However, "firstborn" does not mean "first-created." Rather, the word (Greek: *prototokos*) means "first in rank, heir."

Robert Bowman points out that "Christ, as the Son of God, is the Father's 'heir' because everything that is the Father's is also the Son's. Of course, this is a figure of speech, and should not be pressed too literally (God the Father will never die and 'leave his inheritance' to the Son!). The point is simply that just as we say a man's firstborn son is usually the heir of all his property, so Colossians 1:15 calls Christ the 'firstborn' [heir] of all creation."[12] That Christ is the *heir* of all things is as it should be, since Christ is also the *maker* of all things (Col. 1:16).

Much more could be said on each of these verses. But the above is sufficient to demonstrate that a proper understanding of God's Word supports *and in no case denies* the full deity of Jesus Christ. Only a distortion of these passages will yield the conclusion that Jesus was something less than God.

Appendix F

Important Creeds of Christendom

Throughout church history, a number of important creeds (formal statements of belief based on Scripture) have been formulated as statements of orthodoxy. Several of these relate to our study on the preexistence and eternality of Christ: the Nicene Creed, the Athanasian Creed, the Chalcedonian Creed, and the Westminster Confession of Faith. Below are descriptions and excerpts from each of these.

The Nicene Creed (A.D. 325)

The Council of Nicaea convened in A.D. 325 to settle a dispute regarding the nature of Christ. Arius, a presbyter of Alexandria who was the founder of Arianism, argued that the Son was created from the nonexistent, and was of a *different* substance than the Father. There was a time, Arius argued, when the Son was not. But Christ was the highest of all created beings.

Athanasius of Alexandria, the champion of orthodoxy, stressed the oneness of God while maintaining three distinct persons within the Godhead. He maintained that the Son was the *same* substance as the Father and was hence fully divine. Athanasius argued for the eternal personal existence of the Son.

A third position was set forth by Eusebius of Caesarea. He argued that the Son was of a *similar* substance with the Father.

After considerable debate, Athanasius won out and Christ was recognized by the council as being on a level with the Father as an uncreated being.

The Nicene Creed reads:

I believe in one God the Father Almighty; Maker of heaven and earth, and of all things visible and invisible.

And in one Lord Jesus Christ, the only-begotten Son of God, begotten of the Father before all worlds [God of God], Light of Light, very God of very God, begotten, not made, being of one substance [essence] with the Father; by whom all things were made; who, for us men and for our salvation, came down from heaven, and was incarnate by the Holy Ghost of the Virgin Mary, and was made man; and was crucified also for us under Pontius Pilate; He suffered and was buried; and the third day He rose again, according to the Scriptures; and ascended into heaven, and sitteth on the right hand of the Father; and He shall come again, with glory, to judge both the quick and the dead; whose kingdom shall have no end.

And [I believe] in the Holy Ghost, the Lord and Giver of Life; who proceedeth from the Father [and the Son]; who with the Father and the Son together is worshiped and glorified; who spake by the Prophets. And [I believe] in one Holy Catholic and Apostolic Church. I acknowledge one Baptism for the remission of sins; and I look for the resurrection of the dead, and the life of the world to come. Amen.[1] (This last paragraph was added in A.D. 381.)[2]

The Athanasian Creed (Date: Unknown[3])

The Athanasian Creed is essentially an amplification of the Nicene Creed. It came to be generally adopted among the Western churches. This creed contains the words:

We worship one God in trinity, and trinity in unity, neither confounding the persons nor dividing the substance. For the person of the Father is one; of the Son, another; of the Holy Spirit, another. But the divinity of the Father and of the Son and of the Holy Spirit is one, the glory equal, the majesty equal. Such as is the Father, such also is the Son, and such the Holy Spirit. The Father is uncreated, the Son is uncreated, the Holy Spirit is uncreated. The Father is infinite, the Son is infinite, the Holy Spirit is infinite. The Father is eternal, the Son is eternal, the Holy Spirit is eternal. And yet there are not three eternal Beings, but one eternal Being. So also there are not three uncreated Beings, nor three infinite Beings, but one uncreated and one infinite Being. In like manner, the Father is omnipotent, the Son is omnipotent, and the Holy Spirit is omnipotent. And yet there are not three omnipotent Beings, but one omnipotent Being. Thus the Father is

God, the Son is God, and the Holy Spirit is God. And yet there are not three Gods, but one God only. The Father is Lord, the Son is Lord, and the Holy Spirit is Lord. And yet there are not three Lords, but one Lord only. For as we are compelled by Christian truth to confess each person distinctively to be both God and Lord, we are prohibited by the Catholic religion to say that there are three Gods or Lords. The Father is made by none, nor created, nor begotten. The Son is from the Father alone, not made, not created, but begotten. The Holy Spirit is not created by the Father and the Son, nor begotten, but proceeds. Therefore, there is one Father, not three Fathers; one Son, not three Sons; one Holy Spirit, not three Holy Spirits. And in this Trinity there is nothing prior or posterior, nothing greater or less, but all three persons are coeternal and coequal to themselves. So that through all, as was said above, both unity in trinity and trinity in unity is to be adored. Whoever would be saved, let him thus think concerning the Trinity.[4]

The Chalcedonian Creed (A.D. 451)

Eutyches (the founder of Eutychianism) argued that Christ's human and divine natures merged to form a third composite nature. "The divine nature was so modified and accommodated to the human nature that Christ was not really divine. . . . At the same time the human nature was so modified and changed by assimilation to the divine nature that He was no longer genuinely human."[5] Thus, according to this teaching, Christ was neither fully human nor fully divine. This heretical view was condemned by the Council of Chalcedon in A.D. 451.

The Chalcedonian Creed reads:

We, then, following the holy Fathers, all with one consent, teach men to confess one and the same Son, our Lord Jesus Christ, the same perfect in Godhead and also perfect in manhood; truly God and truly man, of a reasonable [rational] soul and body; consubstantial [co-essential] with the Father according to the Godhead, and consubstantial with us according to the Manhood; in all things like unto us, without sin; begotten before all ages of the Father according to the Godhead, and in these latter days, for us and for our salvation, born of the Virgin Mary, the Mother of God, according to the Manhood; one and the same Christ, Son, Lord, only begotten, to be acknowledged in two natures, inconfusedly, unchangeably, indivisibly, inseparably; the distinction of natures being by no means taken away by the union, but rather the property of each nature being preserved, and concurring in one Person and one Subsistence, not parted or divided into two persons, but one and the same Son, and only begotten, God the Word, the Lord Jesus Christ; as the prophets from the beginning [have declared] concerning Him, and the Lord Jesus Christ Himself has taught us, and the Creed of the holy Fathers has handed down to us.[6]

The Westminster Confession of Faith (A.D. 1646)

The Westminster Confession arose out of the stormy political scene in England during the reign of Charles I. "Charles met with resistance when he attempted to impose episcopacy on the Church of Scotland and to conform its services to the Church of England's Common Book of Prayer. A civil war erupted and Oliver Cromwell led the Puritan forces to victory. Charles I was beheaded in the process. In 1643 the English parliament commissioned the Westminster Assembly to develop the creed of the Church of England. The 121 English Puritan ministers met for 1,163 daily sessions from 1643 to 1649. The Westminster Confession of Faith, completed in 1646, affirmed a strong Calvinistic position and disavowed 'the errors of Arminianism, Roman Catholicism, and sectarianism.'"[7]

Below is the doctrinal statement about God found in the Westminster Confession of Faith:

I. There is but one only living and true God, who is infinite in being and perfection, a most pure spirit, invisible, without body, parts, or passions, immutable, immense, eternal, incomprehensible, almighty, most wise, most holy, most free, most absolute, working all things according to the counsel of His own immutable and most righteous will, for His own glory; most loving, gracious, merciful, long-suffering, abundant in goodness and truth, forgiving iniquity, transgression, and sin; the rewarder of them that diligently seek Him; and withal most just and terrible in His judgments, hating all sin, and who will by no means clear the guilty.

II. God hath all life, glory, goodness, blessedness, in and of Himself; and is alone in and unto Himself all-sufficient, not standing in need of any creatures which He hath made, nor deriving any glory from them, but only manifesting His own glory in, by, unto, and upon them: He is the alone fountain of all being, of whom, through whom, and to whom, are all things; and hath most sovereign dominion over them, to do by them, for them, and upon them, whatsoever Himself pleaseth. In His sight all things are open and manifest; His knowledge is infinite, infallible, and independent upon the creature, so as nothing is to Him contingent or uncertain. He is most holy in all His counsels, in all His works, and in all His commands. To Him is due from angels and men, and every other creature, whatsoever worship, service, or obedience He is pleased to require of them.

In the unity of the Godhead there be three Persons of one substance, power, and eternity; God the Father, God the Son, and God the Holy Ghost. The Father is of none, neither begotten nor proceeding; the Son is eternally begotten of the Father; the Holy Ghost eternally proceeding from the Father and the Son.[8]

Creeds Are Not Infallible

All of the above creeds are helpful statements of orthodoxy. However, it must be emphasized that creeds are man-made documents. None of them is inspired as Scripture is inspired. Neither are they authoritative as Scripture is authoritative. Creeds are orthodox confessions of faith that are true insofar as they accurately reflect what Scripture teaches. They are helpful "measuring sticks" for orthodoxy.

Appendix G

A Catalog of Ancient Errors
on the Person of Christ

In the early centuries of church history, a number of serious errors regarding the person of Christ crept up.[1] Some of these errors involved a denial of Christ's *deity;* others involved a denial or a compromising of Christ's *humanity;* still others involved the idea that the human and divine in Christ merged to form a third compound nature. All of these positions were condemned as being unorthodox by various church councils.

The chart below summarizes some of the main Christological errors that developed early in church history. Following this chart is a more in-depth description of each error.

Table G.1
Christological Errors[2]

Group	Time	Human Nature	Divine Nature	Church Council
Docetists	1st Century	Denied. Christ only *appeared* to be human. Had a phantom-like body.	Affirmed.	
Ebionites	2nd Century	Affirmed.	Denied. Jesus was the natural son of Joseph and Mary. Was elected to be the Son of God at his baptism.	

Arians	4th Century	Affirmed.	Denied. Jesus is not eternal. He was created before world began.	Condemned by the Council of Nicea, A.D. 325.
Apollinarians	4th Century	Compromised. Argued that Jesus had a human body and soul, but said the divine *Logos* replaced the human spirit.	Affirmed.	Condemned by the Council of Constantinople, A.D. 680.
Nestorians	5th Century	Affirmed. Christ was two *persons*—human and divine—in a sympathetic union (not two *natures* in one person).	Affirmed. Christ was two *persons*—human and divine—in a sympathetic union (not two *natures* in one person).	Condemned by the Council of Ephesus, A.D. 431.
Eutychians	5th Century	Diminished. The human and divine in Christ merged to form a third compound nature.	Diminished. The human and divine in Christ merged to form a third compound nature.	Condemned by the Council of Chalcedon, A.D. 451.
Orthodoxy		Affirmed. Perfect and complete humanity.	Affirmed. Perfect and complete deity.	Defined by the Council of Chalcedon, A.D. 451.

The Docetists

The Docetists believed in a form of dualism, the view that matter is evil and spirit is good. Because of this, they believed Jesus couldn't have had a real material human body because that would have involved a union of spirit and matter (good and evil). Jesus therefore must have had a phantom-like body—that is, he only had the *appearance* of flesh, without substance or reality. ("Docetism" comes from a Greek word, *dokeo,* meaning "to seem" or "to appear.")

Jesus' suffering and death on the cross was therefore not real, for it is inconceivable that a Supreme God (spirit) would give himself up to the destructive power of matter (evil).

Bible passages that refute Docetism include Colossians 1:15–18; 2:9; Hebrews 2:14; 1 John 2:22–23; 4:2–6; 5:1–6; and 2 John 7.

The Ebionites

The Ebionites denied the virgin birth and the deity of Jesus Christ. They believed Jesus was a mere man, a prophet who was the natural son of Joseph and Mary. Jesus allegedly distinguished himself by strict observance of the Jewish law, and was accordingly chosen to be the Messiah because of his legal piety. The consciousness that God chose him to be the Messiah came at his baptism, when he received the Holy Spirit. Jesus' mission as the Messiah was not to save humankind, but to call all humanity to obey the law.

The Ebionites refused to recognize the apostleship of Paul, saying that he was an "apostate" from the law. They demanded that all Christians submit to circumcision.

The Arians

According to Arius, the founder of Arianism, Jesus was created out of nothing before the world began and is thus not an eternal being. Arius reasoned that since Jesus was "begotten," he must have had a beginning. And since Jesus was a created being, he couldn't have possessed the same divine essence or substance as the Father. In Arius's thinking, Jesus was simply the first and greatest of all created beings. Jesus was brought into being by the Father so that the world might be created through him.

In view of the above, it seems clear that in Arius's thought Jesus was not God, but he was more than man. He might be considered a pre-temporal, superhuman creature.

Arius was opposed by the highly capable Athanasius of Alexandria. "Athanasius stressed the oneness of God while maintaining three distinct Persons within the Godhead. He also propounded the eternal existence of the Son. Athanasius stands out in the history of the church as one of the brilliant defenders of orthodoxy."[3]

The Apollinarians

The Apollinarians, following the lead of Apollinarius, believed in a trichotomous view of man—that is, they viewed man as having a *body, soul,* and *spirit.* In their view, Jesus possessed a human body and soul, but *not* a human spirit (which Apollinarius considered to be the seat of sin in the human being). In place of a human spirit in Jesus was the divine Logos or divine reason. Jesus was considered human because he possessed a human body and soul; he was considered divine because he possessed divine reason in place of the human spirit. This *Logos* or divine reason was believed to have dominated the passive human body and soul in Jesus.

Apparently, Apollinarius's interest was in securing the unity of the person of Jesus Christ without sacrificing his deity, and to guard the sinlessness of Christ. "The problem with Apollinarius's view was that while retaining the deity of Christ, he denied the genuine humanity of Christ. In Apollinarius's teaching Jesus was less than man."[4]

The Nestorians

According to the Nestorians, Jesus was a mediator consisting of two persons, not just two natures. Instead of two natures in one person, the Nestorians placed two persons—the human and the divine—alongside each other with a mere moral and sympathetic union, but without a *real* union.

Nestorius taught that while Christ suffered in his humanity, his deity was uninvolved. "The teaching was a denial of a real incarnation; instead of affirming Christ as God-man, He was viewed as two persons, God and man, with no [real] union between them. Nestorius believed that because Mary was only the source of Jesus' humanity, He must be two distinct persons."[5]

The Eutychians

The Eutychians taught that the human and divine in Christ merged to form a single composite nature. "The divine nature was so modified and accommodated to the human nature that Christ was not really divine. . . . At the same time the human nature was so modified and changed by assimilation to the divine nature that He was no longer genuinely human."[6] The result of this teaching was that Christ was neither human nor divine.

Notes

Introduction

1. See Charles Hodge, *Systematic Theology*, abridged edition, ed. Edward N. Gross (Grand Rapids: Baker Book House, 1988), p. 177. Also see Leon Morris, *Luke*, Tyndale New Testament Commentaries (Grand Rapids: Wm. B. Eerdmans Publishing, 1983), p. 339.

2. See Robert L. Reymond, *Jesus, Divine Messiah: The Old Testament Witness* (Scotland, Great Britain: Christian Focus Publications, 1990), p. vi.

3. Norman Geisler, *To Understand the Bible Look for Jesus* (Grand Rapids: Baker Book House, 1979), p. 31.

4. Lewis Sperry Chafer, *Systematic Theology*, vol. 2 (Dallas: Dallas Seminary Press, 1978), p. 399; cf. Millard J. Erickson, *The Word Became Flesh: A Modern Incarnational Christology* (Grand Rapids: Baker Book House, 1991), pp. 440–41.

5. Henry Clarence Thiessen, *Lectures in Systematic Theology* (Grand Rapids: Wm. B. Eerdmans Publishing, 1981), p. 210.

6. John F. Walvoord, *Jesus Christ Our Lord* (Chicago: Moody Press, 1980), p. 8.

Chapter 1—Knowing God: Father, Son, and Holy Spirit

1. J. I. Packer, *Knowing God* (Downers Grove, Ill.: InterVarsity Press, 1979), p. 29.

2. Erich Sauer, *From Eternity to Eternity* (Grand Rapids: Wm. B. Eerdmans Publishing, 1979), p. 13.

3. Benjamin B. Warfield, *Biblical and Theological Studies* (Phillipsburg, N.J.: Presbyterian and Reformed Publishing, 1968), p. 30.

4. Louis Berkhof, *Systematic Theology* (Grand Rapids: Wm. B. Eerdmans Publishing, 1982), p. 84.

5. Millard J. Erickson, *Christian Theology* (Grand Rapids: Baker Book House, 1987), p. 322.

6. Ibid.

7. Marcus Rainsford, *Our Lord Prays for His Own* (Chicago: Moody Press, 1978), p. 91.

8. Finite minds will never be able to *fully* grasp how three persons can be in one God. To fully understand this aspect of God would require the *mind* of God. Nevertheless, clarifying what we mean by the word *person* may be of some help.

Many theologians believe today that the term *person*, as related to the Father, Son, and Holy Spirit, is an imperfect expression of what the Bible communicates. Some believe the word tends to distract from the unity of the Trinity. Certainly, in God there are not three separate and distinct individuals such as Peter, James, and Paul who

265

have different "essences" and attributes. Rather, there are three personal self-distinctions or self-consciousnesses within the Godhead.

In applying the term *person* to God, therefore, the word is used in a distinctive sense from its normal use in relation to individual human beings. Though each member of the Godhead manifests the key qualities of personality (such as intellect, emotion, and will), they do not act *independently* as three separate human individuals would act. Nevertheless, the personalities involved in the Trinity are expressed in such terms as "I," "Thou," and "He." As well, the persons of the Godhead address each other as individuals and manifest their individuality in personal acts.

In summary, then, the Father, Son, and Holy Spirit are persons in the sense that they are personal self-distinctions and are self-aware subjects, and have the personal attributes of mind, emotions, and will. Each of the three is aware of the others, speaks to the others, and carries on a loving relationship with the others.

9. H. C. Leupold, *Exposition of Genesis*, vol. 1 (Grand Rapids: Baker Book House, 1980), pp. 86–88.

10. Ibid.

11. Gleason Archer, *Encyclopedia of Bible Difficulties* (Grand Rapids: Zondervan Publishing House, 1982), p. 359.

12. Benjamin B. Warfield, *The Person and Work of Christ* (Philadelphia: Presbyterian and Reformed Publishing, 1950), p. 66.

13. Robert L. Reymond, *Jesus, Divine Messiah: The New Testament Witness* (Phillipsburg, N.J.: Presbyterian and Reformed Publishing, 1990), p. 84.

14. Warfield, *Biblical and Theological Studies*, p. 32.

15. Ibid.

16. Many theologians describe the eternal relationship of the Son to the Father by the term *generation*, and the eternal relationship of the Holy Spirit to the Father *and* the Son by the term *procession*. Without getting too theological, the gist of what is meant by these words is that: (1) The Father begets the Son, and it is he—along *with* the Son—from whom the Holy Spirit proceeds, though the Father is neither begotten nor does he proceed. (2) The Son is begotten of the Father, and it is he—along *with* the Father—from whom the Holy Spirit proceeds, but he neither begets nor proceeds. (3) The Holy Spirit proceeds from both the Father and the Son, but he neither begets nor is he the one from whom any proceed.

Theologian Charles Ryrie notes that "logically (but in no way chronologically), generation of the Son precedes procession of the Spirit. It is fully recognized that both terms are inadequate, but no one has been able to improve on them. What single words could ever express the eternal relationships of the Trinity? Certainly the terms imply no inferiority of one Person to any of the others. Neither do the words *First* and *Second* and *Third* when used of the Persons of the Godhead imply any chronological order. Generation and Procession are attempts to denote *eternal* relationships involving distinctions between equal Persons" (Charles Ryrie, *The Holy Spirit* [Chicago: Moody Press, 1965], p. 21).

17. James Oliver Buswell, *A Systematic Theology of the Christian Religion* (Grand Rapids: Zondervan Publishing House, 1979), 1:105.

18. Charles C. Ryrie, *Basic Theology* (Wheaton, Ill.: Victor Books, 1986), p. 248; cf. Reymond, p. 68.

19. Warfield, *The Person and Work of Christ*, p. 77.

20. See John F. Walvoord, *Jesus Christ Our Lord* (Chicago: Moody Press, 1980), pp. 22–25.

21. C. F. Keil and F. Delitzsch, *Commentary on the Old Testament*, vol. 6 (Grand Rapids: Wm. B. Eerdmans Publishing, 1986), pp. 273–78; Robert Jamieson, A. R. Fausset, and David Brown, *A Commentary—Critical, Experimental, and Practical—on the Old and New Testaments* (Grand Rapids: Wm. B. Eerdmans Publishing, 1973), p. 508.

22. See R. Laird Harris, "Proverbs," in *The Wycliffe Bible Commentary*, eds. Charles F. Pfeiffer and Everett F. Harrison (Chicago: Moody Press, 1974), p. 581.

Chapter 2—The Preexistent, Eternal Christ

1. Charles C. Ryrie, *Basic Theology* (Wheaton, Ill.: Victor Books, 1986), p. 237.

2. R. C. H. Lenski, *Hebrews* (Minneapolis: Augsburg Publishing House, 1961), p. 36.

3. F. F. Bruce, *The Epistle to the Hebrews* (Grand Rapids: Wm. B. Eerdmans Publishing, 1979), p. 4.

4. John MacArthur, *The Superiority of Christ* (Chicago: Moody Press, 1986), p. 33.

5. Harold B. Kuhn, "Creation," in *Basic Christian Doctrines*, ed. Carl F. Henry (Grand Rapids: Baker Book House, 1983), p. 61.

6. Louis Berkhof, *Manual of Christian Doctrine* (Grand Rapids: Wm. B. Eerdmans Publishing, 1983), p. 96.

7. R. C. H. Lenski, *John* (Minneapolis: Augsburg Publishing House, 1961), p. 86.

8. F. F. Bruce, *The Gospel of John* (London: Pickering & Inglis Ltd., 1983), p. 43.

9. See E. W. Hengstenberg, *Christology of the Old Testament* (Grand Rapids: Kregel Publications, 1970), pp. 586–95.

10. John Martin, "Micah," in *The Bible Knowledge Commentary*, Old Testament, eds. John F. Walvoord and Roy B. Zuck (Wheaton, Ill.: Victor Books, 1985), p. 1486.

11. Robert Jamieson, A. R. Fausset, and David Brown, *A Commentary—Critical, Experimental, and Practical—on the Old and New Testaments* (Grand Rapids: Wm. B. Eerdmans Publishing, 1973), p. 600.

12. Martin, p. 1486.

13. Robert L. Reymond, *Jesus, Divine Messiah: The Old Testament Witness* (Scotland, Great Britain: Christian Focus Publications, 1990), p. 61.

14. Charles C. Ryrie, *The Ryrie Study Bible* (Chicago: Moody Press, 1986), p. 1247.

15. Gregory A. Boyd, "Sharing Your Faith with a Oneness Pentecostal," *Christian Research Journal* (Spring 1991), p. 7.

16. Albert Barnes, *Notes on the Old Testament—Isaiah* (Grand Rapids: Baker Book House, 1977), p. 193.

17. Hengstenberg, p. 196.

18. Ibid.

19. John Martin, "Isaiah," in *The Bible Knowledge Commentary*, p. 1053.

20. J. F. Stenning, *The Targum of Isaiah* (London: Oxford Press, 1949), p. 32, italics added.

21. Ryrie, *Basic Theology*, p. 37.

22. Ibid.

23. Zane Hodges, "Hebrews," in *The Bible Knowledge Commentary*, New Testament, eds. John F. Walvoord and Roy B. Zuck (Wheaton, Ill.: Victor Books, 1983), p. 782.

24. John F. Walvoord, *Jesus Christ Our Lord* (Chicago: Moody Press, 1980), p. 30.

25. Ibid., p. 28.

26. See Robert L. Reymond, *Jesus, Divine Messiah: The New Testament Witness* (Phillipsburg, N.J.: Presbyterian and Reformed Publishing, 1990), p. 122.

27. Quoted in Josh McDowell and Bart Larson, *Jesus: A Biblical Defense of His Deity* (San Bernardino, Calif.: Here's Life Publishers, 1983), p. 54.

28. Reymond, *Jesus, Divine Messiah: The New Testament Witness*, p. 122.

29. A. W. Tozer; quoted in Ryrie, *Basic Theology*, p. 42.

30. Reymond, *Jesus, Divine Messiah: The New Testament Witness*, pp. 121–22.

31. Norman L. Geisler, "Colossians," in *The Bible Knowledge Commentary*, p. 672.

32. John MacArthur, *Hebrews* (Chicago: Moody Press, 1983), p. 16.

33. Curtis Vaughan, "Colossians," in *The Expositor's Bible Commentary*, vol. 11, ed. Frank E. Gaebelein (Grand Rapids: Zondervan Publishing House, 1978), p. 182.

34. J. B. Lightfoot, *St. Paul's Epistles to the Colossians and to Philemon* (Grand Rapids: Zondervan Publishing House, 1979), p. 181.

35. Vaughan, p. 199.

36. Benjamin B. Warfield, *The Person and Work of Christ* (Philadelphia: Presbyterian and Reformed Publishing, 1950), p. 46.

37. Quoted in Vaughan, p. 199.

38. Richard C. Trench, quoted in Kenneth S. Wuest, "Ephesians and Colossians in the Greek New Testament," *Wuest's Word Studies* (Grand Rapids: Wm. B. Eerdmans Publishing, 1953), p. 203.

39. A. T. Robertson, quoted in Vaughan, p. 199.

40. Gerald F. Hawthorne, "Hebrews," in *The International Bible Commentary*, ed. F. F. Bruce (Grand Rapids: Zondervan Publishing House, 1979), p. 1506.

41. William R. Newell, *Hebrews: Verse By Verse* (Chicago: Moody Press, 1947), p. 11.

Chapter 3—Christ the Creator

1. Henry M. Morris, *The Biblical Basis for Modern Science* (Grand Rapids: Baker Book House, 1984), p. 156.

2. Ibid.

3. Ibid., p. 158.

4. John MacArthur, *The Superiority of Christ* (Chicago: Moody Press, 1986), pp. 33–34.

5. Erich Sauer, *From Eternity to Eternity* (Grand Rapids: Wm. B. Eerdmans Publishing, 1979), p. 19; cf. John C. Whitcomb, Jr., *The Early Earth* (Grand Rapids: Baker Book House, 1979), p. 58; Morris, p. 163.

6. Whitcomb, p. 58.

7. Harold B. Kuhn, "Creation," in *Basic Christian Doctrines*, ed. Carl F. Henry (Grand Rapids: Baker Book House, 1983), p. 58.

8. There were obviously no human spectators to the creation. And since the first man and woman were placed in an already existing universe, we must accept whatever God has revealed about the creation *by faith*. Otherwise we can know nothing with certainty about the origin of the universe. Hebrews 11:3 tells us, "By faith we understand that the universe was formed at God's command, so that what is seen was not made out of what was visible."

9. Millard J. Erickson, *Christian Theology* (Grand Rapids: Baker Book House, 1987), pp. 372–73.

10. Louis Berkhof, *Systematic Theology* (Grand Rapids: Wm. B. Eerdmans Publishing, 1982), p. 129.

11. Norman Geisler, *Christian Apologetics* (Grand Rapids: Baker Book House, 1976), p. 338.

12. R. C. H. Lenski, *Hebrews* (Minneapolis: Augsburg Publishing House, 1961), p. 35.

13. Ibid., p. 36.

14. John F. Walvoord, *Jesus Christ Our Lord* (Chicago: Moody Press, 1980), p. 38.

15. Whitcomb, pp. 24–25.

16. John Eadie, *A Commentary on the Greek Text of the Epistle of Paul to the Colossians* (Grand Rapids: Baker Book House, 1979), p. 51.

17. H. C. G. Moule, *Studies in Colossians & Philemon* (Grand Rapids: Kregel Publications, 1977), p. 79.

18. Albert Barnes, *Barnes' Notes on the Old & New Testaments* (Grand Rapids: Baker Book House, 1976), p. 248.

19. Curtis Vaughan, "Colossians," in *The Expositor's Bible Commentary*, vol. 11, ed. Frank E. Gaebelein (Grand Rapids: Zondervan Publishing House, 1978), p. 182.

20. MacArthur, pp. 44–49.

21. Robert L. Reymond, *Jesus, Divine Messiah: The Old Testament Witness* (Scotland, Great Britain: Christian Focus Publications, 1990), p. 16.

22. For example, 1 Corinthians 8:6 and Revelation 3:14. The first two of these passages are touched upon elsewhere in the book. In Revelation 3:14, Christ said to the church in Laodicea: "These are the words of the Amen, the faithful and true witness, *the ruler of God's creation*" (italics added). The word *ruler* is unique and indicates "one who begins," "origin," "source," "creator," or "first cause." Commenting on this verse, Henry Alford states that "in Him the whole creation of God is begun and conditioned; He is its source and primary fountainhead" (quoted in John F. Walvoord, *Revelation* [Chicago: Moody Press, 1980], p. 90).

23. Morris, p. 155.

24. Sauer, p. 30.

Chapter 4—Christ the Preserver

1. Charles Hodge, *Systematic Theology*, abridged edition, ed. Edward N. Gross (Grand Rapids: Baker Book House, 1988), p. 215.

2. John MacArthur, *The Superiority of Christ* (Chicago: Moody Press, 1986), p. 37.

3. Ibid.

4. John F. Walvoord, *Jesus Christ Our Lord* (Chicago: Moody Press, 1980), p. 38; cf. Robert L. Reymond, *Jesus, Divine Messiah: The Old Testament Witness* (Scotland, Great Britain: Christian Focus Publications, 1990), p. 100.

5. Walvoord, p. 49.

6. Ibid., pp. 49–50.

7. For example, John A. Martin, "Isaiah," in *The Bible Knowledge Commentary*, Old Testament, eds. John F. Walvoord and Roy B. Zuck (Wheaton, Ill.: Victor Books, 1987), p. 118; Charles C. Ryrie, *The Ryrie Study Bible* (Chicago: Moody Press, 1986), p. 1002; cf. Reymond, p. 4.

8. John Eadie, *A Commentary on the Greek Text of the Epistle of Paul to the Colossians* (Grand Rapids: Baker Book House, 1979), p. 56.

9. Cited in Marvin R. Vincent, *Word Studies in the New Testament*, vol. 3 (Grand Rapids: Wm. B. Eerdmans Publishing, 1975), p. 471.

10. Walvoord, p. 50; J. B. Lightfoot, *St. Paul's Epistles to the Colossians and to Philemon* (Grand Rapids: Zondervan Publishing House, 1979), p. 156.

11. Eadie, p. 57.

12. Walvoord, p. 50.

13. Gerald F. Hawthorne, "Hebrews," in *The International Bible Commentary,* ed. F. F. Bruce (Grand Rapids: Zondervan Publishing House, 1979), p. 1506.

14. Quoted in Paul Enns, *The Moody Handbook of Theology* (Chicago: Moody Press, 1989), p. 226.

15. Brooke Foss Westcott, *The Epistle to the Hebrews* (Grand Rapids: Wm. B. Eerdmans Publishing, 1974), pp. 13–14.

16. Leon Morris, "Hebrews," in *The Expositor's Bible Commentary*, vol. 12, ed. Frank E. Gaebelein (Grand Rapids: Zondervan Publishing House, 1978), p. 14.

17. Ibid.

18. E. Schuyler English, *Studies in the Epistle to the Hebrews* (Neptune, N.J.: Loizeaux Brothers, 1976), p. 45.

19. Robert Jamieson, A. R. Fausset, and David Brown, *A Commentary—Critical, Experimental, and Practical—on the Old and New Testaments* (Grand Rapids: Wm. B. Eerdmans Publishing, 1976), p. 1015; Charles C. Ryrie, *Basic Theology* (Wheaton, Ill.: Victor Books, 1986), p. 239.

20. Paul W. Marsh, "1 Corinthians," in *The International Bible Commentary*, p. 1368.

21. R. C. H. Lenski, *1 Corinthians* (Minneapolis: Augsburg Publishing House, 1961), p. 393.

22. Marsh, p. 1368.

23. Lenski, p. 392.

24. Leon Morris, *The First Epistle of Paul to the Corinthians*, Tyndale New Testament Commentaries (Grand Rapids: Wm. B. Eerdmans Publishing, 1976), p. 142.

25. J. Dwight Pentecost, "Daniel," in *The Bible Knowledge Commentary*, p. 1340. See also John F. Walvoord, *Daniel: The Key to Prophetic Revelation* (Chicago: Moody Press, 1981), p. 93.

26. Robert D. Culver, "Daniel," in *The Wycliffe Bible Commentary*, eds. Charles F. Pfeiffer and Everett F. Harrison (Chicago: Moody Press, 1974), p. 782. See also Matthew Henry, *Commentary on the Whole Bible* (Grand Rapids: Zondervan Publishing House, 1974), p. 1088.

27. Walvoord, *Jesus Christ Our Lord*, p. 51.

28. Eadie, p. 58.

Chapter 5—Christ the Angel of the Lord

1. Paul Enns, *The Moody Handbook of Theology* (Chicago: Moody Press, 1989), p. 216; John F. Walvoord, *Jesus Christ Our Lord* (Chicago: Moody Press, 1980), p. 51.

2. I recognize that other interpretations as to the identity of the Angel of Yahweh have been offered by various scholars. Millard J. Erickson summarizes the three major views: "(1) he is merely an angel with a special commission; (2) he is God himself visible in a humanlike form; (3) he is the Logos, a temporary preincarnate visit by the second person of the Trinity" (*Christian Theology*, unabridged, one-volume edition [Grand Rapids: Baker Book House, 1987], p. 443). Erickson opts for the second view. While this view is possible, I believe it fails to satisfactorily explain the scriptural evidence. The third view seems to me to be much more compatible with trinitarian

theology (see Benjamin B. Warfield, *Biblical and Theological Studies* [Phillipsburg, N.J.: Presbyterian and Reformed Publishing, 1968], p. 30).

3. See Robert L. Reymond, *Jesus, Divine Messiah: The Old Testament Witness* (Scotland, Great Britain: Christian Focus Publications, 1990), p. 3.

4. Ibid., p. 4.

5. See R. Alan Cole, *Exodus: An Introduction and Commentary* (Downers Grove, Ill.: InterVarsity Press, 1973), p. 65.

6. Guy B. Funderburk notes: "[The Angel] was not restricted to executing a single order, but, like Jesus, He spoke with authority as though He were God Himself. Only the Logos, or some other manifest personification of God, would be able to do that" ("Angel," in *The Zondervan Pictorial Encyclopedia of the Bible*, ed. Merrill C. Tenney, vol. 1 [Grand Rapids: Zondervan Publishing House, 1978], p. 163).

7. See H. C. Leupold, *Exposition of Genesis*, vol. 1 (Grand Rapids: Baker Book House, 1980), p. 503.

8. See chapter 9.

9. Geerhardus Vos; quoted in Reymond, p. 2.

10. As Revelation 12:10 indicates, accusing Christians before God's throne is a continual activity of Satan.

11. Reymond, pp. 1, 102.

12. C. F. Keil and Franz Delitzsch, "Zechariah," *Biblical Commentary on the Old Testament* (Grand Rapids: Wm. B. Eerdmans Publishing, 1954), p. 235.

13. This is attested to by many scholars: Charles Hodge, *Systematic Theology*, abridged edition, ed. Edward N. Gross (Grand Rapids: Baker Book House, 1988), p. 178; Robert G. Gromacki, *The Virgin Birth: Doctrine of Deity* (Grand Rapids: Baker Book House, 1984), p. 21; Walvoord, pp. 52–54; J. Dwight Pentecost, "Daniel," in *The Bible Knowledge Commentary*, Old Testament, eds. John F. Walvoord and Roy B. Zuck (Wheaton, Ill.: Victor Books, 1987), p. 1340; Enns, p. 216; and Henry Clarence Thiessen, *Lectures in Systematic Theology* (Grand Rapids: Wm. B. Eerdmans Publishing, 1981), p. 209f.

14. Walvoord notes: "As the Angel of Jehovah characteristically appears in bodily, usually human form, He could not be the Holy Spirit who does not appear bodily, except in the rare instance of appearing in the form of a dove at the baptism of Christ" (*Jesus Christ Our Lord*, p. 46).

15. Ibid., p. 54.

16. Walvoord notes: "As the Angel of Jehovah is the sent One, He could not be the Father for the Father is the Sender." (Ibid., p. 46.)

17. Ibid.

18. Norman Geisler, *To Understand the Bible Look for Jesus* (Grand Rapids: Baker Book House, 1979), p. 67.

19. See, for example, Stanley D. Toussaint, *Behold the King: A Study of Matthew* (Portland, Oreg.: Multnomah Press, 1980), p. 43; Arno C. Gaebelein, *The Gospel of Matthew* (Neptune, N.J.: Loizeaux Brothers, 1977), pp. 29–30; compare with F. F. Bruce, *The Book of Acts* (Grand Rapids: Wm. B. Eerdmans Publishing, 1986), p. 120.

20. Funderburk, p. 163.

21. This chart is adapted from Geisler, p. 50.

22. See Josh McDowell and Bart Larson, *Jesus: A Biblical Defense of His Deity* (San Bernardino, Calif.: Here's Life Publishers, 1983), p. 79.

23. Irenaeus, *Against Heresies* (4.10.1); cited in Walvoord, p. 55.

24. *First Apology*, lxii; lxiii; compare with Martyr's *Dialogue with Trypho*, p. 59; see McDowell and Larson, p. 79.

25. Tertullian, *Against Praxeas*, p. 16; see also Tertullian's *Against Marcion*, 2.27; cited in Walvoord, p. 55.

26. See Richard Watson, *Theological Institutes*, 2 vols., 29th ed. (New York: Nelson & Philipps, 1850), 1:501–2; quoted in Walvoord, p. 55.

27. Hodge, p. 177.

28. Francis Brown, S. R. Driver, and Charles A. Briggs, *A Hebrew and English Lexicon of the Old Testament* (Oxford: Clarendon Press, 1980), p. 521. Also see H. Bietenhard, s.v. "Angel," in *New Testament Theology*, ed. Colin Brown, vol. 1 (Grand Rapids: Zondervan Publishing House, 1979), pp. 101–3.

29. John Calvin, *Institutes of the Christian Religion*, ed. John T. McNeill, trans. Ford Lewis Battles (Philadelphia: The Westminster Press, 1960), vol. 1, p. 133, insert mine, italics added.

30. See John J. Davis, *Moses and the Gods of Egypt* (Grand Rapids: Baker Book House, 1986), p. 69. Davis notes: "Moses recognized the fact that he was in the presence of deity and feared to look upon the face of God (cf. Exod. 33:20; Judg. 6:22–23; 13:22)" (p. 71).

31. Ibid.

32. See Ron Rhodes, *When Servants Suffer: Finding Purpose in Pain* (Wheaton, Ill.: Harold Shaw Publishers, 1989).

33. Pentecost, for example, comments: "Perhaps this Angel, like the One in the fiery furnace with the three young men (3:25), was the preincarnate Christ" (p. 1349). See also *The Expositor's Bible Commentary*, ed. Frank E. Gaebelein, vol. 7 (Grand Rapids: Zondervan Publishing House, 1985), p. 82.

34. Kyle M. Yates, "Genesis," in *The Wycliffe Bible Commentary*, p. 11. For further substantiation for this view, see H. C. Leupold, *Exposition of Genesis*, vol. 1 (Grand Rapids: Baker Book House, 1968), pp. 242–43.

35. Geerhardus Vos, *Biblical Theology: Old and New Testaments* (Grand Rapids: Wm. B. Eerdmans Publishing, 1985), p. 72.

36. Keil and Delitzsch, *Genesis*, p. 125.

37. Jon A. Buell and O. Quentin Hyder, *Jesus: God, Ghost or Guru?* (Grand Rapids: Zondervan Publishing House, 1978), p. 48.

Chapter 6—Christ the Shepherd

1. For example: Norman Geisler, *To Understand the Bible Look for Jesus* (Grand Rapids: Baker Book House, 1979), p. 48, and *A Popular Survey of the Old Testament* (Grand Rapids: Baker Book House, 1978), p. 200; Robert Lightner, *The Saviour and the Scriptures* (Grand Rapids: Baker Book House, 1966), p. 23; Josh McDowell, *Evidence that Demands a Verdict* (Arrowhead Springs: Campus Crusade for Christ International, 1972), p. 100; Lewis Sperry Chafer, *Systematic Theology*, vol. 2 (Wheaton, Ill.: Victor Books, 1988), p. 251; John F. Walvoord, *Jesus Christ Our Lord* (Chicago: Moody Press, 1980), pp. 49, 61, 232–34; Everett F. Harrison, "John," in *The Wycliffe Bible Commentary*, eds. Charles F. Pfeiffer and Everett F. Harrison (Chicago: Moody Press, 1974), p. 1095; Haddon W. Robinson, *Psalm Twenty-Three* (Chicago: Moody Press, 1979), p. 12; Edmund P. Clowney, *The Unfolding Mystery: Discovering Christ in the Old Testament* (Phillipsburg, N.J.: Presbyterian and Reformed Publishing, 1988), p. 163.

2. Walvoord, p. 49.

3. Ibid.; cf. Robinson, pp. 11–12.

4. Zane C. Hodges, *The Hungry Inherit* (Portland, Oreg.: Multnomah Press, 1980), p. 128.

5. That the "Angel" mentioned in these verses is the Angel of the Lord seems more than clear. See Kyle M. Yates, "Genesis," *The Wycliffe Bible Commentary*, p. 45; cf. Derek Kidner, *Genesis: An Introduction and Commentary* (Downers Grove, Ill.: InterVarsity Press, 1967), p. 214.

6. Geisler, *To Understand the Bible Look for Jesus*, pp. 48ff; cf. Millard J. Erickson, *The Word Became Flesh: A Contemporary Incarnational Christology* (Grand Rapids: Baker Book House, 1991), p. 449.

7. Walvoord, p. 61; cf. Chafer, p. 251.

8. This chart is based on McDowell, p. 100; and Geisler, *To Understand the Bible Look for Jesus*, pp. 48–49.

9. Erickson, p. 444.

10. Robinson, p. 19.

11. Ibid., pp. 15–16.

12. Ibid., p. 24.

13. A. T. Robertson, *Word Pictures*, vol. 5 (Nashville: Broadman Press, 1930), p. 63; Zane C. Hodges, *The Gospel Under Siege* (Dallas: Redencion Viva, 1981), p. 13.

14. Robinson, p. 35.

15. Ibid., p. 43.

16. J. Dwight Pentecost, *The Words and Works of Jesus Christ* (Grand Rapids: Zondervan Publishing House, 1982), p. 225.

17. F. F. Bruce, *The Gospel of John* (London: Pickering & Inglis Ltd., 1983), p. 224.

18. Leon Morris, *The Gospel According to John* (Grand Rapids: Wm. B. Eerdmans Publishing, 1987), p. 503.

19. Ibid.

20. Ibid., pp. 506–7.

21. Ibid., p. 508.

22. Bruce, p. 226.

23. Edwin A. Blum, "John," in *The Bible Knowledge Commentary*, New Testament, eds. John F. Walvoord and Roy B. Zuck (Wheaton, Ill.: Victor Books, 1983), p. 310.

24. Phillip Keller, *A Shepherd Looks at Psalm 23* (Grand Rapids: Zondervan Publishing House, 1976), p. 18.

25. Phillip Keller, *A Shepherd Looks at the Good Shepherd and His Sheep* (Grand Rapids: Zondervan Publishing House, 1978), p. 63.

Chapter 7—Christ the Savior

1. Norman Geisler, *To Understand the Bible Look for Jesus* (Grand Rapids: Baker Book House, 1979), p. 32.

2. John F. Walvoord, *Jesus Christ Our Lord* (Chicago: Moody Press, 1980), p. 61.

3. Ibid., p. 58.

4. Charles Hodge, *Systematic Theology*, abridged edition, ed. Edward N. Gross (Grand Rapids: Baker Book House, 1988), p. 346.

5. Robert L. Reymond, *Jesus, Divine Messiah: The New Testament Witness* (Phillipsburg, N.J.: Presbyterian and Reformed Publishing, 1990), p. 121.

6. Geisler, p. 47.

7. Ibid., p. 53.

8. Erich Sauer, *The Dawn of World Redemption* (Grand Rapids: Wm. B. Eerdmans Publishing, 1977), p. 22.

9. See Henry Clarence Thiessen, *Lectures in Systematic Theology* (Grand Rapids: Wm. B. Eerdmans Publishing, 1981), p. 100ff.

10. Charles C. Ryrie, *Basic Theology* (Wheaton, Ill.: Victor Books, 1986), p. 312.

11. Louis Berkhof, *Manual of Christian Doctrine* (Grand Rapids: Wm. B. Eerdmans Publishing, 1983), p. 84.

12. Hodge, pp. 197–98.

13. Thiessen, p. 201.

14. Benjamin B. Warfield, *Biblical and Theological Studies* (Phillipsburg, N.J.: Presbyterian and Reformed Publishing, 1968), p. 171.

15. Robert P. Lightner, *Evangelical Theology* (Grand Rapids: Baker Book House, 1986), p. 193.

16. Erich Sauer, *From Eternity to Eternity* (Grand Rapids: Wm. B. Eerdmans Publishing, 1979), p. 40.

17. John F. Walvoord, *The Holy Spirit* (Grand Rapids: Zondervan Publishing House, 1958), p. 32.

18. Lightner, p. 57.

19. See E. W. Hengstenberg, *Christology of the Old Testament* (Grand Rapids: Kregel Publications, 1970), pp. 28–40.

20. H. C. Leupold, *Exposition of Genesis*, vol. 1 (Grand Rapids: Baker Book House, 1968), p. 155.

21. Kyle M. Yates, "Genesis," in *The Wycliffe Bible Commentary*, eds. Charles F. Pfeiffer and Everett F. Harrison (Chicago: Moody Press, 1974), pp. 7–8.

22. Walvoord, *Jesus Christ Our Lord*, p. 57.

23. Robert Jamieson, A. R. Fausset, and David Brown, "Genesis," in *A Commentary—Critical, Experimental, and Practical—on the Old and New Testaments* (Grand Rapids: Wm. B. Eerdmans Publishing, 1976), p. 16.

24. See John Ankerberg, John Weldon, and Walter C. Kaiser, *The Case for Jesus the Messiah* (Chattanooga: The John Ankerberg Evangelistic Association, 1989), p. 26.

25. Walvoord, *Jesus Christ Our Lord*, p. 58.

26. Job also seems to have had some knowledge of Christ the Redeemer (see Job 19:25; cf. 9:33; 33:23); see Robert L. Reymond, *Jesus, Divine Messiah: The Old Testament Witness* (Scotland, Great Britain: Christian Focus Publications, 1990), pp. 100–102.

27. Walvoord, *Jesus Christ Our Lord*, p. 58.

28. E. Schuyler English, *Studies in the Epistle to the Hebrews* (Neptune, N.J.: Loizeaux Brothers, 1976), p. 405.

29. John MacArthur, *Hebrews* (Chicago: Moody Press, 1983), p. 353.

30. English, p. 406.

31. Hengstenberg, pp. 58–66.

32. Ibid., pp. 60–62.

33. Walvoord, *Jesus Christ Our Lord*, p. 60.

34. Albert Barnes, *Barnes Notes on the Old and New Testaments*, vol. 1 (Grand Rapids: Baker Book House, 1977), p. 24.

35. Matthew Henry, *The Matthew Henry Commentary* (Grand Rapids: Zondervan Publishing House, 1974), pp. 579–80.

36. Walvoord, *Jesus Christ Our Lord*, p. 60.

37. Ibid., pp. 254–55.

38. See, for example, Robert L. Reymond, *Jesus, Divine Messiah: The Old Testament Witness*, p. 101.

39. Quoted in the commentary of Robert Jamieson, A. R. Fausset, and David Brown, in *The Bethany Parallel Commentary on the New Testament* (Minneapolis: Bethany House Publishers, 1983), p. 1368; see also Sauer, *From Eternity to Eternity*, p. 45.

40. Millard J. Erickson, *Christian Theology*, unabridged, one-volume edition (Grand Rapids: Baker Book House, 1987), p. 765, insert mine.

41. R. C. H. Lenski, *First Peter* (Minneapolis: Augsburg Publishing House, 1961), p. 46.

42. Adam Clark, in *The Bethany Parallel Commentary on the New Testament*, p. 1473.

Chapter 8—Christ the Eternal *Logos*

1. See F. F. Bruce, *The Gospel of John* (Grand Rapids: Wm. B. Eerdmans Publishing, 1984), pp. 28–31.

2. Leon Morris, *The Gospel According to John*, The New International Commentary on the New Testament (Grand Rapids: Wm. B. Eerdmans Publishing, 1987), p. 119.

3. J. Dwight Pentecost, *The Words and Works of Jesus Christ* (Grand Rapids: Zondervan Publishing House, 1982), p. 29.

4. Morris, p. 73; Bruce, p. 33; see also Rob Bowman, *Jehovah's Witnesses, Jesus Christ, and the Gospel of John* (Grand Rapids: Baker Book House, 1989), pp. 21–22.

5. Harold B. Kuhn, "Creation," in *Basic Christian Doctrines*, ed. Carl F. Henry (Grand Rapids: Baker Book House, 1983), p. 61.

6. Louis Berkhof, *Manual of Christian Doctrine* (Grand Rapids: Wm. B. Eerdmans Publishing, 1983), p. 96.

7. R. C. H. Lenski, *The Interpretation of St. John's Gospel* (Minneapolis: Augsburg Publishing House, 1961), p. 27.

8. Morris, p. 73.

9. Ibid., p. 77.

10. Benjamin B. Warfield, *The Person and Work of Christ* (Philadelphia: Presbyterian and Reformed Publishing, 1950), p. 53.

11. David J. Ellis, "John," in *The International Bible Commentary*, ed. F. F. Bruce (Grand Rapids: Zondervan Publishing House, 1986), p. 1232.

12. Morris, p. 79.

13. Lenski, p. 33.

14. Ibid., p. 103.

15. Bruce, p. 40.

16. *New Bible Dictionary*, ed. J. D. Douglas (Wheaton, Ill.: Tyndale House Publishers, 1982), p. 1101.

17. Warfield, p. 55.

18. Pentecost, p. 31.

19. Lenski, pp. 71–72.

20. Warfield, p. 55.

21. Morris, p. 83.

22. Pentecost, p. 30.

23. Morris, p. 85; J. W. Shephard agrees with Morris: "The true Light (Logos) was already in continuous existence, lighting by conscience and special revelations in na-

ture, every single man, even before the Incarnation. But the Logos carried His revelation further now by coming into the world" (J. W. Shephard, *The Christ of the Gospels* [Grand Rapids: Wm. B. Eerdmans Publishing, 1975], p. 17).

24. William Hendriksen, *Exposition of the Gospel According to John* (Grand Rapids: Baker Book House, 1976), 22:42.

25. Robert P. Lightner, *The God of the Bible* (Grand Rapids: Baker Book House, 1978), p. 55.

Chapter 9—Christ and His Divine Names

1. See Robert L. Reymond, *Jesus, Divine Messiah: The New Testament Witness* (Phillipsburg, N.J.: Presbyterian and Reformed Publishing, 1990), p. 94.

2. See Robert P. Lightner, *The God of the Bible* (Grand Rapids: Baker Book House, 1978), p. 117.

3. Rob Bowman, *Jehovah's Witnesses, Jesus Christ, and the Gospel of John* (Grand Rapids: Baker Book House, 1989), p. 99.

4. William Barclay, *The Gospel of John*, vol. 2 (Philadelphia: Westminster Press, 1956), pp. 42–43.

5. Philo, "Life of Moses," iii.41; cited by *The Jewish Encyclopedia*, ed. Isidore Singer (New York: Funk and Wagnalls, 1904), vol. 1, p. 201.

6. Josephus, *The Antiquities of the Jews*, in *Complete Works* (Grand Rapids: Kregel Publications, 1974), ii:12, par. 4.

7. Millard J. Erickson, *The Word Became Flesh: A Contemporary Incarnational Christology* (Grand Rapids: Baker Book House, 1991), p. 434.

8. Robert L. Reymond, *Jesus, Divine Messiah: The Old Testament Witness* (Scotland, Great Britain: Christian Focus Publications, 1990), pp. 78–84.

9. Jon A. Buell and O. Quentin Hyder, *Jesus: God, Ghost or Guru?* (Grand Rapids: Zondervan Publishing House, 1978), p. 27; cf. Josh McDowell and Bart Larson, *Jesus: A Biblical Defense of His Deity* (San Bernardino, Calif.: Here's Life Publishers, 1983), pp. 21–24.

10. Reymond, *Jesus, Divine Messiah: The New Testament Witness*, pp. 92–94.

11. Erickson, pp. 28–29.

12. David F. Wells, *The Person of Christ* (Westchester, Ill.: Crossway Books, 1984), pp. 64–65.

13. S. E. Johnson, "Lord (Christ)," *The Interpreter's Dictionary of the Bible* (New York: Abingdon, 1976), 3:151.

14. William G. T. Shedd, *Romans* (New York: Scribner, 1879), p. 318. See also Benjamin B. Warfield, *The Person and Work of Christ* (Philadelphia: Presbyterian and Reformed Publishing, 1950), p. 225.

15. See Lightner, pp. 109–10.

16. Charles C. Ryrie, *Basic Theology* (Wheaton, Ill.: Victor Books, 1986), p. 48; John F. Walvoord notes: "It is apparent that Elohim in the Old Testament is God in the New Testament (Greek, *theos*). Hence all passages in the New Testament referring to Christ by this title link Him with the Elohim of the Old Testament (cf. Rom. 15:6; Eph. 1:3; 5:5, 20; II Peter 1:1)" (John F. Walvoord, *Jesus Christ Our Lord* [Chicago: Moody Press, 1980], pp. 37–38).

17. Robert Reymond notes that "inasmuch as 'appearing' is never referred to the Father but is consistently employed to refer to Christ's return in glory, the *prima facie* conclusion is that the 'appearing of the glory of our great God' refers to Christ's ap-

pearing and not the Father's appearing" (Reymond, *Jesus, Divine Messiah: The New Testament Witness*, p. 276).

18. *The New Bible Dictionary* contains this helpful observation: "The Hebrews, Greeks, and Romans all used their alphabetic letters as numerals, so that 'alpha and omega' could easily stand for 'first and last'" (*The New Bible Dictionary*, ed. J. D. Douglas [Wheaton, Ill.: Tyndale House Publishers, 1982], p. 26).

19. John F. Walvoord, *The Revelation of Jesus Christ* (Chicago: Moody Press, 1980), p. 60.

Chapter 10—The Virgin Birth

1. See J. Gresham Machen, *The Virgin Birth of Christ* (New York: Harper, 1930).

2. See F. F. Bruce, *The Gospel of John* (London: Pickering & Inglis Ltd., 1983), p. 43.

3. Robert L. Reymond, *Jesus, Divine Messiah: The Old Testament Witness* (Scotland, Great Britain: Christian Focus Publications, 1990), p. 93.

4. Bruce, p. 96.

5. J. Dwight Pentecost, *The Words and Works of Jesus Christ* (Grand Rapids: Zondervan Publishing House, 1982), pp. 43–44.

6. John A. Martin, "Luke," in *The Bible Knowledge Commentary*, New Testament, eds. John F. Walvoord and Roy B. Zuck (Wheaton, Ill.: Victor Books, 1983), p. 205.

7. Stanley D. Toussaint, *Behold the King: A Study of Matthew* (Portland, Oreg.: Multnomah Press, 1980), p. 42.

8. Robert L. Reymond, *Jesus, Divine Messiah: The New Testament Witness* (Phillipsburg, N.J.: Presbyterian and Reformed Publishing, 1990), p. 129, insert mine.

9. Ibid., p. 130, insert mine.

10. Laurence E. Porter, "Luke," in *The International Bible Commentary*, ed. F. F. Bruce (Grand Rapids: Zondervan Publishing House, 1986), p. 1188.

11. Martin, p. 205.

12. Pentecost, p. 45.

13. Robert G. Gromacki, *The Virgin Birth: Doctrine of Deity* (Grand Rapids: Baker Book House, 1984), p. 73.

14. Though the text says that *"an* angel of the Lord" appeared to Joseph, this is not the same as *the* Angel of the Lord that was a preexistent appearance of Christ in Old Testament times. See chapter 5.

15. Millard J. Erickson, *The Word Became Flesh: A Contemporary Incarnational Christology* (Grand Rapids: Baker Book House, 1991), p. 24.

16. Pentecost, p. 55.

17. Benjamin B. Warfield, *The Lord of Glory* (Grand Rapids: Baker Book House, 1974), p. 108.

18. Leon Morris, *The Gospel According to St. Luke* (Grand Rapids: Wm. B. Eerdmans Publishing, 1983), p. 86.

19. Louis A. Barbieri, "Matthew," in *The Bible Knowledge Commentary*, p. 22.

20. Pentecost, p. 67.

Chapter 11—Eternal God in Human Flesh

1. Erich Sauer, *The Triumph of the Crucified* (Grand Rapids: Wm. B. Eerdmans Publishing, 1977), p. 13.

2. Robert G. Gromacki, *The Virgin Birth: Doctrine of Deity* (Grand Rapids: Baker Book House, 1981), p. 101.

3. Ibid., p. 102.

4. Ibid., p. 103.

5. Edgar J. Goodspeed, *Modern Apocrypha* (Boston: The Beacon Press, 1956), p. 7.

6. See Norman Geisler, *To Understand the Bible Look for Jesus* (Grand Rapids: Baker Book House, 1979), p. 67.

7. John F. Walvoord, *Jesus Christ Our Lord* (Chicago: Moody Press, 1980), p. 111.

8. See Millard Erickson, *Christian Theology*, unabridged, one-volume edition (Grand Rapids: Baker Book House, 1987), p. 711.

9. Gromacki, p. 103.

10. Charles C. Ryrie, *Basic Theology* (Wheaton, Ill.: Victor Books, 1986), p. 261.

11. Benjamin Warfield, *The Person and Work of Christ* (Philadelphia: Presbyterian and Reformed Publishing, 1950), p. 39.

12. Ibid.

13. Walvoord, p. 138.

14. Ibid., pp. 138–39.

15. Robert L. Reymond, *Jesus, Divine Messiah: The New Testament Witness* (Phillipsburg, N.J.: Presbyterian and Reformed Publishing, 1990), p. 258.

16. See Erickson, p. 734.

17. Walvoord, p. 141.

18. See also Geisler, p. 28.

19. Walvoord, p. 144.

20. Ibid.

21. Robert P. Lightner, "Philippians," in *The Bible Knowledge Commentary*, New Testament, eds. John F. Walvoord and Roy B. Zuck (Wheaton, Ill.: Victor Books, 1983), p. 654.

22. Walvoord, p. 143.

23. Lightner, p. 654.

24. J. I. Packer, *Knowing God* (Downers Grove, Ill.: InterVarsity Press, 1979), p. 50.

25. Louis Berkhof; cited by Gromacki, p. 106.

26. Gromacki, p. 107.

27. Ibid., p. 110.

28. See Reymond, p. 79.

29. Warfield, p. 63.

30. Ibid., p. 80.

31. Gromacki, p. 113.

32. Ibid., p. 114.

33. Ibid., p. 106.

34. Walvoord, p. 115.

35. Robert P. Lightner, *Evangelical Theology* (Grand Rapids: Baker Book House, 1986), p. 82.

36. Walvoord, p. 115.

37. Ryrie, p. 250.

38. Walvoord, p. 116.

39. See Gromacki, p. 109; and Walvoord, p. 115.

40. Walvoord, p. 118.

41. William G. T. Shedd; cited in Gromacki, p. 111.

42. Reymond, p. 80.

Chapter 12—Christ and His Eternal Glory

1. Erich Sauer, *The Dawn of World Redemption* (Grand Rapids: Wm. B. Eerdmans Publishing, 1977), p. 30.

2. *The New International Dictionary of New Testament Theology,* ed. Colin Brown, vol. 2 (Grand Rapids: Zondervan Publishing House, 1979), p. 45.

3. Walter C. Kaiser, *Hard Sayings of the Old Testament* (Downer Grove, Ill.: InterVarsity Press, 1988), p. 83.

4. Ibid.

5. Ibid., p. 84.

6. Ibid.

7. Robert L. Reymond, *Jesus, Divine Messiah: The New Testament Witness* (Phillipsburg, N.J.: Presbyterian and Reformed Publishing, 1990), p. 161.

8. John D. Grassmick, "Mark," in *The Bible Knowledge Commentary,* New Testament, eds. John F. Walvoord and Roy B. Zuck (Wheaton, Ill.: Victor Books, 1983), p. 142.

9. J. Dwight Pentecost, *The Words and Works of Jesus Christ* (Grand Rapids: Zondervan Publishing House, 1982), p. 257.

10. Arno C. Gaebelein, *The Gospel of Matthew* (Neptune, N.J.: Loizeaux Brothers, 1977), p. 363.

11. Pentecost, p. 257. Leon Morris agrees that there is Exodus typology in this verse. He writes: "The Exodus had delivered Israel from bondage. Jesus by His 'exodus' would deliver His people from a far worse bondage" (Leon Morris, *The Gospel According to St. Luke* [Grand Rapids: Wm. B. Eerdmans Publishing, 1983], p. 172).

12. R. C. H. Lenski, *John* (Minneapolis: Augsburg Publishing House, 1961), p. 1127.

13. David J. Ellis, "John," in *The International Bible Commentary,* ed. F. F. Bruce (Grand Rapids: Zondervan Publishing House, 1986), p. 1259.

14. John F. Walvoord, *Jesus Christ Our Lord* (Chicago: Moody Press, 1980), p. 143.

15. Isbon T. Beckwith, *The Apocalypse of John* (Grand Rapids: Baker Book House, 1967), pp. 312–13.

16. Millard Erickson, *Christian Theology,* unabridged, one-volume edition (Grand Rapids: Baker Book House, 1987), p. 1229.

17. Cited in Tim LaHaye, *Revelation: Illustrated and Made Plain* (Grand Rapids: Zondervan Publishing House, 1975), p. 315.

18. Hal Lindsey, *There's A New World Coming* (Santa Ana: Vision House Publishing, 1973), p. 293.

Appendix A: A Glossary of Names, Titles, and Attributes of Christ

1. This chart is adapted from Josh McDowell and Bart Larson, *Jesus: A Biblical Defense of His Deity* (San Bernardino, Calif.: Here's Life Publishers, 1983), pp. 62–64.

Appendix B: Messianic Prophecies Fulfilled in Christ

1. Norman Geisler and Ron Brooks, *When Skeptics Ask* (Wheaton, Ill.: Victor Books, 1990), p. 115.

2. John Ankerberg, John Weldon, and Walter C. Kaiser, *The Case for Jesus the Messiah* (Chattanooga: The John Ankerberg Evangelistic Association, 1989), p. 16.

3. Ibid., p. 91.

4. Robert L. Reymond, *Jesus, Divine Messiah: The New Testament Witness* (Phillipsburg, N.J.: Presbyterian and Reformed Publishing, 1990), p. 47.

Appendix C: Types of Christ in the Old Testament

1. *Webster's New International Dictionary of the English Language,* 2d ed.; cited in John F. Walvoord, *Jesus Christ Our Lord* (Chicago: Moody Press, 1980), p. 62.

2. Donald K. Campbell, "The Interpretation of Types," *Bibliotheca Sacra* (July 1955), p. 250.

3. Walvoord, p. 62; cf. Lewis Sperry Chafer, *Systematic Theology* (Dallas: Dallas Theological Seminary, 1948), 1:30.

4. Paul Lee Tan, *The Interpretation of Prophecy* (Rockville, Md.: Assurance Publishers, 1974), p. 168.

5. See, for example, Bernard Ramm, *Protestant Biblical Interpretation* (Grand Rapids: Baker Book House, 1978), pp. 215–40; and A. Berkeley Mickelsen, *Interpreting the Bible* (Grand Rapids: Wm. B. Eerdmans Publishing, 1977), pp. 236–64.

6. Mickelsen, p. 237.

7. Walvoord, p. 63.

8. Ibid., p. 64.

9. Ibid., p. 65.

10. Ibid.

11. Ibid., p. 67.

12. Ibid.

13. Ibid., p. 68.

14. Ibid., p. 73.

15. Adapted from Norman Geisler, *To Understand the Bible Look for Jesus* (Grand Rapids: Baker Book House, 1979), p. 39.

16. Merrill F. Unger, *Unger's Guide to the Bible* (Wheaton, Ill.: Tyndale House Publishers, 1974), p. 128.

17. Walvoord, p. 75.

18. Ibid., p. 76.

19. Ibid.

20. Ibid.

21. Ibid., p. 77.

22. Unger, p. 129.

Appendix D: Was Melchizedek a Preincarnate Appearance of Christ?

1. F. F. Bruce, *The Epistle to the Hebrews* (Grand Rapids: Wm. B. Eerdmans Publishing, 1979), pp. 137–38, insertions mine.

2. Gleason Archer, *Encyclopedia of Bible Difficulties* (Grand Rapids: Zondervan Publishing House, 1982), pp. 91–92.

3. Ibid.

Appendix E: Rightly Dividing the Word: Interpreting Difficult Passages

1. For a comprehensive treatment of biblical difficulties, see Norman L. Geisler and Thomas Howe, *When Critics Ask* (Wheaton, Ill.: Victor Books, 1992).

2. Leon Morris, *The Gospel According to John* (Grand Rapids: Wm. B. Eerdmans Publishing, 1971), p. 658.

3. Robert M. Bowman, *Why You Should Believe in the Trinity* (Grand Rapids: Baker Book House, 1989), pp. 14–15.

4. Arthur W. Pink, *Exposition of the Gospel of John*, vol. 3 (Swengel, Penn.: Bible Truth Depot, 1945), pp. 281–82, insert mine.

5. Benjamin B. Warfield, *The Person and Work of Christ* (Philadelphia: Presbyterian and Reformed Publishing, 1950), p. 61, inserts mine.

6. See R. H. Lightfoot; cited in Morris, p. 842.

7. Bowman, p. 72; cf. Millard J. Erickson, *The Word Became Flesh: A Contemporary Incarnational Christology* (Grand Rapids: Baker Book House, 1991), pp. 20–21.

8. Josh McDowell and Bart Larson, *Jesus: A Biblical Defense of His Deity* (San Bernardino, Calif.: Here's Life Publishers, 1975), p. 90.

9. Bowman, p. 80.

10. John F. Walvoord, *Jesus Christ Our Lord* (Chicago: Moody Press, 1980), p. 44.

11. Warfield, p. 56.

12. Bowman, p. 62.

Appendix F: Important Creeds of Christendom

1. Philip Schaff, *The Creeds of Christendom* (Grand Rapids: Baker Book House, 1983), 2:58–59.

2. The Council of Constantinople added the clause of the Holy Spirit in A.D. 381.

3. The actual authorship and date of composition of this creed is unknown. Philip Schaff writes: "Since the ninth century it has been ascribed to Athanasius, bishop of Alexandria, the chief defender of the divinity of Christ and the orthodox doctrine of the Trinity (d. 373). . . . Since the middle of the seventeenth century the Athanasian authorship has been abandoned by learned Catholics as well as Protestants. The evidence against it is conclusive" (1:35).

4. Quoted in Charles Hodge, *Systematic Theology*, abridged edition, ed. Edward N. Gross (Grand Rapids: Baker Book House, 1988), pp. 172–73.

5. James Oliver Buswell, *A Systematic Theology of the Christian Religion* (Grand Rapids: Zondervan Publishing House, 1979), 2:51.

6. Schaff, 2:62–63.

7. Paul Enns, *The Moody Handbook of Theology* (Chicago: Moody Press, 1989), pp. 477–78.

8. "Westminster Confession of Faith," chapter 2, *The Constitution of the Presbyterian Church of the United States of America* (Philadelphia: Presbyterian Board of Publication and Sabbath-School Work, 1907), pp. 16–20.

Appendix G: A Catalog of Ancient Errors on the Person of Christ

1. For an excellent discussion of these errors, see Millard J. Erickson, *The Word Became Flesh: A Contemporary Incarnational Christology* (Grand Rapids: Baker Book House, 1991).

2. Adapted from Charles C. Ryrie, *Basic Theology* (Wheaton, Ill.: Victor Books, 1986), p. 253.

3. Paul Enns, *The Moody Handbook of Theology* (Chicago: Moody Press, 1989), p. 420.

4. Ibid., p. 422.

5. Ibid.

6. James Oliver Buswell, *A Systematic Theology of the Christian Religion* (Grand Rapids: Zondervan Publishing House, 1979), 2:51.

Bibliography

Books with an asterisk (*) are especially recommended for further study on Christ's preexistence and eternality, his appearances in Old Testament times, and his specific fulfillment of messianic prophecy.

1. Christology

*Ankerberg, John; Weldon, John; and Kaiser, Walter C. *The Case for Jesus the Messiah.* Chattanooga: John Ankerberg Evangelistic Association, 1989.

Buell, Jon A. and Hyder, O. Quentin. *Jesus: God, Ghost or Guru?* Grand Rapids: Zondervan, 1978.

Clowney, Edmund P. *The Unfolding Mystery: Discovering Christ in the Old Testament.* Phillipsburg, N.J.: Presbyterian and Reformed, 1988.

Erickson, Millard J. *The Word Became Flesh: A Contemporary Incarnational Christology.* Grand Rapids: Baker, 1991.

*Geisler, Norman. *To Understand the Bible Look for Jesus.* Grand Rapids: Baker, 1979.

Gromacki, Robert G. *The Virgin Birth: Doctrine of Deity.* Grand Rapids: Baker, 1984.

*Hengstenberg, E. W. *Christology of the Old Testament.* Grand Rapids: Kregel, 1970.

Lightner, Robert P. *The Death Christ Died.* Schaumburg, Ill.: Regular Baptist Press, 1978.

Machen, J. Gresham. *The Virgin Birth of Christ.* New York: Harper, 1930.

McDowell, Josh, and Bart Larson. *Jesus: A Biblical Defense of His Deity.* San Bernardino, Calif.: Here's Life, 1983.

Norris, Richard A. *The Christological Controversy.* Philadelphia: Fortress, 1982.

*Pentecost, J. Dwight. *The Words and Works of Jesus Christ.* Grand Rapids: Zondervan, 1982.

Rainsford, Marcus. *Our Lord Prays for His Own.* Chicago: Moody, 1978.

*Reymond, Robert L. *Jesus, Divine Messiah: The New Testament Witness.* Phillipsburg, N.J.: Presbyterian and Reformed, 1990.

*_____. *Jesus, Divine Messiah: The Old Testament Witness*. Scotland, Great Britain: Christian Focus, 1990.

Runia, Klaas. *The Present-Day Christological Debate*. Downers Grove, Ill.: InterVarsity, 1984.

Shephard, J. W. *The Christ of the Gospels*. Grand Rapids: Eerdmans, 1975.

*Walvoord, John F. *Jesus Christ Our Lord*. Chicago: Moody, 1980.

*Warfield, Benjamin B. *The Lord of Glory*. Grand Rapids: Baker, 1974.

*_____. *The Person and Work of Christ*. Philadelphia: Presbyterian and Reformed, 1950.

Wells, David F. *The Person of Christ*. Westchester, Ill.: Crossway Books, 1984.

2. General Theology

Basic Christian Doctrines, ed. Carl F. Henry. Grand Rapids: Baker, 1983.

Berkhof, Louis. *Manual of Christian Doctrine*. Grand Rapids: Eerdmans, 1983.

_____. *Systematic Theology*. Grand Rapids: Eerdmans, 1982.

Bowman, Rob. *Why You Should Believe in the Trinity*. Grand Rapids: Baker, 1989.

Buswell, James Oliver. *A Systematic Theology of the Christian Religion*. Grand Rapids: Zondervan, 1979.

Calvin, John. *Institutes of the Christian Religion*, ed. John T. McNeill, trans. Ford Lewis Battles. Philadelphia: Westminster, 1960.

Chafer, Lewis Sperry. *Systematic Theology*. Wheaton, Ill.: Victor Books, 1988.

Enns, Paul. *The Moody Handbook of Theology*. Chicago: Moody, 1989.

Erickson, Millard J. *Christian Theology*, unabridged, one-volume edition. Grand Rapids: Baker, 1987.

Hodge, Charles. *Systematic Theology*, abridged edition, ed. Edward N. Gross. Grand Rapids: Baker, 1988.

Lightner, Robert P. *Evangelical Theology*. Grand Rapids: Baker, 1986.

_____. *The God of the Bible*. Grand Rapids: Baker, 1978.

_____. *The Saviour and the Scriptures*. Grand Rapids: Baker, 1966.

Packer, J. I. *Knowing God*. Downers Grove, Ill.: InterVarsity, 1979.

Ryrie, Charles C. *Basic Theology*. Wheaton, Ill.: Victor Books, 1986.

_____. *The Holy Spirit*. Chicago: Moody, 1965.

Sauer, Erich. *From Eternity to Eternity*. Grand Rapids: Eerdmans, 1979.

_____. *The Dawn of World Redemption*. Grand Rapids: Eerdmans, 1977.

_____. *The Triumph of the Crucified*. Grand Rapids: Eerdmans, 1977.

Thiessen, Henry Clarence. *Lectures in Systematic Theology*. Grand Rapids: Eerdmans, 1981.

Vos, Geerhardus. *Biblical Theology: Old and New Testaments*. Grand Rapids: Eerdmans, 1985.

Walvoord, John F. *The Holy Spirit*. Grand Rapids: Zondervan, 1958.

Warfield, Benjamin B. *Biblical and Theological Studies.* Phillipsburg, N.J.: Presbyterian and Reformed, 1968.

3. General Works

Bowman, Rob. *Jehovah's Witnesses, Jesus Christ, and the Gospel of John.* Grand Rapids: Baker, 1989.

Davis, John J. *Moses and the Gods of Egypt.* Grand Rapids: Baker, 1986.

Geisler, Norman. *A Popular Survey of the Old Testament.* Grand Rapids: Baker, 1978.

_____. *Christian Apologetics.* Grand Rapids: Baker, 1976.

Goodspeed, Edgar J. *Modern Apocrypha.* Boston: Beacon, 1956.

Hodges, Zane C. *The Gospel Under Siege.* Dallas: Redencion Viva, 1981.

_____. *The Hungry Inherit.* Portland, Oreg.: Multnomah, 1980.

Josephus, *The Antiquities of the Jews,* in *Complete Works.* Grand Rapids: Kregel, 1974.

Kaiser, Walter C. *Hard Sayings of the Old Testament.* Downers Grove, Ill.: InterVarsity, 1988.

Keller, Phillip. *A Shepherd Looks at the Good Shepherd and His Sheep.* Grand Rapids: Zondervan, 1978.

McDowell, Josh. *Evidence that Demands a Verdict.* Arrowhead Springs: Campus Crusade for Christ International, 1972.

Mickelsen, A. Berkeley. *Interpreting the Bible.* Grand Rapids: Eerdmans, 1977.

Morris, Henry M. *The Biblical Basis for Modern Science.* Grand Rapids: Baker, 1984.

Ramm, Bernard. *Protestant Biblical Interpretation.* Grand Rapids: Baker, 1978.

Rhodes, Ron. *When Servants Suffer: Finding Purpose in Pain.* Wheaton, Ill.: Harold Shaw, 1989.

Ryrie, Charles C. *The Ryrie Study Bible.* Chicago: Moody, 1986.

Schaff, Philip. *The Creeds of Christendom.* Grand Rapids: Baker, 1983.

Stenning, J. F. *The Targum of Isaiah.* London: Oxford Press, 1949.

Tan, Paul Lee. *The Interpretation of Prophecy.* Rockville, Md.: Assurance, 1974.

The Constitution of the Presbyterian Church of the United States of America. Philadelphia: Presbyterian Board of Publication and Sabbath-School Work, 1907.

Unger, Merrill F. *Unger's Guide to the Bible.* Wheaton, Ill.: Tyndale, 1974.

Whitcomb, John C. *The Early Earth.* Grand Rapids: Baker, 1979.

4. Commentaries

Barclay, William. *The Gospel of John,* vol. 2. Philadelphia: Westminster, 1956.

Barnes, Albert. *Barnes Notes on the Old and New Testaments*. Grand Rapids: Baker, 1977.

Beckwith, Isbon T. *The Apocalypse of John*. Grand Rapids: Baker, 1967.

Bible Knowledge Commentary, The, Old Testament, eds. John F. Walvoord and Roy B. Zuck. Wheaton, Ill.: Victor Books, 1985.

Bruce, F. F. *The Book of Acts*. Grand Rapids: Eerdmans, 1986.

_____. *The Epistle to the Hebrews*. Grand Rapids: Eerdmans, 1979.

_____. *The Gospel of John*. Grand Rapids: Eerdmans, 1984.

Cole, R. Alan. *Exodus: An Introduction and Commentary*. Downers Grove, Ill.: InterVarsity, 1973.

Eadie, John. *A Commentary on the Greek Text of the Epistle of Paul to the Colossians*. Grand Rapids: Baker, 1979.

English, E. Schuyler. *Studies in the Epistle to the Hebrews*. Neptune, N.J.: Loizeaux Brothers, 1976.

Expositor's Bible Commentary, The, ed. Frank E. Gaebelein. Grand Rapids: Zondervan, 1978.

Gaebelein, Arno C. *The Gospel of Matthew*. Neptune, N.J.: Loizeaux Brothers, 1977.

Hendriksen, William. *Exposition of the Gospel According to John*. Grand Rapids: Baker, 1976.

Henry, Matthew. *Commentary on the Whole Bible*. Grand Rapids: Zondervan, 1974.

International Bible Commentary, The, ed. F. F. Bruce. Grand Rapids: Zondervan, 1979.

Jamieson, Robert, A. R. Fausset, and David Brown. *A Commentary—Critical, Experimental, and Practical—on the Old and New Testaments*. Grand Rapids: Eerdmans, 1973.

Keil, C. F., and Franz Delitzsch. *Biblical Commentary on the Old Testament*. Grand Rapids: Eerdmans, 1954.

Keller, Phillip. *A Shepherd Looks at Psalm 23*. Grand Rapids: Zondervan, 1976.

Kidner, Derek. *Genesis: An Introduction and Commentary*. Downers Grove, Ill.: InterVarsity, 1967.

Lenski, R. C. H. *1 Corinthians*. Minneapolis: Augsburg, 1961.

_____. *First Peter*. Minneapolis: Augsburg, 1961.

_____. *Hebrews*. Minneapolis: Augsburg, 1961.

_____. *The Interpretation of St. John's Gospel*. Minneapolis: Augsburg, 1961.

Leupold, H. C. *Exposition of Genesis*, vol. 1. Grand Rapids: Baker, 1968.

Lightfoot, J. B. *St. Paul's Epistles to the Colossians and to Philemon*. Grand Rapids: Zondervan, 1979.

Lindsey, Hal. *There's A New World Coming*. Santa Ana: Vision House, 1973.

MacArthur, John. *Hebrews*. Chicago: Moody, 1983.

_____. *The Superiority of Christ*. Chicago: Moody, 1986.

Morris, Leon. *The First Epistle of Paul to the Corinthians*, Tyndale New Testament Commentaries. Grand Rapids: Eerdmans, 1976.

_____. *The Gospel According to John*. Grand Rapids: Eerdmans, 1971.

_____. *The Gospel According to St. Luke*. Grand Rapids: Eerdmans, 1983.

Moule, H. C. G. *Studies in Colossians & Philemon*. Grand Rapids: Kregel, 1977.

Newell, William R. *Hebrews: Verse By Verse*. Chicago: Moody, 1947.

Pink, Arthur W. *Exposition of the Gospel of John*. Swengel, Penn.: Bible Truth Depot, 1945.

Robertson, A. T. *Word Pictures*. Nashville: Broadman, 1930.

Robinson, Haddon W. *Psalm Twenty-Three*. Chicago: Moody, 1979.

Shedd, William G. T. *Romans*. New York: Scribner, 1879.

Toussaint, Stanley D. *Behold the King: A Study of Matthew*. Portland, Oreg.: Multnomah, 1980.

Vincent, Marvin R. *Word Studies in the New Testament*. Grand Rapids: Eerdmans, 1975.

Walvoord, John F. *Daniel: The Key to Prophetic Revelation*. Chicago: Moody, 1981.

_____. *The Revelation of Jesus Christ*. Chicago: Moody, 1980.

Westcott, Brooke Foss. *The Epistle to the Hebrews*. Grand Rapids: Eerdmans, 1974.

Wuest, Kenneth S. *Wuest's Word Studies*. Grand Rapids: Eerdmans, 1953.

Wycliffe Bible Commentary, The, eds. Charles F. Pfeiffer and Everett F. Harrison. Chicago: Moody, 1974.

5. Reference Works

Archer, Gleason. *Encyclopedia of Bible Difficulties*. Grand Rapids: Zondervan, 1982.

Brown, Francis, S. R. Driver, and Charles A. Briggs. *A Hebrew and English Lexicon of the Old Testament*. Oxford: Clarendon Press, 1980.

Jewish Encyclopedia, The, ed. Isidore Singer. New York: Funk and Wagnalls, 1904.

New Bible Dictionary, The, ed. J. D. Douglas. Wheaton, Ill.: Tyndale, 1982.

New International Dictionary of New Testament Theology, The, ed. Colin Brown. Grand Rapids: Zondervan, 1979.

New Testament Theology, ed. Colin Brown. Grand Rapids: Zondervan, 1979.

Zondervan Pictorial Encyclopedia of the Bible, The, ed. Merrill C. Tenney. Grand Rapids: Zondervan, 1978.

Name and Subject Index
(primary page references are in bold)

Scripture Index